PMI-ACP® Exam Prep

Questions, Answers & Explanations

PMtraining™

www.PMTraining.com

PMI-ACP® Exam Prep

Questions, Answers & Explanations

www.PMTraining.com

Copyrighted Material

Edition 2018.

Published by SSI Logic

ISBN 10: 0989470350
ISBN-13: 978-0989470353

All inquiries should be addressed via email to:
support@pmtraining.com

or by mail post to:
PMTraining
340 S Lemon Ave #9038
Walnut, CA 91789

Table of Contents

Introduction

Practice Exams and Quizzes

INTRODUCTION

Welcome

Thank you for selecting PMTraining's *PMI-ACP® Exam Prep – Questions, Answers, and Explanations* for your PMI-ACP® study needs. The goal of this book is to provide condensed mock exams and practice tests which allow you to become comfortable with the pace, subject matter, and difficulty of the PMI Agile Certified Practitioner (PMI-ACP) exam.

The content in this book is designed to optimize the time you spend studying in multiple ways.

1. Practice exams in this book are condensed to be completed in one hour; allowing you to balance your time between practice tests and other methods of study.

2. Passing score requirements in this book are slightly higher than the real exam; allowing you to naturally adjust to a higher test score requirement.

3. Practice exams included in this book cover the entire scope of the PMI-ACP exam, while shorter quizzes focus only on specific Knowledge Areas outlined in the *PMI-ACP® Examination Content Outline.*

The practice exam content in this book is structured into two general types of exam preparation:

- "Lite" Mock Exams, which allow you to test your knowledge across condensed versions of the PMI-ACP exam; designed to be completed within one hour.

- Knowledge Area Quizzes, which reflect brief practice tests focused on specific exam topic areas, outlined in the *PMI-ACP® Examination Content Outline,* designed to be completed in 25 minutes.

We wish you the best of luck in your pursuit to become a PMI Agile Certified Practitioner (PMI-ACP).

PMI-ACP® Exam Overview

About the PMI Agile Certified Practitioner (PMI-ACP®) Certification

The PMI-ACP certification is managed by the Project Management Institute (PMI®) and is designed for project management practitioners who are using Agile practices in their projects. Since 2011, the PMI-ACP certification has become one of the most widely recognized credentials available, for professionals who implement Agile methodologies.

The latest version of the PMI-ACP exam was released on March 26, 2018 and is the basis for this book.

The PMI-ACP certification is a globally recognized credential, and individuals are encouraged to remain active via PMI's Continuing Certification Requirements (CCRs). Only individuals who maintain active PMI-ACP credentials may refer to themselves as a PMI Agile Certified Practitioner. Individuals do not need to be a member of PMI to earn the PMI-ACP credential.

The minimum requirements in attaining the PMI-ACP certification:

- Education: At a minimum, A high school diploma is required
- General project experience
    - 2000 Hours (a minimum of 12 Months) working on project teams earned within the past 5 years OR a current PMP® or PgMP® certification.
- Agile project experience
    - 1500 hours (a minimum of 8 months) working on agile project teams or in agile methodologies.
- Project Management Education: 21 PMI contact hours of accredited education
- Ethics: Agree to PMI's Code of Ethics and Professional Conduct
- **Pass the PMI-ACP Exam**

PMI-ACP Exam Details

The PMI-ACP exam is designed to objectively assess and measure project management knowledge. Concepts covered in the PMI-ACP exam are derived from the *PMI-ACP Reference List,* comprising 12 different reference texts that articulate Agile practices. This list of reference books can be found on the PMI website.

Most important of these reference texts is PMI's own *Agile Practice Guide* which provides a significant touchpoint of concepts for the current PMI-ACP exam.

The actual exam is offered in a computer based testing (CBT) environment. A summary of the exam structure and passing requirements are as follows:

- There are 120 total multiple choice questions which make up the PMI-ACP exam
- 20 randomly placed "pre-test questions" are included, and do not count towards the pass/fail determination
- Individuals have 3 hours to complete the exam
- Only correct answers count, and a passing score is determined by "sound psychometric analysis". This method indicates that scores reflect the difficulty of the questions answered. *

** For the purposes of this book, a numeric scoring system will be applied, allowing students to easily measure their knowledge.*

The PMI-ACP Exam Content

The PMI-ACP exam covers a variety of agile tools, techniques, knowledge, and skills over the following seven domains:

Domain	% of Exam
I. Agile Principles and Mindset	16
II. Value-driven Delivery	20
III. Stakeholder Engagement	17
IV. Team Performance	16
V. Adaptive Planning	12
VI. Problem Detection and Resolution	10
VII. Continuous Improvement (Product, Process, People)	9

The Project Management Institute further divides the seven domains into sub-domains and tasks to better organize the tools and techniques and knowledge and skills you must master to pass the PMI-ACP exam. For specific details of the sub-domains and tasks, please visit pmi.org.

To improve your chances of becoming an agile certified practitioner, SSI Logic has categorized each question into one of the seven agile domains and noted this categorization in each answer key.

Practice Exams and Quizzes

PMI-ACP Lite Mock Exam 1 Practice Questions

Test Name: PMI-ACP Lite Mock Exam 1
Total Questions: 40
Correct Answers Needed to Pass:
30 (75.00%)
Time Allowed: 60 Minutes

Test Description

This is a cumulative PMI-ACP Mock Exam which can be used as a benchmark for your PMI-ACP aptitude. This practice test includes questions from all exam topic areas, including sections from Agile Tools and Techniques, and all three Agile Knowledge and Skills areas.

Test Questions

1. Which of the following is a collaborative approach to defining requirements and business-oriented functional tests for software products based on capturing and illustrating requirements using realistic examples instead of abstract statements?

A. Work Instructions (WI)

B. Work Breakdown Structure (WBS)

C. Requirements Manual (RM)

D. Specifications by Example (SBE)

2. What is the minimum number of Scrum teams for applying the Scrum of Scrums method?

A. 5

B. 3

C. 4

D. 2

3. The project sponsor has requested a project to be delivered using Agile methods. She has strongly encouraged the use of a product backlog, daily stand-ups, and using Kanban boards for WIP management. She has also designed an "Agile-compliance rewards" program that is supposed to handsomely reward the top performing team members. According to the servant-leadership mindset, what is wrong with this approach?

A. Daily stand-ups; this will introduce management overhead.

B. Use of Kanban boards; Scrum and Kanban methods are being blended.

C. The rewards program; the servant-leadership model encourages creating an environment where everyone can succeed.

D. WIP management; the servant-leader is responsible for the WIP management.

4. A software vendor has recently hired you to manage some of its key projects. During your orientation at the organization you were told that the organization has recently adopted Agile practices for project management. A chart was then shown to you where Agile and Kanban were shown as subset of Lean. What is your view on this?

A. The chart is wrong because Agile, Kanban and Lean are three different approaches to project management.

B. The chart is wrong because Kanban is a subset of Lean while Agile is not.

C. Agile and Kanban are subsets of Lean because they are named instances of Lean thinking.

D. The chart is wrong because Agile is a subset of Lean while Kanban is not.

5. What is a date-driven project?

A. The one that has each project activity tied to a specific date.

B. The one that demands a detailed project schedule and critical paths to be developed.

C. The one that must be released by a certain date but for which the feature set is negotiable.

D. The one that imposes a deadline for all of the features to be delivered.

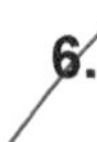

6. Ideally Agile team members should be collocated. However, there could be a number of reasons why this might not be practical. Which of the following are some of the benefits of having a dispersed team instead of a collocated team?

A. Global presence, economy of scale, and reduced costs.

B. Global presence

C. Reduced costs

D. Economy of scale

7. You have been assigned to lead a massive enterprise process reengineering and automation project. Due to the size and complexity of the project a very large team has been formed. You have split the larger team into smaller teams and have asked each team to estimate a subset of stories. However, before each team starts their own estimating, which of the following activities must first be conducted?

A. Start all teams together in a joint planning poker game for an hour or so and have them estimate 10 to 20 stories.

B. Assign one estimating chief for each team and appoint a chief of chiefs.

C. Conduct a detailed feasibility and cost benefit analysis for the project.

D. Decompose all epics and themes into smaller user stories so that they can be more accurately estimated.

8. Which of the following statements regarding Agile retrospectives is correct?

A. Retrospectives help teams groom product backlog.

B. Retrospectives help teams develop release plans.

C. Retrospectives help teams improve.

D. Retrospectives help teams develop iteration plans.

9. A programmer estimated ideal time for the development of a user story to be five days. If the programmer is assigned another project in parallel, what would be the effect of multi-tasking on the ideal time of the user story?

A. The ideal time will increase by 80%.

B. The ideal time will double.

C. The ideal time will not change.

D. The ideal time will decrease to half.

10. What is a starting point of an Agile project?

A. Iteration plan

B. Daily plan

C. Retrospective

D. Release plan

11. What is the purpose of conducting a "Color Code Dots" activity during an iteration retrospective?

A. Show how people experienced events on the timeline.

B. Show resource requirements for completing the backlog items.

C. Show the delays occurred on the project.

D. Show the progress of the project.

12. You are leading a complex Agile project. The team has recently found out that some of the stories selected for the current iteration will not be complete by the end of the iteration. What should you do next?

A. Reduce the scope of the stories.

B. Consult with the product owner.

C. Split the stories into smaller stories.

D. Push the stories to the next iteration.

13. You have recently taken over a project that is halfway through the execution. You are not happy with the team's throughput. You also have noticed that each team member is multi-tasking and has, on average, five concurrently assigned tasks. According to Clark and Wheelwright, what percent of the team's time is currently being wasted and spent on non-value-adding activities?

A. 20 percent

B. 40 percent

C. 60 percent

D. 50 percent

14. Which of the following is critical for delivering finished work in the shortest possible time, with higher quality and without external dependencies?

A. Product owner.

B. Generalists.

C. Cross-functional teams.

D. Team facilitator.

15. Which of the following is generally considered the LAST option to estimate a team's velocity?

A. Making a forecast.

B. Running an iteration.

C. Using historical values.

D. Running a few iterations.

16. You were halfway through your project when the product owner left the company. The new product owner has been assigned to the project but they come from a different part of the business. You were reviewing the product backlog with the new product owner when they requested to reprioritize of some of the backlog items. What should you do?

A. Escalate the conflict to the Agile coach or the higher management.

B. Reprioritize the items as demanded by the product owner.

C. Avoid the confrontation with the product owner and ask the team to negotiate a workable solution with the product owner.

D. Tell the product owner that the current ranking was agreed by the team and the previous product owner.

17. Which of the following is a unit of measure for expressing the overall size of a user story?

A. KLOC

B. Story Points

C. Product backlog

D. Velocity

18. Your organization has announced a major transformation program. You have been selected as the project manager for one of the process improvement projects. You are now selecting your project team. Which of the following should be one of your considerations while selecting your team?

A. Select team members who can either be collocated or are at least 25% available for the project.

B. Select team members who are geographically distributed but 100% available for the project.

C. Select team members who can be collocated and are 100% available for the project.

D. Select team members who can either be collocated or are at least 50% available for the project.

19. Which of the following tools are used by Agile teams to focus product development in small increments?

A. Spikes

B. Retrospectives

C. User stories

D. Kanban boards

20. You have recently noticed that many of the daily team stand-ups are turning into a status meeting and swaying away from the stand-up principles. You think this is more of a facilitation issue than a team issue. Which of the following might help you in this situation?

A. Encourage the project manager to facilitate the stand-ups.

B. Encourage the scrum master to facilitate the stand-ups.

C. Encourage the product owner to facilitate the stand-ups.

D. Encourage team members to facilitate the stand-ups in a round-robin fashion.

21. Some people insist new organizational structures be installed before any cultural shift can begin. Others argue that new organizational structures are only superficial adjustments until the collective culture moves in a meaningful direction. What is your view on this?

A. One cannot progress without the other.

B. Culture first needs to move in a meaningful direction.

C. Organizational structure needs to be installed first.

D. Organizational structure is not related to the organizational culture.

22. Which of the following two Agile meetings can be combined into a single meeting?

A. Portfolio planning and product planning

B. Retrospective and iteration planning

C. Strategic planning and iteration planning

D. Release planning and daily planning

23. Which of the following situation will increase an Agile project's ROI?

A. Releasing the prioritized features sooner than planned.

B. Employing Agile tools such as Kanban board and burndown charts.

C. Investing the unused budget in the stock market.

D. Focusing primarily on the 'Must have" features.

24. "Working software over comprehensive documentation" is one of the key Agile Manifesto values. Which of the following Agile approaches helps in achieving this value?

A. Daily standups

B. Demonstrations and reviews

C. Agile measurements

D. Chartering the project and the team

25. You are estimating a story by estimating the amount of effort required to deliver the story when the team has to focus exclusively on this story and does not face any delays or interruptions. What are you estimating?

A. Run time

B. Ideal time

C. Idle time

D. Real time

26. A fishbowl window can increase a team's productivity by facilitating communications. A fishbowl window reduces the:

A. Collaboration lag

B. Project scope

C. Direct project costs

D. Required coordination

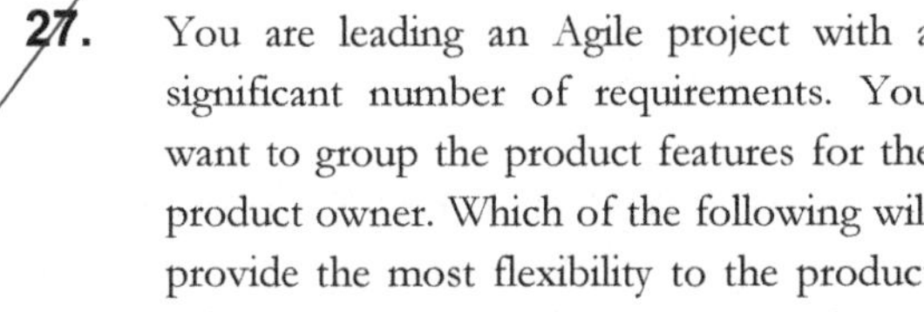

27. You are leading an Agile project with a significant number of requirements. You want to group the product features for the product owner. Which of the following will provide the most flexibility to the product owner in prioritizing the requirements?

A. Features must be grouped by functionality.

B. Features must be sorted based on their story size.

C. Features must be sorted based on business value.

D. Features must be written so as to minimize the technical dependencies between them.

28. In Agile projects, where are project requirements documented?

A. Requirements are documented in the scope management plan.

B. Requirements are documented in the requirements management plan.

C. Requirements are documented in the product backlog.

D. Requirements are documented in the project management plan.

29. Which of the following is the correct representation of the spectrum of project life cycles?

A. Predictive – Agile – Iterative – Incremental

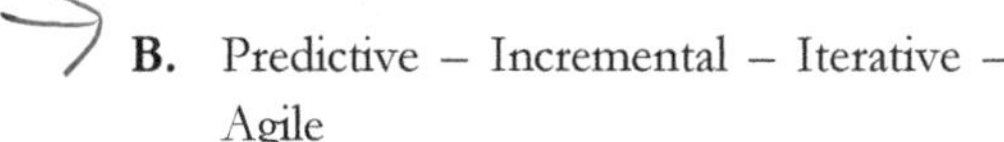

B. Predictive – Incremental – Iterative – Agile

C. Iterative – Agile – Predictive – Incremental

D. Iterative – Agile – Incremental – Predictive

30. You and your Agile team are currently analyzing your project's backlog. You want to identify the stories that have historically delighted the users but now have become their basic requirements. Which Agile techniques are you applying?

A. Fishbone analysis

B. Backlog grooming

C. Value stream mapping

D. Kano analysis

31. Which of the following is regarded as the most collaborative contracting approach?

A. Graduated time and materials

B. Not-to-exceed time and materials

C. Dynamic scope option

D. Team augmentation

32. Which of the following is a critical success factor for Agile teams?

A. Project duration

B. Strong product ownership

C. Cost estimates

D. Requirements complexity

33. An Agile team has recently established a Kanban board to manage its WIP. Kanban board is a visual tool that shows the flow of work and helps in spotting bottlenecks. What technique allows the team to see how to pull work across the board?

A. Response time limits at the top of each column.

B. Velocity at the top of each item.

C. Work in progress limits at the top of each column.

D. Cycle time limits at the top of each item.

34. George is managing a complex financial application development project in an Agile environment. One of the critical success factors for the project is agility and responsiveness to change. In order to foster an Agile environment, George must take a hard look on which of the following processes with an aim to streamline them?

A. Production processes.

B. Agile processes.

C. Lengthy processes, causing bottlenecks.

D. Quality management processes.

35. An Agile team has recently been put together to deliver a system upgrade project. The product owner has provided the product backlog but is hesitant in prioritizing the stories. What should you do?

A. Do not proceed unless the backlog is prioritized by the product owner.

B. Follow a traditional project life cycle on this project.

C. Let the team prioritize the stories if the product owner cannot prioritize them.

D. Educate the product owner regarding the importance of prioritization in Agile projects.

36. Which of the following is NOT a recognized Agile metric for user stories?

A. Cycle time

B. Ideal time

C. Story points

D. Conditions of satisfaction

37. You are leading a traditional to Agile transformation initiative for your organization. Which of the following is the best way of using a Kanban board on this project?

A. Showing new approaches already in use as "tested", those being tried as "in-tray" and those still waiting to be introduced as "out-tray".

B. Showing new approaches already in use as "in-tray", those being tried as "tested" and those still waiting to be introduced as "ready".

C. Showing new approaches already in use as "in progress", those being tried as "in trial" and those still waiting to be introduced as "to do".

D. Showing new approaches already in use as "done", those being tried as "in progress" and those still waiting to be introduced as "to do".

38. Which of the following requires system-level testing for end-to-end information, unit testing for the building blocks, and, in between, determines if there is a need for integration testing?

A. Test at all levels.

B. Continuous integration.

C. Acceptance Test Driven Development (ATDD).

D. Behavior Driven Development (BDD).

39. When Agile teams, together with product owners, prioritize backlog items, which Agile technique are they relying on?

A. Subjective prioritization

B. Qualitative prioritization

C. Relative prioritization

D. Quantitative prioritization

40. The Manifesto for Agile Software Development was published in:

A. 2003

B. 2002

C. 2004

D. 2001

PMI-ACP Lite Mock Exam 1 Answer Key and Explanations

1. D - Specifications by Example (SBE) is a collaborative approach to defining requirements and business-oriented functional tests for software products based on capturing and illustrating requirements using realistic examples instead of abstract statements. [Agile Practice Guide, 1st edition, Page 154] [Adaptive Planning]

2. B - There has to be a minimum of three teams to apply the Scrum of Scrums method; two base teams plus an overarching team. [Agile Practice Guide, 1st edition, Page 111] [Value-driven Delivery]

3. C - The servant-leadership model encourages creating an environment where everyone can succeed. The rewards program will create a competing environment which doesn't help in ensuring everyone succeeds. [Agile Practice Guide, 1st edition, Page 33] [Agile Principles and Mindset]

4. C - Agile and Kanban are subsets of Lean because they are named instances of Lean thinking that share Lean concepts such as "focus on value", "small batch sizes", and "elimination of waste". [Agile Practice Guide, 1st edition, Page 11] [Agile Principles and Mindset]

5. C - Many project are either date-driven or feature-driven. A date-driven project is one that must be released by a certain date but for which the feature set is negotiable. A feature-driven project is one where the release date is as soon as possible but the completion of a set of features is more important. [Cohn, M., 2006. Agile Estimating and Planning. 1st ed. Massachusetts: Pearson Education. Page 133] [Adaptive Planning]

6. A - There can be multiple factors (or constraints) that can limit forming a collocated Agile team. Such factors include requirement for global presence and opportunities for economy of scale and reduced costs. [Agile Practice Guide, 1st edition, Page 40] [Team Performance]

7. A - If the project is already underway and being estimated, this implies that a feasibility study would have already been performed for such a large and complex project prior to commencement. Decomposing all epics and themes is not recommended unless some of these are being planned for the next few iterations. The risk with multiple teams estimating user stories is inconsistent estimates. It is recommended that all teams start together in a joint planning poker game for an hour or so and have them estimate 10 to 20 stories. Then make sure each team has a copy of these stories and their estimates and that they use them as baselines for estimating the stories they are given to estimate. [Cohn, M., 2006. Agile Estimating and Planning. 1st ed. Massachusetts: Pearson Education. Page 58] [Problem Detection and Resolution]

8. C - Retrospectives allow Agile teams to learn about, improve, and adapt their processes. Retrospectives help teams–even great ones–keep improving. [Derby, E. and Larsen, D., 2006. Agile Retrospectives: Making Good Teams Great. 1st ed. Texas: Pragmatic Bookshelf, Page 1] [Continuous Improvement]

9. C - Ideal time is the amount of time that something takes when stripped of all peripheral activities including waiting time.

Multi-tasking will not impact the ideal time for the user story. However, the elapsed time (actual duration from start to finish) will be impacted. [Cohn, M., 2006. Agile Estimating and Planning. 1st ed. Massachusetts: Pearson Education. Page 43] [Adaptive Planning]

10. D - The release plan is developed first, followed by the iteration plan. During the iteration the team develops and refines the daily plan. The retrospective is usually conducted at the end of the iteration. [Cohn, M., 2006. Agile Estimating and Planning. 1st ed. Massachusetts: Pearson Education. Page 28] [Adaptive Planning]

11. A - A "Color Code Dots" activity is used in conjunction with a timeline to gather data about feelings in a longer iteration, release, or project retrospective. This activity is used to show how people experienced events on the timeline. [Derby, E. and Larsen, D., 2006. Agile Retrospectives: Making Good Teams Great. 1st ed. Texas: Pragmatic Bookshelf, Page 59] [Continuous Improvement]

12. B - If, during an iteration, a story is found to be larger than expected, then it needs to be brought to the attention of the product owner. The product owner, in collaboration with the team, can then find a way to split the story or reduce its scope such that a portion can hopefully still be completed within the iteration with the remainder moved to a future iteration. [Cohn, M., 2006. Agile Estimating and Planning. 1st ed. Massachusetts: Pearson Education. Page 212] [Problem Detection and Resolution]

13. C - According to Clark and Wheelwright (1993), an individual only spends 40% of his/her time on value-adding tasks when he/she is working on five concurrent tasks. Since all team members are multi-tasking on five tasks on average, this implies that 60% of the team time is being lost in "task switching" which is non-value-adding and considered a waste. [Cohn, M., 2006. Agile Estimating and Planning. 1st ed. Massachusetts: Pearson Education. Page 15] [Team Performance]

14. C - Cross-functional teams consists of team members with all the skills necessary to produce a working product. Cross-functional teams are critical because they can deliver finished work in the shortest possible time, with higher quality, without external dependencies. [Agile Practice Guide, 1st edition, Page 41] [Team Performance]

15. A - There are times when we don't have historical values and it is just not feasible to run a few iterations in order to observe velocity. In cases like these, we need to forecast velocity. However, forecasting velocity is the last resort. [Cohn, M., 2006. Agile Estimating and Planning. 1st ed. Massachusetts: Pearson Education. Page 179] [Team Performance]

16. B - The product owner is the owner of the product backlog and is ultimately accountable for the outcome of the project. At this stage, it is critical for you to review the entire backlog with the new product owner and ensure that they agree with the current ranking of stories. [Agile Practice Guide, 1st edition, Page 41] [Problem Detection and Resolution]

17. B - Story points are a unit of measure for expressing the overall size of a user story, feature, or other piece of work. [Cohn, M., 2006. Agile Estimating and Planning. 1st ed. Massachusetts: Pearson Education. Page 36] [Adaptive Planning]

18. C - In practice, the most effective Agile teams are collocated and are made 100% available for the project. [Agile Practice Guide, 1st edition, Page 39] [Value-driven Delivery]

19. C - Agile teams focus on completing and delivering user-valued features. One of the best ways to do this is to work with user stories, which are a lightweight technique for expressing product requirements. [Cohn, M., 2006. Agile Estimating and Planning. 1st ed. Massachusetts: Pearson Education. Page 25] [Adaptive Planning]

20. D - Encouraging team members to facilitate the stand-ups instead of the project manager or the leader ensures the stand-ups do not turn into status meetings, but instead are used as a time for the team to self-organize and make commitments to each other. [Agile Practice Guide, 1st edition, Page 54] [Problem Detection and Resolution]

21. A - In reality, one cannot progress without the other. Project leaders wanting to achieve agility should consider the current and future states of both of these aspects in their organization. [Agile Practice Guide, 1st edition, Page 77] [Value-driven Delivery]

22. B - It doesn't make sense to combine two planning meetings at different levels. Since iteration retrospectives and iteration planning are at the same level, these can be combined if the Agile team deems fit. [Cohn, M., 2006. Agile Estimating and Planning. 1st ed. Massachusetts: Pearson Education. Page 28] [Continuous Improvement]

23. A - Agile projects increase ROIs by releasing higher value features before the lower value features. If somehow, prioritized features can be released earlier than planned, this can further increase the ROI. [Agile Practice Guide, 1st edition, Page 61] [Value-driven Delivery]

24. B - Agile teams use prototypes, demonstrations and reviews to understand and refine project scope which enables rapid delivery of a working product. [Agile Practice Guide, 1st edition, Page 97] [Agile Principles and Mindset]

25. B - Ideal time is the amount of time that something takes when stripped of all peripheral activities. Elapsed time is the amount of time from the start to finish of an activity. It is almost always far easier and accurate to predict the duration of an event in ideal time than in elapsed time. [Cohn, M., 2006. Agile Estimating and Planning. 1st ed. Massachusetts: Pearson Education. Page 43] [Adaptive Planning]

26. A - A Fishbowl window is a long-lived video conferencing link between various locations. People start the link at the beginning of a workday and close it at the end. In this way, people can see and engage spontaneously with each other, reducing the collaboration lag otherwise inherent in the geographical separation. An effective communication tool may reduce the risk of scope creep but doesn't reduce the project scope. This might increase the direct project costs (due to the use of technology) but, at the same time, might reduce the indirect project costs (due to efficient WIP management). [Agile Practice Guide, 1st edition, Page 46] [Team Performance]

27. D - Features will be sorted based on business value once the product owner prioritizes them. The question is asking for a condition that offers the maximum flexibility to the product owner to choose any feature they think is of high value. The only thing that can prevent this are technical dependencies between features. In order for the product owner to have the most flexibility in prioritizing, features must be written so as to minimize the technical dependencies between them. [Cohn, M., 2006. Agile Estimating and Planning. 1st ed. Massachusetts: Pearson Education. Page 25] [Adaptive Planning]

28. C - In Agile projects, the project requirements are documented in the project backlog. The rest of the choices relate to traditional approaches to scope management. [Agile Practice Guide, 1st edition, Page 91] [Adaptive Planning]

29. B - One way to understand how project life cycles vary is by using a continuum ranging from predictive cycles on one end, to Agile cycles on the other end, with more iterative or incremental cycles in the middle. [Agile Practice Guide, 1st edition, Page 18] [Agile Principles and Mindset]

30. D - The Kano model gives us an approach to separate feature into three categories: must-have features, linear features, and delighters. According to Kano model, features that delight customers eventually become their basic requirements. [Cohn, M., 2006. Agile Estimating and Planning. 1st ed. Massachusetts: Pearson Education. Page 110] [Stakeholder Engagement]

31. D - The team augmentation arrangement is regarded as the most collaborative contracting approach as this embeds the supplier's services directly into the customer organization. Funding teams instead of a specific scope preserves the customer's strategic discretion on what work should actually be done. [Agile Practice Guide, 1st edition, Page 78] [Value-driven Delivery]

32. B - Cost estimates, project duration, and requirements are progressively elaborated as the project progresses. These are project attributes and not critical success factors. The critical success factor is product ownership; without attention to the highest value for the customer, the Agile team may create unwanted features. [Agile Practice Guide, 1st edition, Page 41] [Agile Principles and Mindset]

33. C - The work in progress (WIP) limits at the top of each column on a Kanban board allows the team to see how to pull work across the board. [Agile Practice Guide, 1st edition, Page 66] [Value-driven Delivery]

34. C - The scenario doesn't give enough context to determine if there are any issues with the production or quality management processes. George needs to focus on processes that are impeding the team's agility and progress. Lengthy processes that are causing bottlenecks is the best response to this question. [Agile Practice Guide, 1st edition, Page 35] [Problem Detection and Resolution]

35. D - Prioritization is critical for Agile projects. You need to educate the product owner regarding the importance of prioritization in Agile projects and help them prioritize the backlog. [Agile Practice Guide, 1st edition, Page 52] [Problem Detection and Resolution]

36. D - Conditions of satisfaction are the criteria user stories need to meet in order to mark them as complete. This is not an Agile metric. Metrics such as ideal time, story points and cycle time can be quantified. [Cohn, M., 2006. Agile Estimating and Planning. 1st ed. Massachusetts: Pearson Education. Pages 34, 246] [Value-driven Delivery]

37. D - The best answer is showing new approaches already in use as "done", those being tried as "in progress" and those still waiting to be introduced as "to do". Other choices are incorrectly mapped to categories. [Agile Practice Guide, 1st edition, Page 84] [Value-driven Delivery]

38. A - "Test at all levels" employs system-level testing for end-to-end information, unit testing for the building blocks, and, in between, determines if there is a need for integration testing. [Agile Practice Guide, 1st edition, Page 56] [Value-driven Delivery]

39. C - Agile teams prioritize stories based on their business value. Agile teams use a simple prioritization technique: the ranking of stories is done based on their relative business value. [Cohn, M., 2006. Agile Estimating and Planning. 1st ed. Massachusetts: Pearson Education. Page 36] [Value-driven Delivery]

40. D - Thought leaders in the software industry formalized the Agile movement in 2001 with the publication of the Manifesto for Agile Software Development. [Agile Practice Guide, 1st edition, Page 8] [Agile Principles and Mindset]

PMI-ACP Lite Mock Exam 2 Practice Questions

Test Name: PMI-ACP Lite Mock Exam 2
Total Questions: 40
Correct Answers Needed to Pass:
30 (75.00%)
Time Allowed: 60 Minutes

Test Description

This is a cumulative PMI-ACP Mock Exam which can be used as a benchmark for your PMI-ACP aptitude. This practice test includes questions from all exam topic areas, including sections from Agile Tools and Techniques, and all three Agile Knowledge and Skills areas.

Test Questions

1. Your project manager has called a team meeting. The meeting agenda is to obtain team's consensus on multiple items such as, what "ready" means, what "done" means, how time-box will be respected, and what work in process limits will be used. What is the project manager trying to develop?

A. Working agreement

B. Project charter

C. Iteration plan

D. Kanban board

2. A software vendor on your project is hoping to be awarded a contract providing software for another project at your company. You are not leading the other project. However, the vendor offers you tickets to an upcoming professional sports event if you will "put in a good word" for his company to the vendor selection team of the other project. What do you do?

A. Decline the tickets and notify appropriate management of the situation.

B. Accept the tickets if company policy allows it and provide a recommendation for that vendor to the other project team.

C. Fire the vendor.

D. Decline the tickets but provide a recommendation for the vendor.

3. Which of the following statements regarding planning poker is incorrect?

A. Planning poker brings together multiple expert opinions to do the estimating.

B. Cross-functional representation in the estimation team is recommended.

C. Planning poker is played by senior team representatives and the product owner.

D. A lively dialogue ensues during planning poker and estimators are called upon to justify their estimates.

4. When is the ideal time to conduct team check-ins during an iteration retrospective?

A. Somewhere during the retrospective.

B. At the end of the retrospective.

C. After reviewing the goal and agenda.

D. After welcoming the participants.

5. An Agile team measures story points without completing the actual feature or story. What is the problem with this approach?

A. Ineffective use of a Kanban board.

B. Increased response time.

C. Violation of Agile Principles.

D. Decrease of team's velocity.

6. Your organization has a standing ethics review committee, and you are a member of this committee. A complaint has been filed against a project leader for allegedly violating a number of company policies. If the allegations are proved, they would be terminated for cause. During the investigation, their boss has been uncooperative. He asked the committee investigators not to contact his employee directly and has tried to slow down the process of investigation. What should you do?

A. Check into the nature of relationship between the project leader and the boss.

B. Conduct a more detailed investigation.

C. Call the project leader for an interview.

D. Refer the issue to the appropriate management.

7. You need to understand how satisfied team members are with a particular focus area on the project. You collect this information in an iteration retrospective and now want to show this visually. What do you need to develop?

A. Fulfilment line-chart

B. Satisfaction histogram

C. Kano model

D. Normal distribution

8. In contrast to waterfall teams, Agile teams do not report a percentage of completion of each WIP item. Which of the following is the biggest problem associated with traditional status reporting?

A. Predictive measurements often do not reflect reality.

B. Projects are never completed on time.

C. Project scope can change anytime.

D. Status reporting encourages documentation which is not an Agile way to solve problems.

9. In Agile communities, people with expertise in one domain, less-developed skills in associated areas and good collaboration skills are known as:

A. U-shaped people

B. I-shaped people

C. H-shaped people

D. T-shaped people

10. Which of the following is a term used for a person who has various depths of

specialization in multiple skills required by the team?

A. I-Shaped

B. Broken Comb

C. Super Specialist

D. T-Shaped

11. You are leading an Agile team developing a factory automation system. From time to time, you rely on customer feedback to validate the functionality of the system being developed. Which Agile event is used to capture this feedback?

A. Backlog grooming

B. Retrospective

C. Spike event

D. Iteration demonstration

12. A variation between story points completed and the story points planned on a burndown chart can indicate a number of things. Which of the following is usually not a cause of such variations?

A. Duration of the iteration.

B. Effect of team members multi-tasking.

C. Effect of large stories.

D. Team members out of the office.

13. You are managing a complex project that requires a lot of knowledge work. The project's objectives are known but the scope cannot be articulated in great detail. You need to hire some experts from a consulting firm to help you with some of the knowledge work. Which of the following contracting approaches would you recommend if the customer wants to have full control over scope variation and cost without exposing the supplier to any financial risk?

A. Cost plus fixed fee arrangement with the consulting firm.

B. Team augmentation arrangement with the consulting firm.

C. Early cancellation option in a fixed-price arrangement.

D. Fixed-price arrangement with the consulting firm.

14. You have recently been hired as a senior business analyst on a complex system integration project. The chief programmer has asked you to review the project BRD prior to arranging a meeting with him. What is a BRD?

A. High level schedule of a project.

B. Collection of user stories sorted by themes.

C. Listing of all requirements for a specific project.

D. Business risk document.

15. An Agile team has a firm release date. As a result of this constraint, not all of the identified features will be developed. In such a situation, which of the following features would you recommend to be dropped from the release plan?

A. High risk and low value.

B. High risk and high value.

C. Low risk and low value.

D. Low risk and high value.

16. Recently a handful of defects have been reported on the product. Fixing these defects during the current iteration would add significant workload. What do you recommend?

A. Fixing all defects in the iteration once they are discovered.

B. Scheduling all defect repair for the next iteration.

C. Scheduling all defect repair for the last iteration.

D. Ignoring the defects until project closure.

17. During a planning poker meeting, on the second round of estimating a particular user story, four estimators give you five, five, five, and three. Which of the following is not recommended in this case?

A. Ask the low estimator if they are OK with an estimate of five.

B. Ignore the three as five has got the majority vote.

C. Ask the low estimator to explain their estimate.

D. Proceed to the third round.

18. Which of the following can be classified as one specialized form of cadence?

A. Rolling Wave Planning

B. Kanban

C. Time-boxing

D. Story estimating

19. An Agile project has a total of 700 story points and each project iteration has a fixed duration of three weeks. At the end of the 4th iteration, the team had successfully delivered 76 story points. The team was able to successfully address some improvement opportunities and during the 5th iteration the team was able to deliver an additional 24 story points. Assuming that the team will not be able to maintain its current velocity and revert back to the velocity the team was at by the end of the 4th iteration, and no more story points are added to the project, how many more weeks are required to complete the project?

A. 75 weeks

B. 90 weeks

C. 96 weeks

D. 87 weeks

20. An Agile team is currently working with the product owner in defining project requirements. Some of the features would not be developed in the near future. It was recommended to write one much larger user story for such features rather than multiple fine-grained user stories. Such stories are called:

A. Macro-stories

B. Epics

C. Micro-stories

D. Tales

21. How is a project selection decision taken based on its expected NPV value?

A. Projects with positive NPV should be rejected.

B. Projects with negative NPV should be accepted.

C. The project with the highest NPV should be selected.

D. NPV alone cannot provide any information that helps in the selection decision.

22. You are responsible for designing a new lessons learned management system for an organization. As a part of the project, you need to consult with a number of senior stakeholders and assess their needs and requirements. You then have to facilitate consensus on the system features, workflows, processes and procedures. Once the system is developed, it has to be rolled out across the organization and all employees have to be trained in effective use of the system. You have chosen to use a hybrid project life cycle. Which of the following life cycles should be adopted for the user training phase of the project?

A. Predictive

B. Iterative

C. Incremental

D. Agile

23. Your Agile team is dispersed in three different time zones. You have decided to deploy fishbowl windows at each work location. What is a fishbowl window?

A. A management report.

B. A video conferencing link.

C. An information radiator.

D. An online document management system.

24. In Scrum, who is responsible for exploring Scrum tools and techniques and select the right ones to be used by the team?

A. Product owner

B. Scrum master

C. Agile team

D. Agile coach

25. You are managing a 20-member Agile team on a complex project. You have noticed that the daily standups are not very effective. Due to the range of issues discussed, the team is not able to focus. What should you do?

A. Ask the team to take notes during the meeting.

B. Limit the number of issues discussed.

C. Divide the team into smaller teams.

D. Increase the duration of the daily standups.

26. You are managing an ecommerce-enabled website for a retailing giant. Both the project team and the client organization are happy with the clarity of the original functional and non-functional requirements set out in the contract's SOW. You have recommended the Agile project management approach to the client and they are happy with any management approach as long as they receive a working product. You and your team have a tough decision to make regarding sprint durations. A sprint duration of two weeks would add a lot of pressure on the team as complex requirements will be tough to build in a single sprint. A sprint duration of six weeks would make the project less Agile but the project might get finished early as the customer won't get to see many prototypes. What sprint size should be selected?

A. Six weeks should be selected since the project would get finished early and satisfy the customer.

B. Two weeks should be selected since Agile Manifesto mandates frequent delivery of working software.

C. A sprint size needs to be determined that maximizes customer value and satisfaction.

D. Four weeks should be selected as that is the average of two numbers.

27. When new stories are added throughout the project, the typical line-based burndown chart doesn't reflect the true team's performance. In such cases, the use of a bar chart is recommended and all scope additions are shown below the horizontal axis. When using such a chart, which of the following is NOT recommended:

A. When work is removed, the bottom is raised.

B. Any time work is completed, the top is raised.

C. When work is re-estimated, the top is moved up or down.

D. When new work is added, the bottom is lowered.

28. Which of the following is an Agile technique that regularly checks the effectiveness of the quality process, looks for the root cause of issues, and suggest trials of new approaches to improve quality?

A. User stories

B. Sprints

C. Retrospectives

D. Backlog

29. What are the typical five W's on a fishbone diagram?

A. What, Who, When, Where, and Why

B. Work, Workflows, Waste, Weather, and When

C. Defects, Overproduction, Transportation, Waiting, and Inventory

D. Plan, Do, Check, Act and Confirm

30. You are forming the first Agile team in your company that will deliver a complex human resources management system. Which of the following should be your top most challenge?

A. Establishing efficient communication and collaboration tools for a geographically dispersed team.

B. Prioritizing system features based on strategic value.

C. Building a foundational trust, a safe work environment and an Agile Mindset.

D. Acquire a cross-functional team that is 100% dedicated to the project.

31. Which of the following actions is NOT recommended when planning a large project with multiple Agile teams?

A. Adding a detail to user stories as soon as possible.

B. Look-ahead planning

C. Incorporating feeding buffers into the plan.

D. Allowing each team to establish its own basis of estimates.

32. Agile approaches do not encourage working simultaneously on multiple tasks. In an Agile community, multi-tasking is considered to exact a horrible toll on productivity. According to Clark and Wheelwright, which of the following statements is correct?

A. Productivity increases as the number of concurrent assigned tasks decreases until the optimal point is reached when an individual only performs a single task.

B. 80% efficiency is achieved when an individual doesn't multi-task.

C. 20% or more time is wasted when an individual multi-tasks.

D. There is no direct relationship between productivity and the number of concurrent tasks.

33. You are leading a complex Agile project that is expected to last two years. You have a huge list of features to be prioritized. If you have a large number of stakeholders, which of the following techniques should you use to prioritize these features?

A. Process analysis

B. Meetings

C. Questionnaires

D. Kanban board

34. Which of the following methodology involves a system design and validation practice that uses test-first principles and English-like scripts?

A. Behavior-Driven Development (BDD)

B. Kanban method

C. Agile Unified Process

D. Acceptance Test-Driven Development (ATDD)

35. The amount of time something takes to go from the start of a process to the end of the process is known as:

A. Takt time

B. Cycle time

C. Lag time

D. Lead time

36. Which of the following correctly describes the Five Whys technique?

A. The team determines five mutually exclusive events that can cause a situation.

B. The team determines five solutions to a given problem.

C. The team asks "Why?" five times to get beyond habitual thinking.

D. The team designs five experiments to reduce the project risk.

37. Unlike financial measures such as IRR and NPV, the primary disadvantage to the payback period is that it fails to take into account the time value of money. Which of the following financial measures eliminates this drawback of the payback period calculation?

A. Time-valued Payback Period.

B. Adjusted Payback Period.

C. Modified Payback Period.

D. Discounted Payback Period.

38. An Agile team has performed several Agile projects in the past and has been very consistent with their estimating. On their last project, the team was able to achieve a velocity of 30 story points per iteration, which was about 10% higher than their velocity on their second-to-last project. Recently the team has been assigned a new project that involves some state-of-the-art technology. If the team has no experience in this technology, what would be your team's velocity estimate for this project?

A. 33 story points per iteration

B. Team's velocity cannot be determined until they complete a few iterations.

C. 30 story points per iteration

D. 27 story points per iteration

39. Agile teams identify project risks and determine respective mitigation actions during which of the following events?

A. Daily standups and retrospectives

B. Daily standups, retrospectives and demonstrations.

C. Retrospectives

D. Daily standups

40. You are about to complete the first iteration of your project. You want to invite the product owner and a couple of other key stakeholders to obtain their feedback on your current progress. Which of the following Agile events should you schedule?

A. Retrospective

B. Demonstration

C. Planning poker

D. Spike

PMI-ACP Lite Mock Exam 2 Answer Key and Explanations

1. A - The project manager is trying to develop a team working agreement. This typically includes items such as, what "ready" means, what "done" means, how time-box will be respected, and what work in process limits will be used. [Agile Practice Guide, 1st edition, Page 50] [Team Performance]

2. A - Do not accept the tickets that are offered and notify the appropriate management of the situation. By offering an incentive to you to help the vendor win more business from your company, the vendor has effectively offered a bribe. PMI's Code of Ethics prohibits Agile practitioners from accepting bribes, and further requires them to notify the appropriate management of any unethical conduct. [PMI Code of Ethics and Professional Conduct] [Stakeholder Engagement]

3. C - Planning poker is played by the entire team and not just by the senior team members. The rest of the statements are correct. [Cohn, M., 2006. Agile Estimating and Planning. 1st ed. Massachusetts: Pearson Education. Pages 58, 59] [Adaptive Planning]

4. C - After welcoming the participants and reviewing the goal and agenda, the retrospective leader asks one brief question for the check-ins and each person answers in round-robin fashion. [Derby, E. and Larsen, D., 2006. Agile Retrospectives: Making Good Teams Great. 1st ed. Texas: Pragmatic Bookshelf, Page 41] [Continuous Improvement]

5. C - Measuring story points is not the same as measuring completed stories or features. Some teams attempt to measure story points without completing the actual feature or story. When teams measure only story points, they measure capacity not finished work which violates the Agile Principle of "the primary measure of progress is working software". [Agile Practice Guide, 1st edition, Page 66] [Agile Principles and Mindset]

6. D - Escalate the issue to the appropriate management. PMI requires Agile practitioners to report known instances of wrong doing to the appropriate management. However, the actions that are taken by the organization investigating the complaint must be in line with that organization's own policies. Only the management of the organization can interpret or apply those rules. [PMI Code of Ethics and Professional Conduct] [Stakeholder Engagement]

7. B - The correct response is Satisfaction Histogram. Such histograms highlight how satisfied team members are with a focus area and provide a visual picture of the current status in the area to help the team have deeper discussions and analysis. [Derby, E. and Larsen, D., 2006. Agile Retrospectives: Making Good Teams Great. 1st ed. Texas: Pragmatic Bookshelf, Page 66] [Continuous Improvement]

8. A - The problem with predictive measurements is that they often do not reflect reality. It often happens that a project status light is green up until the last month when the release is due; this is sometimes referred to as a watermelon project (green on the outside, red on the inside). [Agile Practice Guide, 1st edition, Page 60] [Team Performance]

9. D - In Agile communities, people with expertise in one domain, less-developed skills in associated areas and good collaboration skills are known as T-shaped people. [Agile Practice Guide, 1st edition, Page 42] [Value-driven Delivery]

10. B - Broken Comb is a person who has various depths of specialization in multiple skills required by the team. [Agile Practice Guide, 1st edition, Page 150] [Value-driven Delivery]

11. D - The first part of delivery is a demonstration. Demonstrations or reviews are a necessary part of the Agile project flow. Agile teams use prototypes, demonstrations and reviews to understand and refine project scope which enables rapid delivery of a working product. [Agile Practice Guide, 1st edition, Page 57] [Value-driven Delivery]

12. A - Duration of the iteration should not have any effect on the variation as iterations with both shorter and longer iterations can face variations. Variations can occur due to either underestimation or waste. Multi-tasking, and team unavailability can cause waste. Large and complex stories can be underestimated. [Agile Practice Guide, 1st edition, Page 63] [Team Performance]

13. B - The fixed-price arrangement, with or without the early cancellation option will introduce financial risk for the supplier. The cost plus arrangement will introduce financial risk for the customer. A team augmentation arrangement with the consulting firm will be the most collaborative contracting approach in this case. [Agile Practice Guide, 1st edition, Page 78] [Value-driven Delivery]

14. C - A Business Requirement Document (BRD) lists all requirements for a specific project. [Agile Practice Guide, 1st edition, Page 150] [Adaptive Planning]

15. A - High value features cannot be dropped, this eliminates two of the choices. For the low value ones, the low risk ones are easier to develop. In this situation, the high risk and low value stories can be dropped from the release plan. [Cohn, M., 2006. Agile Estimating and Planning. 1st ed. Massachusetts: Pearson Education. Page 80] [Problem Detection and Resolution]

16. A - An Agile team has the goal of fixing all defects in the iteration once they are discovered. [Cohn, M., 2006. Agile Estimating and Planning. 1st ed. Massachusetts: Pearson Education. Page 152] [Problem Detection and Resolution]

17. B - Ignoring a minority vote is not recommended. The low estimator can be asked to explain their estimate. They can be asked if they are OK with an estimate of five or a third round can be conducted. [Cohn, M., 2006. Agile Estimating and Planning. 1st ed. Massachusetts: Pearson Education. Page 57] [Adaptive Planning]

18. C - Cadence means rhythm of execution. Time-boxing is one specialized form of cadence. The time box of a sprint helps to create a regular cadence for the development team, management team, customer, etc. This rhythm helps to keep everyone in sync and keep the process moving. [Agile Practice Guide, 1st edition, Page 151] [Adaptive Planning]

19. C - Velocity = average story points per iteration. At the end of the 4th iteration, the team delivered 76 story points in total. The velocity at the end of the 4th iteration was 76/4 = 19 story points per iteration on average. At the end of the 5th iteration, the team delivered 100 story points in total (76+24). The current velocity is 100/5 = 20 story points per iteration on average. Since 600 story points are remaining (700 – 100), at the 4th iteration velocity of 19 stories per iteration, the team would require additional 32 (31.58) iterations to complete the project. Since each iteration duration is three weeks, the team need additional 96 weeks (32 x 3) to complete the project. [Agile Practice Guide, 1st edition, Page 61] [Team Performance]

20. B - Larger user stories are known as epics. [Cohn, M., 2006. Agile Estimating and Planning. 1st ed. Massachusetts: Pearson Education. Page 53] [Adaptive Planning]

21. C - The project with the highest NPV should be selected. [Cohn, M., 2006. Agile Estimating and Planning. 1st ed. Massachusetts: Pearson Education. Page 100] [Value-driven Delivery]

22. A - Once the system is successfully designed and built, user training may be an extensive task but this can well be planned in advance. Predictive life cycle should be the most structured approach for this phase of the project. [Agile Practice Guide, 1st edition, Page 26] [Agile Principles and Mindset]

23. B - A fishbowl window is a long-lived video conferencing link between two or more locations. [Agile Practice Guide, 1st edition, Page 46] [Team Performance]

24. B - Scrum master is responsible for identifying the most suitable Scrum tools and techniques to be used on the project. On the other hand, the Agile team is responsible to select the right tools and techniques to build the product. [Agile Practice Guide, 1st edition, Page 101] [Value-driven Delivery]

25. C - Agile teams are usually small teams. It is advisable to divide the bigger team into smaller Agile teams and conduct separate daily standups. If the teams are divided by their specialization, they will be able to focus more. [Cohn, M., 2006. Agile Estimating and Planning. 1st ed. Massachusetts: Pearson Education. Page 57] [Problem Detection and Resolution]

26. C - The highest priority is to satisfy the customer through early and continuous delivery of valuable software. A sprint size needs to be determined that maximizes customer value and satisfaction. More information would be required to determine the best duration. [Agile Practice Guide, 1st edition, Page 9] [Value-driven Delivery]

27. B - Anytime work is completed, the top is lowered (not raised). The rest of the choices are correct. [Cohn, M., 2006. Agile Estimating and Planning. 1st ed. Massachusetts: Pearson Education. Page 216] [Team Performance]

28. C - Recurring retrospectives regularly check on the effectiveness of the quality process. They look for the root cause of issues then suggest trials of new approaches to improve quality. [Derby, E. and Larsen, D., 2006. Agile Retrospectives: Making Good Teams Great. 1st ed. Texas: Pragmatic Bookshelf, Page xvii] [Continuous Improvement]

29. A - The typical five W's on a fishbone diagram are: what, who, when, where, and why. [Derby, E. and Larsen, D., 2006. Agile Retrospectives: Making Good Teams Great. 1st ed. Texas: Pragmatic Bookshelf, Page 87] [Continuous Improvement]

30. C - The top most challenge for you is to build a foundational trust, a safe work environment and an Agile Mindset – all other challenges and risks can be mitigated. [Agile Practice Guide, 1st edition, Page 47] [Agile Principles and Mindset]

31. D - When working with multiple teams, it is important to establish a common basis of estimates rather than allowing each team to work out their own basis of estimates. Estimates have to be consistent throughout the project. [Cohn, M., 2006. Agile Estimating and Planning. 1st ed. Massachusetts: Pearson Education. Page 199] [Adaptive Planning]

32. C - Multi-tasking exacts a horrible toll on productivity. Clark and Wheelwright (1993) studied the effect of multi-tasking and found that the time an individual spends on value-adding work drops rapidly when the individual is working on more than two tasks. With two value-adding tasks, if a team member becomes blocked on one task, he/she can switch to the other task. Productivity increases as the number of concurrent assigned tasks decreases until the optimal point is reached (80% productivity) when an individual only performs two independent value-adding tasks. (Note that observed productivity while performing a single task is only 70%.) [Cohn, M., 2006. Agile Estimating and Planning. 1st ed. Massachusetts: Pearson Education. Page 15] [Team Performance]

33. C - A questionnaire is the right tool to be used if you have a large population base and you need to quickly identify which features are valued more than the others. [Cohn, M., 2006. Agile Estimating and Planning. 1st ed. Massachusetts: Pearson Education. Page 112] [Problem Detection and Resolution]

34. A - Behavior-Driven Development (BDD) involves a system design and validation practice that uses test-first principles and English-like scripts. [Agile Practice Guide, 1st edition, Page 150] [Value-driven Delivery]

35. B - The amount of time something takes to go from the start of a process to the end of the process is known as cycle time. For Agile stories, it is the time taken by a story in the "ready" state to move to the "complete" state. [Cohn, M., 2006. Agile Estimating and Planning. 1st ed. Massachusetts: Pearson Education. Page 246] [Adaptive Planning]

36. C - The Five Whys technique is used to discover underlying conditions that contribute to an issue. Team members work in pairs or small groups to look at issues. They ask "Why?" five times to get beyond habitual thinking. [Derby, E. and Larsen, D., 2006. Agile Retrospectives: Making Good Teams Great. 1st ed. Texas: Pragmatic Bookshelf, Page 85] [Continuous Improvement]

37. D - The discounted payback period method removes the primary disadvantage of the payback period method by applying appropriate discount factors to each item in the cash flow stream. All other choices are made-up terms. [Cohn, M., 2006. Agile Estimating and Planning. 1st ed. Massachusetts: Pearson Education. Page 105] [Value-driven Delivery]

38. B - If the technology or business domain has changed dramatically, it may not be appropriate to use a team's past velocity to estimate the team's velocity on the new project. [Cohn, M., 2006. Agile Estimating and Planning. 1st ed. Massachusetts: Pearson Education. Page 134] [Team Performance]

39. B - Risks can be identified at any time: daily standups, retrospectives and/or demonstrations. [Cohn, M., 2006. Agile Estimating and Planning. 1st ed. Massachusetts: Pearson Education. Page 5] [Team Performance]

40. B - In iteration-based Agile, the team demonstrates all completed work items at the end of the iteration. [Agile Practice Guide, 1st edition, Page 55] [Value-driven Delivery]

PMI-ACP Knowledge Area Quiz: Team Performance Practice Questions

Test Name: Knowledge Area Test: Communications
Total Questions: 15
Correct Answers Needed to Pass: 11 (73.33%)
Time Allowed: 25 Minutes

Test Description

This practice quiz specifically targets your knowledge of the Communications exam topic area.

Test Questions

1. Which of the following statements is true for Agile projects?

   A. Earned value management is tailored to fit Agile projects.

   B. Agile favors empirical and value-based measurements.

   C. Agile values predictive measurements.

   D. Project percentage of completion is the critical success factor for Agile projects.

2. An Agile project has a total of 700 story points and each project iteration has a fixed duration of three weeks. At the end of the 4th iteration, the team had successfully delivered 76 story points. The team was able to successfully address some improvement opportunities and during the 5th iteration the team was able to deliver an additional 24 story points. Assuming that the team maintains its current velocity and no more story points are added to the project, how many more weeks are required to complete the project?

   A. 96 weeks

   B. 75 weeks

   C. 90 weeks

   D. 87 weeks

3. An Agile team is currently working on a system development project for a major local retailer. Recently a couple of programmers have been hired and assigned on this project. How should the addition of new team members affect the number of story points for the next iteration?

   A. The story points should be increased.

   B. The story points should not be changed.

   C. The story points should be decreased.

   D. The team should reevaluate its capacity and determine the number of story points.

4. Which of the following statements regarding multi-tasking is incorrect?

   A. It is optimal to assign two concurrent tasks to each team member.

   B. Multi-tasking, beyond two concurrent tasks exacts a horrible toll on productivity.

   C. Multi-tasking extends the completion date of work and leaves work in process longer.

D. Multi-tasking should always be avoided and no team member should work on more than one task at a time.

5. Which of the following conditions is not healthy for Agile teams?

A. Project team is not collocated.

B. Product owner attends daily standups.

C. Project team consists of 20 or more members.

D. Project manager schedules, assigns and tracks project tasks.

6. The first iteration on your project completed the first two stories of the project. Each story had three points so the team's velocity after the first iteration was six story points. The team is not happy with the value and asks you to double the story points so that the overall velocity becomes 12 story points. What should be your response?

A. The absolute value of story points does not matter as long as all stories were relatively estimated.

B. You cannot increase story points for completed features.

C. Double the story points of all stories on the project.

D. Increase the story points as the Agile team has demanded.

7. You are leading an Agile project heading into its third sprint. The third sprint contains 15 stories with an average story size of 3 points. The observed velocities for the first and second sprints were 30 and 35 story points respectively. Based on this information, which of the following statements is correct?

A. The expected velocity for the third sprint is 45 story points.

B. The expected velocity for the third sprint is 30 story points.

C. The expected velocity for the third sprint is 32.5 story points.

D. The expected velocity for the third sprint is 35 story points.

8. Which of the following conditions promises the fastest possible team throughput?

A. There are no change requests on the project.

B. All of the user stories have been identified at the start of the project.

C. Team is 100% dedicated to the project.

D. The project's budget is uncapped.

9. Your organization has recently adopted Agile practices and all new internal projects are being managed using Agile methods. If you want to compare the performance of three projects, which of the following measures cannot be used?

A. Velocity

B. SPI & CPI

C. Actual cost

D. Percent-completion

10. You are leading an Agile team developing a new operating system of a handheld device. During the integration testing you realize that the system has some performance issues. How would you improve the code without altering the functionality of the operating system?

A. Refactoring

B. Kanban

C. Pair Working

D. Scrum of Scrums

11. Which of the following is not considered a standup anti-pattern?

A. Reporting project status during standups.

B. Adding issues to a parking lot.

C. Solving problems during standups.

D. Scrum master assigning project tasks to team.

12. An Agile team was not able to complete any stories during the fourth iteration. How would this be reflected on a burndown chart?

A. The burndown chart will fall down to zero story points.

B. The slope of the burndown chart will become negative.

C. The slope of the burndown chart will become positive.

D. The burndown for the iteration will remain flat at the number of story points remaining at the start of the iteration.

13. During which of the following conditions does a team not need a formal chartering process?

A. As long as the team has worked with each other in the past.

B. As long as the team understands how to work together on this project.

C. If it has been a while since the team has transitioned from traditional approaches.

D. As long as the project is managed using Agile approaches.

14. Moving stories from the "ready" state to the "work in process" state such that 100% resource utilization is achieved will most likely result in:

A. Increased velocity for the iteration.

B. Increased costs.

C. Reduced cycle time.

D. Reduced team's throughput.

15. If two of the senior programmers in your team are not collocated and you want to reap the benefits of pair-programming, which of the following techniques can help you obtain some of those benefits?

A. Ask the partners to call each other before developing any new module.

B. Email automatic screen-shot to the two partners at every half an hour.

C. Set up remote pairing

D. Schedule hourly status meeting

PMI-ACP Knowledge Area Quiz: Team Performance Answer Key and Explanations

1. B - Agile favors empirical and value-based measurements instead of predictive measurements such as POC and earned value management techniques. Agile measures what the team delivers, not what the team predicts it will deliver. [Agile Practice Guide, 1st edition, Page 61] [Team Performance]

2. C - Velocity = average story points per iteration. At the end of the 4th iteration, the team delivered 76 story points in total. The velocity at the end of the 4th iteration was 76/4 = 19 story points per iteration on average. At the end of the 5th iteration, the team delivered 100 story points in total (76+24). The current velocity is 100/5 = 20 story points per iteration on average. Since 600 story points are remaining (700 – 100), at the current velocity of 20 stories per iteration, the team would require an additional 30 iterations to complete the project. Since each iteration duration is three weeks, the team needs an additional 90 weeks (30 x 3) to complete the project. [Agile Practice Guide, 1st edition, Page 61] [Team Performance]

3. D - Each team has its own capacity. When a team uses story points, the number of story points a team can complete in a given time is unique to that team. Addition of the new team members should affect the capacity and the number of story points should be reevaluated by the team in line with nature and type of work remaining on the project. [Agile Practice Guide, 1st edition, Page 66] [Team Performance]

4. D - Multi-tasking exacts a horrible toll on productivity. Clark and Wheelwright (1993) studied the effect of multi-tasking and found that the time an individual spends on value-adding work drops rapidly when the individual is working on more than two tasks. With two value-adding tasks, if a team member becomes blocked on one task, he/she can switch to the other task. It is recommended that you assign tasks in a way that each team member has "two independent tasks" to perform at any given point in time. [Cohn, M., 2006. Agile Estimating and Planning. 1st ed. Massachusetts: Pearson Education. Pages 15, 16] [Team Performance]

5. D - It is desirable that an Agile team is small and collocated. However complex projects might require bigger than ideal team size and geographical distribution of team members. Various Agile techniques can be used to help the team in such situations. Daily standups are team events and product owner's participation is not required; however the participation doesn't harm the team. Agile team are expected to be self-organizing units; command and control by a project manager is not considered healthy for an Agile team. [Agile Practice Guide, 1st edition, Page 34] [Team Performance]

6. A - The absolute value of story points does not matter as long as all stories were relatively estimated. If you increase the story points to show increased velocity, you would also have to increase the story points for all user stories proportionally, which will not add any value. For example, in this case the velocity might get doubled, but so will be the total story points on the project, but the number of iterations and required effort will not change. [Cohn, M., 2006. Agile Estimating and Planning. 1st ed.

Massachusetts: Pearson Education. Page 62] [Team Performance]

7. A - Since the team has planned to complete 45 story points in the third iteration (i.e. 15 x 3), the team is expecting to achieve a velocity of 45 story points in the third iteration. The team would have already considered their past performance when planning for the next sprint and the historic information provided is irrelevant if the sprint has already been planned. [Agile Practice Guide, 1st edition, Page 61] [Team Performance]

8. C - Multi-tasking slows the progress of the entire team, because team members waste time context switching and/or waiting for each other to finish other work. When people are 100% dedicated to the team, the team has the fastest possible throughput. [Agile Practice Guide, 1st edition, Page 44] [Team Performance]

9. A - Any measure can be used to compare performance as long as the measure is used consistently on all projects. There is no issue with actual cost as that will be absolute values. Percent-completion, regardless of how that is measured, can be used for comparison; i.e., which project is near completion, etc. SPI and CPI are ratios and can be used for comparison. However, velocity is relative. Velocity is measured as story points delivered per iteration on average. Since there is no universal measure for story points and different teams measure user stories differently, similar effort user stories can have different story points on two projects. Neither story points nor velocity can be used for comparison. [Cohn, M., 2006. Agile Estimating and Planning. 1st ed. Massachusetts: Pearson Education. Page 36] [Team Performance]

10. A - Refactoring is a product quality technique whereby the design of a product is improved by enhancing its maintainability and other desired attributes without altering its expected behavior. [Agile Practice Guide, 1st edition, Page 153] [Team Performance]

11. B - Reporting project status during standups, solving problems during standups, and task assignments by the scrum master are all examples of standup anti-patterns. However, parking issues to a parking lot is an acceptable practice. [Agile Practice Guide, 1st edition, Page 54] [Team Performance]

12. D - A burndown chart shows a team's progress by showing the number of story points remaining in the project. The vertical axis shows the number of story points remaining and the iterations are shown across the horizontal axis. The linear trend of a burndown chart is downward sloping. However, if no story points are delivered during a particular iteration, the burndown chart will remain flat for that iteration. [Cohn, M., 2006. Agile Estimating and Planning. 1st ed. Massachusetts: Pearson Education. Page 213] [Team Performance]

13. B - Every project needs a project charter so the project team knows why this project matters, where the team is headed and what the project objective is. Teams do not need a formal process for chartering as long as the team understands how to work together. [Agile Practice Guide, 1st edition, Pages 49, 50] [Team Performance]

14. D - Achieving a high level of resource utilization on the project rather than maintaining sufficient slack to cope with the inherent variability in typical project tasks reduces a team's productivity. Loading everyone to 100% of capacity has the same effect as loading a highway to 100% of capacity; no one can make any forward progress. [Cohn, M., 2006. Agile Estimating and Planning. 1st ed. Massachusetts: Pearson Education. Page 16] [Team Performance]

15. C - Setup remote pairing by using virtual conferencing tools to share screens, including voice and video link. As long as the time zone differences are accounted for, this may prove almost as effective as face-to-face pairing. [Agile Practice Guide, 1st edition, Page 46] [Team Performance]

PMI-ACP Lite Mock Exam 3 Practice Questions

Test Name: PMI-ACP Lite Mock Exam 3
Total Questions: 40
Correct Answers Needed to Pass:
30 (75.00%)
Time Allowed: 60 Minutes

Test Description

This is a cumulative PMI-ACP Mock Exam which can be used as a benchmark for your PMI-ACP aptitude. This practice test includes questions from all exam topic areas, including sections from Agile Tools and Techniques, and all three Agile Knowledge and Skills areas.

Test Questions

1. The product design your project team developed was extremely well-received by the customer. There were two key contributors to this design who went above and beyond the call of duty. The customer calls you to tell you how pleased he is with the design. What do you tell him?

A. Tell the customer you worked very hard on the design, and you are happy he is pleased.

B. Thank the customer.

C. Ask to negotiate a bonus payment.

D. Thank him on behalf of the team and call out the contributions two of the team members made.

2. You have recently been asked to design and build a "complex" project that is supposed to somehow reduce the production costs by 20% or more. Although the project's vision is clear, the project requirements are not. You and team need to understand the high level project requirements to start project work. How should you proceed?

A. Develop a project charter followed by a team charter.

B. Develop a team charter followed by a project charter.

C. Build a product roadmap using user story mapping and impact mapping.

D. Groom the product backlog and select the high-value requirements.

3. Which of the following statements regarding the Net Present Value (NPV) is incorrect?

A. NPV calculations take the time value of money into consideration.

B. NPV is the ideal financial benefit measurement method.

C. NPV values are highly dependent on the magnitude of the project.

D. Projects with negative NPV values do not yield any financial benefit.

4. Which of the following measures determines the interest rate of a cash flow stream?

A. ROI

B. DCF

C. NPV

D. IRR

5. On Agile projects, the product backlog serves as the prime documentation of a project's scope. A Scope Statement, on the other hand, documents the project's scope on predictive traditional projects. The product backlog, in contrast to scope statements on traditional projects, is considered to be more:

A. Dynamic and complete

B. Static and complete

C. Dynamic and incomplete

D. Static and incomplete

6. You have recently taken charge of an Agile project. While observing the release burndown chart you saw a burnup during the third iteration of the project. What can be the possible cause of this?

A. New scope has been added to the project.

B. The observed velocity is less than the expected velocity.

C. This is a plotting error as burndown charts always go downwards.

D. Epics were decomposed into smaller stories but the overall story points didn't increase.

7. You have analyzed all the themes of your project and have assigned each one of them to one of the four quadrants of a risk-value matrix that has a risk rating (high and low) on the y-axis, and a business value rating (high and low) on the x-axis. What is the recommend approach to be taken for the themes that fell under the "Low Risk" and "High Value" quadrant?

A. Do first

B. Avoid

C. Do second

D. Do last

8. You are conducting an iteration demonstration to a group of stakeholders when the CFO expresses their displeasure over the missing reporting module. You explain to the CFO why the module was rescheduled to be developed in a later iteration. How could you have better managed this?

A. By including a prototype of the module in the demonstration.

B. By deferring the demonstration until the module was complete.

C. By taking the CFO in confidence when the team took the rescheduling decision.

D. By not rescheduling the module development.

9. Which of the following statement is incorrect regarding Agile approaches:

A. Agile is a blanket term for a unique approach.

B. Agile is based on a values driven mindset.

C. Lean is a superset of Agile.

D. Agile includes many approaches such as Scrum, XP, FDD, etc.

10. A task included in an iteration plan that is being undertaken specifically to gain knowledge or answer a question is known as:

A. Workaround

B. Epic

C. Spike

D. Sprint

11. Agile teams usually limit their estimation to the next few week because:

A. Planning for shorter time periods eliminates multi-tasking.

B. Planning for shorter time periods is more accurate.

C. Planning for shorter time periods is easier.

D. Planning for shorter time periods results in higher ROI.

12. Which of the following are the six primary roles on a Feature-Driven Development project?

A. Project manager, project coordinator, developer, project sponsor, client and user.

B. Project manager, chief architect, development manager, chief programmer, class owner and domain expert.

C. Business analyst, project manager, Agile team, Scrum master, and product owner.

D. Agile coach, servant-leader, Scrum master, development team, and testing team.

13. In Agile settings, what is the ideal frequency for conducting product demonstrations?

A. The ideal frequency for conducting product demonstrations is three weeks.

B. The ideal frequency for conducting product demonstrations is two weeks.

C. The ideal frequency for conducting product demonstrations is one week.

D. There is no ideal frequency, but rather a general guideline of conducting demonstrations at least once every two weeks.

14. The "Triple Nickels" activity is designed to:

A. Reduce project risk.

B. Generate ideas for actions or recommendations.

C. Prioritize and schedule ideas.

D. Analyze ideas to identify opportunities.

15. The Kanban method is less prescriptive than some Agile approaches and less disruptive to being implemented. Organizations can begin applying the Kanban method with relative ease. A Kanban board is a:

A. Low-tech, low-touch technology.

B. Low-tech, high-touch technology.

C. High-tech, high-touch technology.

D. High-tech, low-touch technology.

16. Which of the following events might call for early termination of a sprint in an iteration-based Agile project?

A. A significant number of new features have been requested.

B. The features currently being developed are no longer required.

C. A project is no longer required.

D. A significant number of change request against release features have been lodged.

17. Which of the following Agile techniques help in managing the cost of quality and changes on a project?

A. Backlog grooming

B. Small batch size

C. Kanban board

D. Collocation

18. Return on investment (ROI) is commonly used to measure the financial benefits of an investment. Economists and financial analysts, especially for long-term investments, generally do not prefer this method because:

A. The formula doesn't factor in the demand and supply rule.

B. The formula doesn't factor in the behavioral aspects of the investors.

C. The formula doesn't factor in the time value of money.

D. The formula doesn't factor in the risk associated with the investment.

19. Once you collect all product requirements, you applied the MoSCoW method. Which of the following MoSCoW results will help you define a minimum viable product (MVP)?

A. "Must have" and "Should have"

B. "Must have", "Should have", "Could have", and "Won't have"

C. "Must have"

D. "Must have", "Should have", and "Could have"

20. Which of the following statements doesn't correctly depict Agile values?

A. Quality must be designed.

B. Quality must be planned.

C. Quality must be inspected-in.

D. Quality must be built-in.

21. Lucy is the lead programmer on your project. She wasn't successful in getting selected for another project that involved some state-of-the-art technology. You feel that, due to this reason, she hasn't been pulling her weight. Which ESVP role closely relates to her behavior?

A. Vacationers

B. Explorers

C. Shoppers

D. Prisoners

22. Which of the following Agile techniques can be used in conjunction with a timeline to gather data about feelings in a longer iteration, release, or project retrospective?

A. Color Code Dots

B. Sticky Notes

C. Kanban

D. Six Sigma

23. A key influence on cycle time is the variability in the time it takes to develop a new feature. One of the best ways to reduce variability is to:

A. Work with reasonable small and similarly-sized stories.

B. Cycle time variability is inevitable and cannot be reduced.

C. Grouping relates stories into themes and prioritizing based on theme desirability.

D. Decomposing stories into tasks and estimating tasks instead of estimating stories.

24. Which of the following would you avoid during retrospectives?

A. Identifying small improvements.

B. Identifying major breakthroughs.

C. Learning from previous work.

D. Blame game.

25. If $250,000 is invested at 8% with annual compounding. How much will this money be worth in 15 years?

A. 78810

B. 1000000

C. 793042

D. 550000

26. You are leading an XP project. The analytics expert is of the view that he should single-handedly develop the analytics module since nobody else on the team has the subject matter knowledge. How should you react?

A. Request the expert to train another person on the team.

B. Encourage using a pair programming approach.

C. Hire another analytics expert on the team.

D. Acknowledge the dedication of the analytics expert.

27. Which of the following statements regarding iteration planning is correct?

A. An Agile project can do without iteration plans if a detailed release plan has been developed.

B. The release plan extends the iteration plan by including more detailed cost and schedule estimates.

C. The primary purpose of iteration planning is to refine suppositions made in the more coarse-grained release plan.

D. While the release plan is focused on the project management processes, the iteration plan is more focused on the product development.

28. You are attending a retrospective as the team's servant-leader. What is your responsibility during this event?

A. Ensure that the meeting ends with a workable iteration plan.

B. Observe the team identifying improvement opportunities and create action plans.

C. Ensure that the meeting ends with a workable release plan.

D. Participate in identifying improvement opportunities and creating action plans.

29. How do Agile approaches produce a more valuable product without formal change control procedures?

A. By relying on the Agile teams to deliver a higher quality product.

B. By establishing self-managed teams who are capable of making changes themselves.

C. By delivering in increments and incorporating feedback into future work.

D. By relying on the Agile coach to ensure the product meets all quality standards.

30. Which of the following is the best strategy for forming an Agile team?

A. Team of specialists

B. Team of generalists

C. Team of versatilists

D. Mixed team of generalists and specialists

31. What is the "Payback Period"?

A. The amount of time it takes for the annual revenues to equal annual expenses.

B. The amount of time it takes the project's interest rate to reach MRR.

C. The day a project start to recover and yield a profit.

D. The amount of time required to earn back the initial investment.

32. On your project, you are not required to meet a precise deadline with a precise set of delivered functionality. Instead, you are required to deliver a high-quality software as fast as possible over a sustained period. How should you add buffers to your project?

A. Don't add any buffers.

B. Add feature buffers.

C. Add schedule buffers.

D. Add both the feature and schedule buffers.

33. What is Hoshin Kanri?

A. A strategy or policy deployment method.

B. Visual feedback system.

C. A philosophy that reminds us to get out of our offices and spend time on the plant floor.

D. Part of the manufacturing process limiting the overall throughput.

34. In projects following Scrum framework, who is responsible for ensuring the Scrum process is upheld and works to ensure the Scrum team adheres to the practices and rules?

A. Product owner

B. Scrum master

C. Development team

D. Business analyst

35. Which of the following Agile techniques requires that multiple team members focus simultaneously and coordinate their contributions on a particular work item?

A. Kanban

B. Mobbing

C. Bullying

D. Mura

36. You are leading an Agile project. A big number of features need to be developed and due to the uncertainty involved the effort level required to develop each feature cannot be reliably estimated. If all of the identified features have to be developed, which of the following techniques can protect the on-time completion of the overall project?

A. Schedule buffer

B. Cycle time

C. Feature buffer

D. Ideal time

37. Which of the following is the correct way of assigning story points to user stories in a product backlog?

A. Sort the user stories by descending order of effort required and assign sequential story points from the selected range.

B. Sort the user stories by ascending order of effort required and assign sequential story points from the selected range.

C. Select a medium-sized story and assign it a number somewhere in the middle of the range you expect to use. For the rest of the stories, assign relative values from the range.

D. Calculate the effort required in person-hours for each user story and map that to the selected range of story points.

38. Which of the following is a critical consideration for Agile teams?

A. Eliminating the need for servant-leadership.

B. Using correct Agile lexicon.

C. Planning on following the "perfect" Agile process.

D. Tailoring Agile processes to ensure positive outcomes.

39. Kanban board are used by Agile teams to manage WIP. For what is WIP an abbreviation?

A. Work inventory plan.

B. Work in progress.

C. Work input parameter.

D. Work integrating people.

40. You are leading an Agile project that will introduce a disruptive technology to the market. The team and the product owner have brainstormed together to define a huge list of features. These features were then classified according to the Kano model. If the project budget and duration are critical considerations, which of the following approaches is NOT advisable?

A. Developing as many linear features as possible.

B. Developing at least a few delighters.

C. Developing all of the must-have features.

D. Developing all of the identified features.

PMI-ACP Lite Mock Exam 3 Answer Key and Explanations

1. D - Thank the customer on behalf of the team and cite the contributions made by two of the team members. PMI's Code of Ethics and Professional Conduct requires project managers to act fairly and truthfully. Accepting the credit due to another person or failing to denote where credit is actually due is dishonest and a violation of this code. [Reference: PMI Code of Ethics and Professional Conduct] [Stakeholder Engagement]

2. C - Consider building a product roadmap using specifications, user story mapping, and impact mapping. Then, bring the team and product owner together to clarify the expectations and value of captured requirements. [Agile Practice Guide, 1st edition, Page 58] [Problem Detection and Resolution]

3. B - NPV alone is not the ideal financial benefit measurement method. NPV values are highly dependent on the magnitude of the project. Usually NPV measurements are presented along with the project IRR or the initial investment estimates to demonstrate the financial feasibility of a project. [Cohn, M., 2006. Agile Estimating and Planning. 1st ed. Massachusetts: Pearson Education. Page 102] [Value-driven Delivery]

4. D - IRR determines the interest rate of a cash flow stream at which the present value of the cash flow stream becomes zero. [Cohn, M., 2006. Agile Estimating and Planning. 1st ed. Massachusetts: Pearson Education. Page 104] [Value-driven Delivery]

5. C - The product backlog is dynamic and incomplete; it is a live project artifact. [Agile Practice Guide, 1st edition, Page 52] [Adaptive Planning]

6. A - A burnup on a burndown charts means an increase of the total story points to be delivered. This means new scope of work was added to the project during the third iteration. [Cohn, M., 2006. Agile Estimating and Planning. 1st ed. Massachusetts: Pearson Education. Page 214] [Team Performance]

7. C - "Do second" is recommended for themes that have been classified as "Low Risk" and "High Value". [Cohn, M., 2006. Agile Estimating and Planning. 1st ed. Massachusetts: Pearson Education. Page 85] [Problem Detection and Resolution]

8. C - The scenario doesn't give enough data to determine what triggered the rescheduling. It will be safe to assume that the team would have valid grounds to reschedule the module development. In that case, you should have taken the CFO in confidence when this decision was being taken. [Agile Practice Guide, 1st edition, Page 34] [Stakeholder Engagement]

9. A - Agile is a blanket term for "many" approaches such as Scrum, XP, FDD, DSDM etc. [Agile Practice Guide, 1st edition, Page 11] [Agile Principles and Mindset]

10. C - A spike is a task included in an iteration plan that is being undertaken specifically to gain knowledge or answer a question. [Cohn, M., 2006. Agile Estimating and Planning. 1st ed. Massachusetts: Pearson Education. Page 154] [Continuous Improvement]

11. B - Planning for shorter time periods do not have any direct relationship with a project's ROI or multi-tasking. Although planning for shorter time periods is easier, this is not the reason why Agile teams plan for the next few weeks at the most. Planning for shorter time periods is more accurate because work for the next few weeks is more predictable. There is evidence, that the smaller the chunk of work, the more likely people are to deliver it. [Agile Practice Guide, 1st edition, Page 61] [Adaptive Planning]

12. B - The six primary roles on a Feature-Driven Development project are: Project manager, chief architect, development manager, chief programmer, class owner and domain expert. [Agile Practice Guide, 1st edition, Page 108] [Value-driven Delivery]

13. D - There is no ideal frequency, but rather a general guideline of conducting demonstrations at least once every two weeks. [Agile Practice Guide, 1st edition, Page 55] [Value-driven Delivery]

14. B - The purpose of the "Triple Nickels" activity is to generate ideas for actions or recommendations and uncover important topics about the project history. [Derby, E. and Larsen, D., 2006. Agile Retrospectives: Making Good Teams Great. 1st ed. Texas: Pragmatic Bookshelf, Page 56] [Continuous Improvement]

15. B - Kanban boards are a low-tech, high-touch technology that may seem overly simplistic at first, but those using them soon realize their power. [Agile Practice Guide, 1st edition, Page 105] [Value-driven Delivery]

16. C - Sprints, or iterations are time-boxed and are never terminated early. If the features being developed are suddenly not required, these will be replaced with other high priority features in the backlog. However, if the project is terminated, that would terminate the iteration. [Agile Practice Guide, 1st edition, Page 25] [Agile Principles and Mindset]

17. B - Kanban boards help teams manage the work in progress. Backlog grooming helps in delivering higher value to the organization. Collocation facilitates agility. Small batch systems aim to uncover inconsistencies and quality issues earlier in the project life cycle when the overall cost of change is lower. [Agile Practice Guide, 1st edition, Page 93] [Adaptive Planning]

18. C - Economists and financial analysts generally use alternative approaches to measure financial benefits such as IRR and NPV since the ROI measure doesn't factor in the time value of money. [Cohn, M., 2006. Agile Estimating and Planning. 1st ed. Massachusetts: Pearson Education. Page 100] [Value-driven Delivery]

19. C - Completeness and delivery are subjective. A team may choose to deliver a minimum viable product (MVP) by developing only the "must have" features. Applying MoSCoW rules to project requirements ensure that the highest valued business requirements/features are developed first. [Agile Practice Guide, 1st edition, Pages 23; Cohn, M., 2006. Agile Estimating and Planning. 1st ed. Massachusetts: Pearson Education. Page 187] [Value-driven Delivery]

20. C - Quality should be planned, designed and built-in. Quality is not merely inspected-in in Agile approaches. [Agile Practice Guide, 1st edition, Page 9] [Agile Principles and Mindset]

21. D - Prisoners feel that they've been forced to attend and would rather be doing something else. [Derby, E. and Larsen, D., 2006. Agile Retrospectives: Making Good Teams Great. 1st ed. Texas: Pragmatic Bookshelf, Page 45] [Continuous Improvement]

22. A - "Color Code Dots" activity is used in conjunction with a timeline to gather data about feelings in a longer iteration, release, or project retrospective. [Derby, E. and Larsen, D., 2006. Agile Retrospectives: Making Good Teams Great. 1st ed. Texas: Pragmatic Bookshelf, Page 59] [Continuous Improvement]

23. A - A key influence on cycle time is the variability in the time it takes to develop a new feature. One of the best ways to reduce variability is to work with reasonable small and similarly-sized units of work. Working at the task level can further reduce the variability but compromise the Agile principles. Agile approaches are focused at the feature or story level. [Cohn, M., 2006. Agile Estimating and Planning. 1st ed. Massachusetts: Pearson Education. Page 246] [Problem Detection and Resolution]

24. D - First and foremost, a retrospect is not about blame; the retrospective is a time for the team to learn from previous work and make small improvements. Major breakthroughs are usually not expected but are welcomed. [Agile Practice Guide, 1st edition, Page 51] [Continuous Improvement]

25. C - You need to calculate the Future Value of 250,000 at 8% for 15 years. The formula for Future Value is FV = PV * (1+r)^n. So to calculate, FV = 250,000 * (1 + 0.08)^15 = $793,042. [Cohn, M., 2006. Agile Estimating and Planning. 1st ed. Massachusetts: Pearson Education. Page 100] [Value-driven Delivery]

26. B - On XP projects, we apply the pair programming approach. Even if the analytics expert is the only person to perform a specific task, pair programming must be encouraged. All of the other choices are irrelevant to the problem at hand. [Agile Practice Guide, 1st edition, Page 153] [Problem Detection and Resolution]

27. C - The primary purpose of iteration planning is to refine suppositions made in the more coarse-grained release plan. [Cohn, M., 2006. Agile Estimating and Planning. 1st ed. Massachusetts: Pearson Education. Page 146] [Adaptive Planning]

28. D - Iteration or release plans are not developed during retrospectives. Your responsibility, as the servant-leader, is to fully participate in identifying improvement opportunities and creating action plans. [Agile Practice Guide, 1st edition, Page 35] [Continuous Improvement]

29. C - With an Agile approach to estimating and planning, teams reduce uncertainty about the product ultimately being built as product increments are shown to potential users and other stakeholders at the end of each iteration. Their feedback and responses are used to fine-tune future plans. [Cohn, M., 2006. Agile Estimating and Planning. 1st ed.

Massachusetts: Pearson Education. Page 247] [Value-driven Delivery]

30. D - A cross-functional Agile team is a mixed team of generalists and specialists. [Agile Practice Guide, 1st edition, Page 40] [Agile Principles and Mindset]

31. D - The payback period is the amount of time required to earn back the initial investment. [Cohn, M., 2006. Agile Estimating and Planning. 1st ed. Massachusetts: Pearson Education. Page 104] [Value-driven Delivery]

32. A - In this situation, you are not recommended to take on the small extra work of adding buffers to your project. [Cohn, M., 2006. Agile Estimating and Planning. 1st ed. Massachusetts: Pearson Education. Page 197] [Problem Detection and Resolution]

33. A - Hoshin Kanri is a strategy or policy deployment method. It involves aligning the goals of the company (strategy), with the plans of middle management (tactics) and the work performed on the floor (action). [Agile Practice Guide, 1st edition, Page 152] [Stakeholder Engagement]

34. B - The scrum master is responsible for ensuring the Scrum process is upheld and works to ensure the Scrum team adheres to the practices and rules as well as coaches the team on removing impediments. [Agile Practice Guide, 1st edition, Page 101] [Value-driven Delivery]

35. B - Mobbing requires multiple team members focus simultaneously and coordinate their contributions on a particular work item. Mobbing has a WIP limit of one for an entire team with one keyboard. [Agile Practice Guide, 1st edition, Page 152] [Value-driven Delivery]

36. A - Ideal time and cycle time are irrelevant. Both feature and schedule buffering help in managing scheduling risks. However in this scenario, feature buffering is not applicable as all features need to be developed. [Cohn, M., 2006. Agile Estimating and Planning. 1st ed. Massachusetts: Pearson Education. Page 188] [Adaptive Planning]

37. C - There are two common ways to assign story points. The first approach is to select a story that you expect to be one of the smallest stories you'll work with and say that story is estimated at one story point. The second approach is instead to select a story that seems somewhat medium-sized and give it a number somewhere in the middle of the range you expect to use. Once you have fairly arbitrarily assigned a story point to the first story, each additional story is estimated by comparing it to the first story or to any others that have been estimated. [Cohn, M., 2006. Agile Estimating and Planning. 1st ed. Massachusetts: Pearson Education. Page 36] [Adaptive Planning]

38. D - Do not plan on following the "perfect" Agile process, but instead look for the results. When a cross-functional team delivers finished value often and reflects on the product and process, the team is agile. It does not matter what the team calls its process. Servant-leadership is a critical element of Agile approaches. [Agile Practice Guide, 1st edition, Page 33] [Agile Principles and Mindset]

39. B - WIP is an abbreviation for work in progress. [Agile Practice Guide, 1st edition, Page 66] [Value-driven Delivery]

40. D - If project budget and duration are constraints, the recommended approach is to develop all of the must-have features, as many linear features as possible, and at least a few delighters. [Cohn, M., 2006. Agile Estimating and Planning. 1st ed. Massachusetts: Pearson Education. Page 111] [Problem Detection and Resolution]

PMI-ACP Lite Mock Exam 4 Practice Questions

Test Name: PMI-ACP Lite Mock Exam 4
Total Questions: 40
Correct Answers Needed to Pass:
30 (75.00%)
Time Allowed: 60 Minutes

Test Description

This is a cumulative PMI-ACP Mock Exam which can be used as a benchmark for your PMI-ACP aptitude. This practice test includes questions from all exam topic areas, including sections from Agile Tools and Techniques, and all three Agile Knowledge and Skills areas.

Test Questions

1. You have recently been assigned to an ongoing Agile project. During the sprint retrospective, the project manager asked all of the team members to put sticky dots on the project timeline to show events where emotions ran high or low. What activity is this?

A. Color Code Dots

B. Pareto Charts

C. Affinity diagrams

D. Dalmatian

2. Which of the following financial measures help us look at a cash flow stream as a single, present value amount?

A. NPV

B. Payback Period

C. ROI

D. IRR

3. Which of the following Agile techniques would you recommend if an Agile team wants to prioritize the top issues, ideas or proposals?

A. Planning Poker

B. Prioritize with Dots

C. Hoshin Kanri

D. Ishikawa Diagram

4. How do Agile projects manage quality?

A. Quality review is conducted during recurring retrospectives and daily standups regularly check on the effectiveness of the quality processes.

B. Quality control is conducted during recurring retrospectives and quality assurance is conducted at the end of the project.

C. Quality review is conducted during daily standups and recurring retrospectives regularly check on the effectiveness of the quality processes.

D. Quality and review steps are built in throughout the project and recurring retrospectives regularly check on the effectiveness of the quality processes.

5. It's easy to tell when a feature is 0% done (we haven't started it) and it's relatively easy to tell when we're 100% done (all tests passed for all the product owner's conditions of satisfaction). It is often hard to measure the progress anywhere in between. How should you report progress when faced with such a situation?

A. Stick with 0% for work in progress and 100% complete once all conditions of satisfactions are met.

B. Decompose stories into tasks and sub-tasks and do a bottom-up percentage of completion estimation.

C. Mark the feature 50% complete upon completion of development and 100% complete when the conditions of satisfactions are met.

D. Mark the feature 80% complete upon completion of development and 100% complete when the conditions of satisfactions are met.

6. Which of the following Agile approaches is known best because of its emphasis on constraint-driven delivery?

A. XP

B. DSDM

C. Lean

D. Scrum

7. On traditional projects, a change control board is usually established to authorize change requests. Who is responsible to authorize changes on an Agile project?

A. Scrum master

B. Product owner

C. Agile team

D. End users

8. What is the highest priority of an Agile team?

A. Abandon traditional project management.

B. Whole hearted acceptance to change.

C. Relying less on documentation.

D. Early and continuous delivery of valuable product.

9. You and your team are responsible for delivering an enterprise-wide automation project. Due to the complexity of the project, multiple Agile teams need to be formed. Team size is an important consideration while forming Agile teams. What is the ideal team size in Agile environments?

A. Ten to twenty-five members

B. Three to nine members

C. Fifteen to fifty members

D. Five to twenty members

10. What is the "response time" of an item?

A. The time required to process an item.

B. The total time it takes to deliver including the waiting time.

C. The time that an item waits until the work starts.

D. Average story points per iteration.

11. On a Scrum project, who is responsible for helping the team remove project impediments?

A. Scrum master

B. Project sponsor

C. Product owner

D. Agile coach

12. Which of the following statements regarding Agile release planning is incorrect?

A. Agile release planning focuses on features that will be released by the end of each project iteration.

B. Release planning is the process of creating a very high-level plan that covers a period longer than an iteration.

C. The product owner and the whole team decide how much must be developed and how long that will take before they have a releasable product.

D. A typical release plan will cover perhaps three to six months and maybe three to twelve or more iterations.

13. What does Agile MoSCoW stand for?

A. Capital of Russia.

B. Must Have, Should Have, Could Have, and Won't Have.

C. Motivational Science of Work.

D. Materials, Supply Chain, and Work Order.

14. Your Agile project team is currently having communication issues. You underestimated these risks earlier and did not establish clear ground rules and group norms upfront in the project. Which document typically includes these items?

A. Sprint backlog

B. Team charter

C. Agile Manifesto

D. Product backlog

15. Which of the following Agile techniques uses polling to collect data about how people view their participation in the retrospective?

A. Brainstorming

B. Check-in

C. ESVP

D. Focus on/Focus off

16. Agile contracting best practices require structuring milestones and payment terms on:

A. Stage gates

B. Fixed milestones

C. Phase gates

D. Value-driven deliverables.

17. You are invited to lunch by the manager of a seller organization. Your organization does

not permit receipt of gifts from vendors. You should:

A. Insist on paying for your lunch.

B. Avoid going out to lunch with anyone from the seller organization.

C. Accept the offer since it has a very small value.

D. Go out for lunch and refrain from informing your managers about the lunch.

18. You are leading a 500 story date-driven project that should produce the final release in six months. If the expected velocity is 25 story points per three-week iteration. How many iterations will be required to complete the project?

A. 20

B. 75

C. 167

D. 9

19. You have been hired as a consultant by a manufacturing firm. You have been asked to develop a standardized project management approach for the organization. You are currently considering the entire continuum of project management which is Agile on one end and waterfall on the other. Before you can decide which model to select, you need to conduct a/an:

A. Impact assessment

B. Organization culture assessment

C. Root cause analysis

D. Feasibility analysis

20. The Agile Unified Process (AgileUP) performs iterative cycles across seven key disciplines and incorporates the associated feedback before formal delivery. Which of the following is NOT one of these seven disciplines?

A. Environment

B. Project management

C. Scope creep

D. Configuration management

21. Which of the following is generally known as the best Agile estimating technique?

A. Disaggregation

B. Analogy

C. Planning poker

D. Expert opinion

22. What is the primary benefit of incremental delivery?

A. Reduced change requests

B. Shorter project duration

C. Higher ROI

D. Lower costs

23. You are managing an Agile team developing a high-tech gadget for the organization. The gadget will monitor and report on different aspects of the business and report performance. If you want to assume a servant-leader role, how should you respond to team conflicts?

A. Develop a structured conflict management approach.

B. Escalate all conflicts to higher management.

C. Becoming an impartial bridge-builder.

D. Withdraw from the conflicts and let the team resolve them.

24. You are leading an Agile project. The team has proposed using a Kanban board to manage the team's work in progress and spot bottlenecks. The following work flow has been agreed on for the Kanban board: Ready -> Develop and Unit Test -> Dev-Done -> System Test -> Done. According to this Kanban board, the lead time of an item is the:

A. The time an item enters the "Ready" bin till the time it exits the "Done" bin.

B. The time an item enters the "Develop and Unit Test" bin till the time it exits the "Done" bin.

C. The time an item enters the "Develop and Unit Test" bin till the time it enters the "Done" bin.

D. The time an item enters the "Ready" bin till the time it enters the "Done" bin.

25. When does an Agile team reconfirm its commitments and identify project impediments?

A. Release planning

B. Iteration planning

C. Retrospectives

D. Daily standups

26. Most projects with multiple teams benefit from establishing a common estimating baseline at the start of the project. Which of the following approaches would you recommend for establishing a common estimating baseline?

A. Collaboratively estimating an assortment of new user stories.

B. Both approaches are recommended; benchmarking on user stories from the past project and collaboratively estimating new stories.

C. Select some user stories from the past project and agree on the estimates for them.

D. Each Agile team chooses its own estimating approach.

27. A servant-leader gives colored sticky dots to the team and asks them to put these on a poster containing team issues. The team then starts placing their dots next to the items under consideration. What is this team doing?

A. Conducting a root cause analysis.

B. Developing a fishbone diagram.

C. Identifying issues.

D. Prioritizing issues.

28. Traditional teams govern vendor relationships by fixed milestones or phase gates focused on intermediate artifacts, rather than a full deliverable of incremental business value. What is the challenge associated with this approach?

A. This decreases the team's morale.

B. This limits the use of feedback to improve the product.

C. This increases the size and the number of features in a product.

D. This decreases a project team's throughput.

29. Before starting to plan a release, it is important to know the criteria by which the project will be evaluated as a success or a failure. This is captured in the:

A. Scope baseline

B. Resource utilization

C. Conditions of satisfaction

D. Schedule baseline

30. You are leading a major automation project for an external client. So far over a thousand user stories have been captured by your business analyst. Due to the number and the limited functionality of each user story, the product owner is struggling to prioritize them. How should you resolve this issue?

A. Estimate relative story points and prioritize user stories by their sizes.

B. Merging related stories into larger epics and then prioritize the themes relative to one another.

C. Estimate ideal days and prioritize user stories by their sizes.

D. Combine related stories into larger themes and then prioritize the themes relative to one another.

31. When introducing Agile methods to an organization that has historically managed all its project using predictive life cycles, which of the following approaches is more likely to succeed?

A. Trying the new techniques on high-value projects.

B. Trying the new techniques on completed projects.

C. Trying the new techniques on a less risky pilot project.

D. Trying the new techniques on ongoing projects.

32. Which of the following is not a typical component of an Agile project charter?

A. Feasibility Study

B. Intended flow of work

C. Project vision

D. Release criteria

33. Which of the following is not an Agile approach to project management?

A. Front-loaded planning.

B. Avoiding work in order to focus on high-priority items.

C. Obtaining early feedback.

D. Acting in a transparent manner.

34. Which project attribute determines the right Crystal method to be selected for a project?

A. Expected velocity

B. Team size

C. Number of user stories

D. Duration of the sprint

35. Which of the following project conditions leads to increased cycle times?

A. Decrease in work in progress.

B. Increase in number of features.

C. Decrease in number of features.

D. Increase in work in process.

36. Traditional project management stresses the importance of project integration management and expects the project manager to be in control of the detailed product planning and integrating different aspects of project integration with each other. In an Agile setting who is primarily responsible for integration management?

A. Servant-leader

B. Product owner

C. Agile coach

D. Agile team

37. Selection of the right project management approach is dependent on the team size in which of the following Agile approaches?

A. XP

B. Kanban

C. Scrum

D. Crystal

38. On a burndown chart, the intersection of the work remaining trend line and the horizontal axis indicates the:

A. Cutover date

B. Handover date

C. Completion deadline

D. Most probable completion of work

39. Why do Agile approaches recommend forming dedicated project teams?

A. Flexibility in dealing with change.

B. Increased focus and productivity.

C. Reduced project cost.

D. Out of the box thinking.

40. You are managing a complex project. The project objectives are known but the exact scope of work cannot be defined. Which of the following provisions can allow you to withdraw from a contractual relationship halfway through the project?

A. Early cancellation clause

B. No-contest clause

C. Force majeure clause

D. Non-compete clause

PMI-ACP Lite Mock Exam 4 Answer Key and Explanations

1. A - A "Color Code Dots" activity is used in conjunction with a timeline to gather data about feelings in a longer iteration, release, or project retrospective. This activity is used to show how people experienced events on the timeline. Team members use sticky dots to show events on the timeline where emotions ran high or low. [Derby, E. and Larsen, D., 2006. Agile Retrospectives: Making Good Teams Great. 1st ed. Texas: Pragmatic Bookshelf, Page 59] [Continuous Improvement]

2. A - NPV helps us look at a cash flow stream as a single, present value amount. [Cohn, M., 2006. Agile Estimating and Planning. 1st ed. Massachusetts: Pearson Education. Page 104] [Value-driven Delivery]

3. B - Prioritize with Dots is an Agile technique that helps teams prioritize their top issues, ideas, or proposals. Planning poker is a user story estimating technique. Hoshin Kanri and Ishikawa Diagrams are not prioritization techniques. [Derby, E. and Larsen, D., 2006. Agile Retrospectives: Making Good Teams Great. 1st ed. Texas: Pragmatic Bookshelf, Page 92] [Continuous Improvement]

4. D - In order to navigate changes, Agile methods call for frequent quality and review steps built in throughout the project rather than toward the end of the project. Recurring retrospectives regularly check on the effectiveness of the quality processes. [Agile Practice Guide, 1st edition, Page 93] [Agile Principles and Mindset]

5. A - When determining the work in process percentage of completion is difficult, it is highly recommended to stick with what you know for sure, 0% and 100%; 0% for work in progress and 100% complete once all conditions of satisfactions are met. [Cohn, M., 2006. Agile Estimating and Planning. 1st ed. Massachusetts: Pearson Education. Page 250] [Stakeholder Engagement]

6. B - Dynamic Systems Development Method (DSDM) is known best because of its emphasis on constraint-driven delivery. [Agile Practice Guide, 1st edition, Page 110] [Value-driven Delivery]

7. B - Product owners have the ultimate responsibility of the project success. They prioritize the project backlog and authorize change requests on an Agile project. [Agile Practice Guide, 1st edition, Page 41] [Agile Principles and Mindset]

8. D - According to the 12 principles of Agile, the highest priority of any Agile team is to satisfy the customer through early and continuous delivery of valuable software. [Agile Practice Guide, 1st edition, Page 9] [Agile Principles and Mindset]

9. B - In practice, the most effective Agile teams tend to range in size from three to nine members. [Agile Practice Guide, 1st edition, Page 39] [Value-driven Delivery]

10. C - Response time is the time that an item waits until work starts. [Agile Practice Guide, 1st edition, Pages 61, 64] [Value-driven Delivery]

11. A - On Scrum projects, it's the responsibility of the Scrum master to help the team remove impediments from the project. [Agile Practice Guide, 1st edition, Page 41] [Agile Principles and Mindset]

12. A - Agile release planning doesn't focus on releases at the end of each project iteration. Instead, the product owner and the whole team decide how much must be developed and how long that will take before they have a releasable product. [Cohn, M., 2006. Agile Estimating and Planning. 1st ed. Massachusetts: Pearson Education. Page 131] [Adaptive Planning]

13. B - On DSDM (Dynamic Systems Development Method) projects, requirements are sorted into four categories: must have, should have, could have, and won't have. DSDM refers to this sorting as the MoSCoW rules. [Cohn, M., 2006. Agile Estimating and Planning. 1st ed. Massachusetts: Pearson Education. Page 187] [Value-driven Delivery]

14. B - Teams do not need a formal process for chartering as long as the teams understand how to work together. Some teams benefit from a team chartering process. Team ground rules and norms are typically included in a team charter. [Agile Practice Guide, 1st edition, Page 50] [Value-driven Delivery]

15. C - During an ESVP activity, each participant anonymously reports his or her attitude toward the retrospective as an Explorer, Shopper, Vacationer, or Prisoner. A histogram of this data is then created and used to guide a discussion about what the results mean for the group. [Derby, E. and Larsen, D., 2006. Agile Retrospectives: Making Good Teams Great. 1st ed. Texas: Pragmatic Bookshelf, Page 45] [Continuous Improvement]

16. D - Traditional approaches to contracting structure milestones and payment terms on fixed milestones, phase gates and stage gates. Agile contracting best practices require structuring milestones and payment terms on value-driven deliverables. [Agile Practice Guide, 1st edition, Page 77] [Value-driven Delivery]

17. A - The correct action is for the Agile practitioner is to insist on paying for your own lunch. Avoiding going out to lunch with anyone from the seller organization is drastic, as such a lunch may be an opportunity to build relationships and to understand the seller's position on a project better. Going out to lunch and not informing a manager about the lunch is unethical. Allowing the seller organization to pay for an inexpensive lunch may be acceptable in certain organizations. For example, some organizations have placed a limit on the value of gifts that may be received by their employees, and permit gifts that do not exceed a certain value (e.g., $50). In such a case, a lunch may be within acceptable limits. However, in the current situation, the buyer organization does not permit its employees to receive any gifts from vendors. Therefore, this option is not acceptable. [PMI Code of Ethics and Professional Conduct] [Stakeholder Engagement]

18. D - If the project is date-driven, we have a deadline to finish the project with as many features as possible. A six-month completion period means we have 26 weeks on the project. With an iteration length of three weeks, this means we would get nine iterations to deliver as many features as possible. [Cohn, M., 2006. Agile Estimating and Planning. 1st ed. Massachusetts:

Pearson Education. Page 135] [Team Performance]

19. B - The first thing you need to do is conduct the organization's culture assessment. Impact assessment should be conducted only once the new approach has been selected and approved. Root cause and feasibility analysis are irrelevant to the problem at hand and are rather related to issues and individual projects respectively. [Agile Practice Guide, 1st edition, Page 75] [Agile Principles and Mindset]

20. C - The seven key disciplines of AgileUP are: model, implementation, test, deployment, configuration management, project management, and environment. [Agile Practice Guide, 1st edition, Page 111] [Value-driven Delivery]

21. C - Planning poker is generally recognized as the best Agile estimating technique. Planning poker combines expert opinion, analogy, and disaggregation into an enjoyable approach to estimating that results in quick but reliable estimates. [Cohn, M., 2006. Agile Estimating and Planning. 1st ed. Massachusetts: Pearson Education. Page 56] [Adaptive Planning]

22. C - Incremental delivery results in higher return on investment (ROI) as higher priority stories are delivered well before the others, maximizing the return on investment. [Agile Practice Guide, 1st edition, Page 19] [Value-driven Delivery]

23. C - Developing a structured conflict management approach is not Agile. Withdrawing or escalating all conflicts is not in line with philosophy of servant-leadership. Servant-leaders should become impartial bridge-builders and coaches, rather than making decisions for which others should be responsible. [Agile Practice Guide, 1st edition, Page 35] [Agile Principles and Mindset]

24. A - Lead time is from the time you put an item on the board until you deliver it. This will be represented by the time an item enters the "Ready" bin till the time it exits the "Done" bin. Exiting the "Done" bin implies delivery to the customer. [Agile Practice Guide, 1st edition, Page 65] [Value-driven Delivery]

25. D - Reconfirming commitment and impediment identification is part of the daily standup meetings. [Agile Practice Guide, 1st edition, Page 53] [Team Performance]

26. B - Both approaches are recommended; benchmarking on user stories from the past project and collaboratively estimating new stories. [Cohn, M., 2006. Agile Estimating and Planning. 1st ed. Massachusetts: Pearson Education. Page 200] [Adaptive Planning]

27. D - Prioritize with Dots is an Agile technique that helps teams prioritize their top issues, ideas, or proposals. Planning poker is a user story estimating technique. Hoshin Kanri and Ishikawa Diagrams are not prioritization techniques. [Derby, E. and Larsen, D., 2006. Agile Retrospectives: Making Good Teams Great. 1st ed. Texas: Pragmatic Bookshelf, Page 92] [Problem Detection and Resolution]

28. B - Many vendor relationships are governed by fixed milestones or phase gates focused on intermediate artifacts, rather than a full deliverable of incremental business value.

Often, these controls limit the use of feedback to improve the product. [Agile Practice Guide, 1st edition, Page 77] [Value-driven Delivery]

29. C - As leading indicators of whether a project is likely to achieve its goals, most projects use the triumvirate of schedule, scope and resources. For most projects, this means that the product owner's conditions of satisfaction are defined by a combination of schedule, scope, and resource goals. The conditions of satisfaction is the correct answer to the question because it overarches all three attributes and more. [Cohn, M., 2006. Agile Estimating and Planning. 1st ed. Massachusetts: Pearson Education. Page 133] [Adaptive Planning]

30. D - User story prioritization should be based on their value rather than their size. Merging user stories into larger epics could help in prioritization but you would then lose individual user stories. It is recommended that you combine related stories into larger themes and then prioritize the themes relative to each other. [Cohn, M., 2006. Agile Estimating and Planning. 1st ed. Massachusetts: Pearson Education. Page 79] [Problem Detection and Resolution]

31. C - Trying the new techniques on a less risky project with a medium to low degree of uncertainty is advisable. The lower the risk, more the chances of success. You need some quick wins to help smooth transition to the new approaches. [Agile Practice Guide, 1st edition, Page 30] [Problem Detection and Resolution]

32. A - A pre-project feasibility study is usually considered a critical component of traditional life cycles. In Agile projects, feasibility determination is built into Agile approaches. The rest of the choices are typical components of an Agile project charter. [Agile Practice Guide, 1st edition, Page 49] [Value-driven Delivery]

33. A - Agile implementation strategy includes addressing questions such as how the team can obtain early feedback, how the team can act in a transparent manner, and how work can be avoided to focus on high-priority items. Front-loaded planning is not an Agile approach. [Agile Practice Guide, 1st edition, Page 33] [Agile Principles and Mindset]

34. B - Crystal methodologies are designed to scale and provide a selection of methodology rigor based on the number of people involved in the project and the criticality of the project. [Agile Practice Guide, 1st edition, Page 106] [Value-driven Delivery]

35. D - The more work in process there is, the longer any new feature will take to develop as the new feature must follow along behind the already started work. So an increase in work in process will directly result in the increase of cycle times. [Cohn, M., 2006. Agile Estimating and Planning. 1st ed. Massachusetts: Pearson Education. Page 246] [Problem Detection and Resolution]

36. D - In an Agile setting, the team member determines how plans and components should integrate. [Agile Practice Guide, 1st edition, Page 91] [Agile Principles and Mindset]

37. D - The selection of an appropriate method from the Crystal Family is based on the team size. [Agile Practice Guide, 1st edition, Page 106] [Value-driven Delivery]

38. D - On a burndown chart, the intersection of the work remaining trend line, a projection of the current velocity, and the horizontal axis indicates the most likely completion date. However, as this date is not fixed and the estimate changes with the change in velocity, this intersection does not point to any specific date or deadline. [Agile Practice Guide, 1st edition, Page 62] [Team Performance]

39. B - Agile approaches recommend forming dedicated project teams as this enables the team members to focus on the project which results in increased productivity. [Agile Practice Guide, 1st edition, Page 40] [Agile Principles and Mindset]

40. A - When an Agile supplier delivers sufficient value with only half of the scope completed, the early cancellation clause allows the customer to withdraw from the relationship. [Agile Practice Guide, 1st edition, Page 78] [Value-driven Delivery]

PMI-ACP Knowledge Area Quiz: Continuous Improvement Practice Questions

Test Name: Knowledge Area Test: Planning, Monitoring, and Adapting
Total Questions: 15
Correct Answers Needed to Pass: 11 (73.33%)
Time Allowed: 25 Minutes

Test Description

This practice quiz specifically targets your knowledge of the Planning, Monitoring, and Adapting exam topic area.

Test Questions

1. An Agile team benefits from traditional project management approaches such as lessons learned gathering, analysis and documentation; and Lean approaches such as Kaizen (continuous improvement) during:

A. User stories documentation

B. Retrospectives

C. Team chartering

D. Backlog grooming

2. An Agile team is currently planning the next project iteration and breaking down user stories into tasks. Some of these tasks cannot be estimated accurately due to uncertainty and some knowledge work is required to gain further knowledge. What do you recommend?

A. Drop complex tasks from the iteration plan.

B. Do nothing and let the team cross the bridge when they get to it.

C. Schedule spikes.

D. Drop entire user stories that contain complicated tasks.

3. During a retrospective, you have asked your team to write cards to represent memorable, personally meaningful, or otherwise significant events during the iteration and then post them in a chronological order. What have you asked your team to develop?

A. Timeline

B. Groom the backlog

C. Project closure document

D. Lessons learned

4. Regardless of the size and complexity of a project, which of the following provides a platform to an Agile team to learn about, improve, and adapt its processes?

A. Product owner

B. Sprints

C. Servant-leader

D. Retrospectives

5. Which of the following is a root cause analysis technique?

A. Affinity Diagrams

B. Five Whys

C. Statistical sampling

D. Scatter diagrams

6. You are leading an iteration retrospective. Each participant has anonymously reported his or her attitude toward the retrospective as an Explorer, Shopper, Vacationer, or Prisoner. What should you do next with this data?

A. Ask the prisoners to leave the retrospective.

B. Create a histogram of this data and guide a discussion about what the results mean for the group.

C. Pair the explorers with vacationers and shoppers with prisoners.

D. Divide the group based on their chosen attitude and select group leaders for each of the groups.

7. Prioritization matrices are an important quality planning tool. They provide a way to rank a diverse set of ideas by order of business value. How this list is usually obtained?

A. Through control charts

B. Through variance analysis

C. Through brainstorming

D. Through ANOVA analysis

8. You have asked your team to conduct a brainstorming session to generate ideas for effective behaviors at work and then choose five to seven principles to guide team interactions or processes. What are you developing?

A. Retrospective charter

B. Communications plan

C. Iteration plan

D. Working agreements

9. A team is performing a complex Agile project for the first time and going through a steep learning curve. Which of the following Agile events would you recommend to be frequently scheduled?

A. Iteration planning

B. Spike

C. Daily stand-ups

D. Retrospectives

10. According to the Agile Manifesto, project teams should continuously review the project processes to determine their effectiveness and optimize them. An Agile team implements this principle through:

A. Backlog grooming

B. Sprints aka iteration (faster)

C. Retrospectives

D. Time-boxing

11. Once the problem (variation) has been identified, the next step is to uncover the underlying root cause (source). Fishbone diagrams break down the causes of the problem statement into discrete branches, helping to identify the main or root cause of the problem. The fishbone diagram starts with recording the problem or issue at the fish's:

A. Fins

B. Head

C. Body

D. Tail

12. Your project team has been stuck in the "storming" stage of team development for some time now. You're starting to see signs of interpersonal friction on the team as the team hasn't been able to sort out its inter-team operating processes. Which of the following Agile tools can help you move the team on to the next stage?

A. Spikes

B. Value chains

C. Backlog grooming

D. Retrospectives

13. During an ESVP activity, each participant anonymously reports his or her attitude toward the retrospective as an Explorer, Shopper, Vacationer, or Prisoner. Who are the prisoners?

A. People who are working part-time on the project and have other competing priorities.

B. People who feel that they've been forced to attend and would rather be doing something else.

C. People who are dedicated and committed to the project.

D. People who are micromanaged by their managers.

14. During an ESVP activity, each participant anonymously reports his or her attitude toward the retrospective as an Explorer, Shopper, Vacationer, or Prisoner. Who are the shoppers?

A. People who are accountable for the project finances.

B. People who would like to evaluate ideas and pay for the costs of development of selected ideas.

C. People who are not satisfied or happy with the progress of the project.

D. People who want to look over all the available information and will be happy to go home with one useful new idea.

15. During a retrospective meeting, the Scrum Master announces, "Let's look at what's happening in our group. You can contribute in any of the sections, but participation is voluntary. The aim is to hear from others, so no commenting on another's contribution." She then points to a poster containing five sections (Appreciations, New Information, Puzzles, Complaints, Hopes and Wishes) and allows time for people to comment. What technique is the Scrum Master applying?

A. Temperature Reading

B. Value Stream Mapping

C. Critical Chain Analysis

D. Kano Analysis

Follow your first mind....

PMI-ACP Knowledge Area Quiz: Continuous Improvement Answer Key and Explanations

1. B - An Agile team benefits from traditional project management approaches such as lessons learned gathering, analysis and documentation; and Lean approaches such as Kaizen (continuous improvement) during retrospectives. [Agile Practice Guide, 1st edition, Page 51] [Continuous Improvement]

2. C - The recommendation is to schedule spikes for each knowledge work activity. A spike is a task included in an iteration plan that is being undertaken specifically to gain knowledge or answer a question. [Cohn, M., 2006. Agile Estimating and Planning. 1st ed. Massachusetts: Pearson Education. Page 154] [Continuous Improvement]

3. A - You are developing a timeline of the proceedings so far on the project. Such timelines are used by retrospective leaders to discuss the events and to understand facts and feelings during the iteration, release, or project. [Derby, E. and Larsen, D., 2006. Agile Retrospectives: Making Good Teams Great. 1st ed. Texas: Pragmatic Bookshelf, Page 51] [Continuous Improvement]

4. D - Retrospectives allow Agile teams to learn about, improve, and adapt their processes. [Agile Practice Guide, 1st edition, Page 50] [Continuous Improvement]

5. B - The "Five Whys?" technique helps in discovering underlying conditions that contribute to an issue. Team members ask "Why?" five times to get beyond habitual thinking. The rest of the choices are not root cause analysis techniques. [Derby, E. and Larsen, D., 2006. Agile Retrospectives: Making Good Teams Great. 1st ed. Texas: Pragmatic Bookshelf, Page 85] [Continuous Improvement]

6. B - You are using the ESVP technique. Once the information has been collected, you need to create a histogram of this data and guide a discussion about what the results mean for the group. [Derby, E. and Larsen, D., 2006. Agile Retrospectives: Making Good Teams Great. 1st ed. Texas: Pragmatic Bookshelf, Page 45] [Continuous Improvement]

7. C - Prioritization matrices provide a way of ranking a set of ideas that are usually generated through brainstorming. The other choices are not valid idea generation techniques. [Derby, E. and Larsen, D., 2006. Agile Retrospectives: Making Good Teams Great. 1st ed. Texas: Pragmatic Bookshelf, Page 78] [Continuous Improvement]

8. D - You are clearly developing a team working agreement which requires team members to work together and generate ideas for effective behaviors at work. [Derby, E. and Larsen, D., 2006. Agile Retrospectives: Making Good Teams Great. 1st ed. Texas: Pragmatic Bookshelf, Page 48] [Continuous Improvement]

9. D - The single most important practice is the retrospective because it allows the team to learn about, improve, and adapt its process. Retrospectives help the team learn from its previous work on the product and its process. For a team new to Agile, frequent retrospectives are recommended. [Agile Practice Guide, 1st edition, Page 62] [Continuous Improvement]

10. C - Retrospectives help the team learn from its previous work on the product and its processes. [Agile Practice Guide, 1st edition, Page 50] [Continuous Improvement]

11. B - The fishbone diagram starts with recording the problem or issue at the fish's head. [Derby, E. and Larsen, D., 2006. Agile Retrospectives: Making Good Teams Great. 1st ed. Texas: Pragmatic Bookshelf, Page 87] [Continuous Improvement]

12. D - You know you need to adapt your practices and ease the interpersonal tension before things get worse. You want to introduce retrospectives to your team. The rest of the choices are of little help in this case. [Derby, E. and Larsen, D., 2006. Agile Retrospectives: Making Good Teams Great. 1st ed. Texas: Pragmatic Bookshelf, Page xvi] [Continuous Improvement]

13. B - Prisoners feel that they've been forced to attend and would rather be doing something else. [Derby, E. and Larsen, D., 2006. Agile Retrospectives: Making Good Teams Great. 1st ed. Texas: Pragmatic Bookshelf, Page 45] [Continuous Improvement]

14. D - Shoppers want to look over all the available information and will be happy to go home with one useful new idea. [Derby, E. and Larsen, D., 2006. Agile Retrospectives: Making Good Teams Great. 1st ed. Texas: Pragmatic Bookshelf, Page 45] [Continuous Improvement]

15. A - This is an example of a "Temperature Reading" activity. Temperature Reading allows people to include aspects of group life that are usually ignored: appreciations, puzzles, and hopes and wishes. [Derby, E. and Larsen, D., 2006. Agile Retrospectives: Making Good Teams Great. 1st ed. Texas: Pragmatic Bookshelf, Page 119] [Continuous Improvement]

PMI-ACP Lite Mock Exam 5 Practice Questions

Test Name: PMI-ACP Lite Mock Exam 5
Total Questions: 40
Correct Answers Needed to Pass:
30 (75.00%)
Time Allowed: 60 Minutes

Test Description

This is a cumulative PMI-ACP Mock Exam which can be used as a benchmark for your PMI-ACP aptitude. This practice test includes questions from all exam topic areas, including sections from Agile Tools and Techniques, and all three Agile Knowledge and Skills areas.

Test Questions

1. When a project manager assumes the role of a coach and a facilitator for the project team, in an Agile environment, this role is known as:

A. Servant-leader

B. Project sponsor

C. Domain expert

D. Product owner

2. According to Clark and Wheelwright, an individual's percent of time spent on value-adding tasks is maximized when the person performs:

A. 4 tasks

B. 2 tasks

C. 8 tasks

D. 6 tasks

3. Which of the following is the management framework that emerges when teams employ Scrum as the chosen way of working and use the Kanban Method as a lens through which to view, understand, and continuously improve how they work?

A. Scrum of Kanban

B. WIP

C. Task Board

D. Scrumban

4. Which of the following graphical tools shows a team's progress by showing the number of story points remaining in the project?

A. Sensitivity diagram

B. Waterfall chart

C. Release burndown chart

D. Fishbone diagram

5. Which of these techniques is used during the retrospective closing that helps generate feedback on the retrospective process and gauge the effectiveness of the session from the team members' perspectives?

A. ROTI

B. IRR

C. ROI

D. NPV

6. Which of the following is a technique used during retrospectives to identify team strengths and improvement opportunities?

A. Delta

B. Gamma

C. Beta

D. Alpha

7. An Agile team is currently analyzing the project timeline. The team is marking the time when everything was going smoothly and then the energy dropped. The objective is to analyze this information for patterns of events, behaviors or feelings that cause a shift. What activity is this?

A. Working Agreements

B. Sensitivity Analysis

C. Patterns and Shifts

D. Kaizen

8. You have recently setup a daily team stand-up. For the first few days, the stand-ups were flowing smoothly, until today when a number of issues have been reported by the team. What should be done next?

A. Park the issues and create another meeting to solve them.

B. Ask the team members to follow the change control process.

C. Tell the team members that they can't report issues during daily stand-ups.

D. Resolve the issues and park them so that everyone can see them.

9. You have recently taken over an Agile team that is half way through the project. You noticed that the team is developing a work breakdown structure of the project scope during the first retrospective meeting. What would you recommend to the team?

A. Do not forget to sequence the work packages.

B. Do not forget to include control accounts.

C. Do not forget to develop data dictionaries.

D. Do not develop the work breakdown structure.

10. You have recently taken over a complex technological project and are surprised to find out each team member is 100% (of capacity) allocated to project tasks. What should be your main concern?

A. A high level of resource utilization has been achieved and the project cannot be further fast-tracked.

B. Resource capacities have incorrectly been calculated.

C. Inherent variability in typical project tasks might cause bottlenecks on the project.

D. Resources are overbooked and this is against the company's health and safety policy.

11. Your team is currently struggling with keeping up with the number of stories in WIP state. Which of the following tools can help in this situation?

A. Planning poker

B. Kanban

C. Burndown chart

D. Information radiator

12. You are the servant-leader on an Agile team developing a new financial application for an insurance company. You need to identify the stories to be developed for the first iteration. Which of the following is not a recommended action at this stage?

A. The product owner is asked to select the stories for the iteration.

B. The Agile team estimates the size of the stories.

C. The Agile team decides the sprint duration and expected velocity.

D. You help the team analyze the stories and decide the priorities of the items.

13. "Responding to change over following a plan" doesn't imply that:

A. Agile teams value change management.

B. Agile teams acknowledge that change is inevitable.

C. Agile teams highly value responding to change.

D. Agile teams do not value planning.

14. Your firm, a tunnel construction company, has recently won a contract to construct a network of underground tunnels for a new metro project in the city. The project site contains a network of interconnected geysers and hot springs. These network paths cannot be accurately mapped due to the complexity of the terrain and available technology. Which of the following is the best approach to be used on this project?

A. Deliver the project in increments, one line at a time and adjust the designs as new information becomes available.

B. Do a detailed design before commencing project work and keep the costs under budget.

C. Given the complexities, the project needs to be abandoned.

D. Start all lines at the same time and be prepared to tackle probable flooding of the lines.

15. If the amount of new functionality to be developed is fixed, how should a good release plan account for the project uncertainties?

A. By providing a date range for project completion.

B. By keeping the project open-ended.

C. By providing an estimate of standard deviation along with the deadline estimate.

D. By keeping the completion estimates within the team.

16. One of the challenges of planning a release is estimating the velocity of the team. Which of the following is NOT a valid Agile approach to estimate a team's velocity?

A. Making a forecast.

B. Using historical values.

C. Running an iteration.

D. Conducting a sensitivity analysis.

17. Which of the following statements regarding Agile planning is incorrect?

A. Agile plans are changed as new knowledge becomes available.

B. Agile plans do not cover all of a project's planning at the outset.

C. Agile planning is spread more or less evenly across the duration of a project.

D. Agile planning focuses more on change rather than project objectives.

18. Which of the following scheduling techniques is typically used on Agile projects?

A. Critical chain method

B. Critical path method

C. Iterative, on-demand, or pull-based scheduling

D. Precedence diagraming method

19. Which of the following user stories can be best estimated?

A. Those that are within one order of magnitude in size.

B. Those that are part of the highest valued theme.

C. Those that fulfil the non-functional requirements of a product.

D. Those that involve state-of-the-art technology.

20. You have been assigned to lead a complex project. Which of the following types of people would be your LAST choice to be included in your team?

A. Paint-Drip

B. Broken Comb

C. T-shaped

D. I-shaped

21. A steadily declining burndown chart indicates that?

A. The velocity is increasing.

B. The velocity is constant.

C. The velocity is decreasing.

D. The velocity is zero.

22. Which of the following Agile concepts implies "smallest possible deliverable that meets customer requirements"?

A. User story

B. Minimum viable product

C. Theme

D. Epic

23. Agile approaches promise better user experience of project deliverables in comparison to the traditional waterfall-based approaches. This is due to:

A. Early and continual involvement of users.

B. Early development of an exhaustive product backlog.

C. Relying less on documentation and more on processes.

D. Relying less on processes and more on documentation.

24. You have been assigned as the Agile coach for an Agile team. Which of the following is your correct role?

A. Mentor

B. Facilitator

C. Problem solver

D. Information radiator

25. A project team is currently struggling due to frequent interruptions by various delays and impediments. During the sprint retrospective, it was agreed to adopt some form of visual management that can help with work-in-process management and improve the flow. Which of the following tools should be used to facilitate this?

A. Formal change management process

B. Ground rules

C. Kanban board

D. Silos

26. If you are conducting an ESVP activity to set the stage of a retrospective, you need to be careful about:

A. Converting the polling results into a frequency-based histogram.

B. Limit the polling to the permanent team members.

C. Non-disclosing polling results.

D. Conducting anonymous polling.

27. The amount of effort required to deliver a user story is known as:

A. Sprint duration

B. Developer-hours

C. Story size

D. Iteration risk

28. What do we mean by "backlog grooming"?

A. Adding, removing and reprioritizing items in the feature list.

B. Estimating user stories using story points.

C. Arranging work packages into a logical sequence.

D. Developing Agile team and helping them perform.

29. You just found out that a team doesn't conduct daily stand-ups. You were able to successfully convey the advantages of daily stand-ups as these help teams to micro-commit to each other, uncover problems, and ensure the work flows smoothly through the team. What should be the ideal duration for these meetings?

A. 30 minutes

B. 45 minutes

C. 15 minutes

D. 1 hour

30. A project team is currently building a warehouse management system. Due to the complexity of the project and ambiguous requirements, the team decided to adopt an Agile management approach. If a higher rate of management process improvement is required by the project team, which of the following can help achieve this objective?

A. Deferring the development until all requirements have been collected.

B. Using a Kanban board to enable visual management.

C. Frequent retrospection and selecting improvements.

D. Adopting XP for the development phase.

31. If an Agile project's SPI is greater than the project's CPI, and the CPI is greater than 1.0, what can you infer about the project's schedule performance?

A. The project is behind schedule.

B. Agile projects do not have Earned Value measurements.

C. The project is ahead of schedule.

D. This cannot be determined with the given data.

32. If the size of a task cannot be reliability estimated, which of the following Agile actions is recommended?

A. Using PERT estimates adjusted by the estimate standard deviation.

B. Assigning a random duration estimate to the task.

C. Using Monte Carlo analysis to simulate task duration.

D. Adding a spike and a task placeholder with a rough duration estimate.

33. Which of the following determines which life cycle is the best fit of any given project?

A. Required change control

B. Project's inherent characteristics

C. Complexity of requirements

D. Speed of deliveries

34. In Agile teams, a single person's throughput is not relevant. Focusing on a single person's throughput may be risky because it might:

A. Increase the chances of scope creep.

B. Increase the cost of the project.

C. Increase the sprint duration.

D. Create a bottleneck for the rest of the team.

35. You are managing an ERP system design and development project. The business and system analysts are based in the US, while the developers and testers are based in China. Due to time zone difference you cannot conduct daily morning Scrums. What should you do?

A. Conduct the standups during Chinese working hours and send the recording over to the US.

B. Divide the team into smaller teams.

C. Abolish conducting daily Scrums in this environment.

D. Alternately schedule the daily Scrums between Chinese and American working hours.

36. You are an Agile process analyst and are assigned to work for Anu who is leading a complex Student Services Design project for a university. Anu insists that the team create highly detailed project plans before commencing the work. What should you do?

A. Brush up your resume and start applying for external jobs.

B. Show Anu how you have had success in the past using Agile approaches and why they are better.

C. Escalate the issue to the project sponsor.

D. Put your foot down and don't compromise on Agile values and principles.

37. You are leading an Agile team developing an inventory management and control system for a major retailer in your country. Halfway during the iteration you discover that the predictive analytics module that is currently being developed is no longer required by the customer. What should you do?

A. Freeze the iteration and immediately call a retrospective meeting.

B. Continue developing the feature until a minimum viable product is developed.

C. Delete the code and return the story to the backlog.

D. Reprioritize the backlog and start developing the next priority item.

38. Which of the following Agile approaches encourages sitting together and pair working?

A. Lean

B. XP

C. Scrum

D. Kanban

39. Which of the following is NOT a considered a good planning practice during iteration planning?

A. Looking ahead only the length of one iteration.

B. The tasks on the iteration plan are estimated in ideal hours.

C. Allocating stories to team members.

D. Decomposing user stories into tasks.

40. You are leading a complex project and are currently doing some high-level planning. You want to schedule retrospectives so that each team member's calendar gets booked. How should you schedule these events?

A. When more than a few weeks have passed since the previous retrospective.

B. At the end of each release.

C. You should not schedule these events well in advance, the project team decides when to call a retrospective.

D. At the end of each sprint.

PMI-ACP Lite Mock Exam 5 Answer Key and Explanations

1. A - In an Agile environment, project managers are servant-leaders, changing their emphasis to coaching people who want help, fostering greater collaboration on the team, and aligning stakeholder needs. [Agile Practice Guide, 1st edition, Page 38] [Agile Principles and Mindset]

2. B - Multi-tasking exacts a horrible toll on productivity. Clark and Wheelwright (1993) studied the effect of multi-tasking and found that the time an individual spends on value-adding work drops rapidly when the individual is working on more than two tasks. [Cohn, M., 2006. Agile Estimating and Planning. 1st ed. Massachusetts: Pearson Education. Page 15] [Team Performance]

3. D - Scrumban is an Agile approach originally designed as a way to transition from Scrum to Kanban. As additional Agile frameworks and methodologies emerged, it became an evolving hybrid framework in and of itself where teams use Scrum as a framework and Kanban for process improvement. [Agile Practice Guide, 1st edition, Page 108] [Value-driven Delivery]

4. C - A release burndown chart shows a team's progress by showing the number of story points remaining in the project. The vertical axis shows the number of story points remaining and the iterations are shown across the horizontal axis. [Cohn, M., 2006. Agile Estimating and Planning. 1st ed. Massachusetts: Pearson Education. Page 212] [Team Performance]

5. A - ROTI stands for Return on Time Invested. This technique is used in the closing retrospective phase for iteration or release retrospectives. It helps generate feedback on the retrospective process and gauge the effectiveness of the session from the team members' perspectives. [Derby, E. and Larsen, D., 2006. Agile Retrospectives: Making Good Teams Great. 1st ed. Texas: Pragmatic Bookshelf, Page 124] [Team Performance]

6. A - The Delta activity is used during team retrospective meetings to identify team strengths and improvement opportunities. [Derby, E. and Larsen, D., 2006. Agile Retrospectives: Making Good Teams Great. 1st ed. Texas: Pragmatic Bookshelf, Page 114] [Continuous Improvement]

7. C - This is an example of Patterns and Shifts activity. The team looks for links and connections between facts and feelings and guides the group in recognizing and naming patterns that contribute to current issues. [Derby, E. and Larsen, D., 2006. Agile Retrospectives: Making Good Teams Great. 1st ed. Texas: Pragmatic Bookshelf, Page 90] [Continuous Improvement]

8. A - An anti-pattern typically seen in stand-ups is that the team begins to solve problems as they become apparent. Stand-ups are for realizing there are problems – not for solving them. Add the issues to a parking lot, and then create another meeting, which might be right after the stand-up, and solve problems there. [Agile Practice Guide, 1st edition, Page 54] [Problem Detection and Resolution]

9. D - Work breakdown structures are not developed in Agile projects. Further, retrospectives are team reflection events and not planning events. [Cohn, M., 2006. Agile Estimating and Planning. 1st ed.

Massachusetts: Pearson Education. Page 12] [Problem Detection and Resolution]

10. C - No information on health and safety policy or the capacities calculation method has been provided. These two choices can thus be eliminated. Achieving a high level of resource utilization on the project rather than on maintaining sufficient slack to cope with the inherent variability in typical project tasks typically reduces team's productivity. Loading everyone to 100% of capacity has the same effect as loading a highway to 100% of capacity; no one can make any forward progress. [Cohn, M., 2006. Agile Estimating and Planning. 1st ed. Massachusetts: Pearson Education. Page 16] [Team Performance]

11. B - A Kanban board is a WIP management tool. It helps the team boost performance by limiting the Work in Process (WIP). [Agile Practice Guide, 1st edition, Page 103] [Team Performance]

12. D - A servant-leader facilitates an Agile team and doesn't make decisions for the team. [Agile Practice Guide, 1st edition, Page 34] [Value-driven Delivery]

13. D - "Responding to change over following a plan" implies that while Agile teams do value the act of planning, they focus on responding to changing conditions rather than sticking to up-front plans. [Agile Practice Guide, 1st edition, Page 8] [Agile Principles and Mindset]

14. A - According to the scenario, since the network of geysers and hot springs cannot be accurately mapped, freezing the design upfront is not recommended. Delivering the project in small increments can manage this risk. This might require design changes as new information becomes available. [Agile Practice Guide, 1st edition, Page 16] [Value-driven Delivery]

15. A - If the amount of new functionality is fixed, state your uncertainty as a date range rather than providing a single completion date estimate. The rest of the choices are not recommended Agile practices. [Cohn, M., 2006. Agile Estimating and Planning. 1st ed. Massachusetts: Pearson Education. Page 248] [Adaptive Planning]

16. D - Sensitivity analysis is a risk analysis technique and cannot help in forecasting a team's velocity. The rest of the choices are valid approaches. [Cohn, M., 2006. Agile Estimating and Planning. 1st ed. Massachusetts: Pearson Education. Page 175] [Problem Detection and Resolution]

17. D - Although Agile teams are not only willing but anxious to change, Agile teams do not change plans just for the sake of changing. Agile planning accommodates changes but is still focused on project objectives. [Cohn, M., 2006. Agile Estimating and Planning. 1st ed. Massachusetts: Pearson Education. Page 9] [Adaptive Planning]

18. C - Critical path method, critical chain method, and precedence diagramming method are scheduling techniques used in predictive approaches. Agile approaches include iterative scheduling, on-demand scheduling, and pull-based scheduling. [Agile Practice Guide, 1st edition, Page 92] [Adaptive Planning]

19. A - Agile teams are best at estimating work that is all within one order of magnitude in size. Working with user stories that fall within these ranges will provide the best combination of effort and accuracy. [Cohn, M., 2006. Agile Estimating and Planning. 1st ed. Massachusetts: Pearson Education. Page 249] [Adaptive Planning]

20. D - Broken Comb, also known as Paint-Drip, is a person who has various depths of specialization in multiple skills required by the team. A T-shaped person is the one who has deep area of specialization and broad ability in the rest of the skills required by the team. These are the kinds of people you would like to have in your team in order to form a cross-functional Agile team. [Agile Practice Guide, 1st edition, Pages 150, 153, 155] [Team Performance]

21. B - A burndown chart shows a team's progress by showing the number of story points remaining in the project. The vertical axis shows the number of story points remaining and the iterations are shown across the horizontal axis. A steadily declining burndown chart indicates that the velocity is constant; the same number of story points are being delivered in each project iteration. [Cohn, M., 2006. Agile Estimating and Planning. 1st ed. Massachusetts: Pearson Education. Page 212] [Team Performance]

22. B - A minimum viable product (MVP) is a product or a project outcome that contains sufficient features to satisfy project stakeholders. [Agile Practice Guide, 1st edition, Page 23] [Stakeholder Engagement]

23. A - Exhaustive product backlogs are not developed in Agile projects that would be a waterfall approach. Documentation and processes are both lesser valued than a working product. Agile approaches promise better user experience of project deliverables by early and continual involvement of users. [Agile Practice Guide, 1st edition, Page 58] [Value-driven Delivery]

24. A - Agile coaches play the role of mentors for Agile teams. The servant-leader (project manager or the Scrum master) is responsible for facilitating and removing impediments. [Agile Practice Guide, 1st edition, Page 150] [Agile Principles and Mindset]

25. C - The team should consider making work visible using Kanban boards and experimenting with limits for the various areas of the work process in order to improve flow. [Agile Practice Guide, 1st edition, Page 32] [Problem Detection and Resolution]

26. D - With the ESVP activity, you need to be careful about conducting anonymous polling. If voters fear that their names will be called out, they might not cast an honest vote, especially the prisoners and the vacationers. [Derby, E. and Larsen, D., 2006. Agile Retrospectives: Making Good Teams Great. 1st ed. Texas: Pragmatic Bookshelf, Page 45] [Continuous Improvement]

27. C - The amount of effort required to deliver a user story is known as story size. Teams consider story size so that they do not try to commit to more stories than there is team capacity. [Agile Practice Guide, 1st edition, Page 55] [Adaptive Planning]

28. A - Backlog grooming, also known as backlog refining, involves adding, removing, and prioritizing stories in the product backlog. The purpose of refinement is to help the team understand what the stories are and how large the stories are in relation to each other. [Agile Practice Guide, 1st edition, Page 52] [Adaptive Planning]

29. C - Ideally, the stand-ups should not take more than 15 minutes. [Agile Practice Guide, 1st edition, Page 53] [Adaptive Planning]

30. C - Deferring the development until the design is complete is a waterfall approach. Using a Kanban board can help managing the work but frequent retrospectives can really facilitate process improvement by allowing the team to brainstorm on what went well and what went wrong. [Agile Practice Guide, 1st edition, Page 32] [Problem Detection and Resolution]

31. C - In this case, if the CPI is greater than 1.0, then the SPI will also be greater than 1.0 (since it is greater than the CPI). This implies that the project is ahead of schedule. [Agile Practice Guide, 1st edition, Page 69] [Team Performance]

32. D - An Agile approach should provide a quick fix rather than asking for any laborious method. In this situation, it is recommended to add a spike task for the knowledge work and a task placeholder with a rough duration estimate. A spike is a task included in an iteration plan that is being undertaken specifically to gain knowledge or answer a question. [Cohn, M., 2006. Agile Estimating and Planning. 1st ed. Massachusetts: Pearson Education. Page 154] [Continuous Improvement]

33. B - No project is completely devoid of considerations around requirements, delivery, change and goals. A project's inherent characteristics determine which life cycle is the best fit for that project. [Agile Practice Guide, 1st edition, Page 18] [Agile Principles and Mindset]

34. D - The throughput of a single team member should not affect the project scope, sprint duration or the cost of the project. However, it might create a bottleneck for the rest of the team members due to the difference in individual throughputs. [Agile Practice Guide, 1st edition, Page 42] [Team Performance]

35. B - Agile teams, ideally, should be small teams. It is advisable to divide the bigger team into smaller Agile teams and conduct separate daily standups. For the coordination between the two teams, a Scrum of Scrums should be arranged. [Cohn, M., 2006. Agile Estimating and Planning. 1st ed. Massachusetts: Pearson Education. Page 57] [Problem Detection and Resolution]

36. B - The best thing to be done at this stage is help the project manager understand and realize the benefits of Agile approaches and why these are better than traditional approaches if there is a significant degree of change associated with the project work. [Agile Practice Guide, 1st edition, Page 7] [Stakeholder Engagement]

37. D - If a feature is not required, the development of that feature needs to stop. The code might be deleted or archived, but the story should not be returned to the backlog. Freezing the iteration is not a rational choice for this situation. Such issues are generally discussed first in the daily planning events. [Cohn, M., 2006. Agile Estimating and Planning. 1st ed. Massachusetts: Pearson Education. Page 28] [Problem Detection and Resolution]

38. B - Sitting together and pair working are XP techniques. [Agile Practice Guide, 1st edition, Page 102] [Value-driven Delivery]

39. C - The iteration plan looks ahead only the length of one iteration, usually one to four weeks. The user stories of the release plan are decomposed into tasks in the iteration plan. Where the user stories of a release plan are estimated in story points or ideal days, the tasks on the iteration plan are estimated in ideal hours. It is not recommended to allocate tasks during the iteration planning. [Cohn, M., 2006. Agile Estimating and Planning. 1st ed. Massachusetts: Pearson Education. Pages 145, 146] [Adaptive Planning]

40. C - You should not schedule these events well in advance, the project team decides when to call a retrospective. Retrospectives can be scheduled on different occasions, such as the end of sprint, completion of a release, achievement of some milestone, or whenever the team gets stuck with the project work. [Agile Practice Guide, 1st edition, Page 51] [Continuous Improvement]

PMI-ACP Lite Mock Exam 6 Practice Questions

Test Name: PMI-ACP Lite Mock Exam 6
Total Questions: 40
Correct Answers Needed to Pass:
30 (75.00%)
Time Allowed: 60 Minutes

Test Description

This is a cumulative PMI-ACP Mock Exam which can be used as a benchmark for your PMI-ACP aptitude. This practice test includes questions from all exam topic areas, including sections from Agile Tools and Techniques, and all three Agile Knowledge and Skills areas.

Test Questions

1. If a team has planned 50 story points to be completed in the upcoming project sprint, this implies that the:

A. Benchmark velocity is 50 story points.

B. Actual velocity is 50 story points.

C. Aspirational velocity is 50 story points.

D. Expected velocity is 50 story points.

2. You are leading a complex project with a huge list of features. Due to schedule and budget constraints, you might not be able to develop all of the features. Which of the following would help in developing the feature set that maximizes business value?

A. Decision tree analysis

B. MoSCoW analysis

C. Analysis of variance

D. Feasibility analysis

3. Which of the following Agile plans is generally the most precise?

A. Release

B. Task

C. Iteration

D. Daily

4. Your project team has recently completed the 3rd iteration on the project. So far 45 story points have been successfully delivered to the customer. For this project, the iteration size is fixed at three weeks. The team (six team members) is dedicated to working five days per week. Looking at the backlog, you have 150 story points remaining to be delivered. How many more weeks are required to complete the project?

A. 10

B. 30

C. 15

D. 1

5. Which of the following roles is responsible for helping the management of an organization to understand the advantages of Agile practices, tools and techniques?

A. Product owner

B. Agile coach

C. Scrum master

D. Agile manager

6. You have been hired as an Agile coach by an organization that has recently decided to transition to Agile approaches. Which of the following Agile approaches can help the in shifting a team's focus from creating a perfect plan at the start of the project to creating a plan that is more useful in the short term?

A. Re-planning frequently.

B. Selecting no more than 30 story points per iteration.

C. Creating smaller Agile teams.

D. Replacing the project manager with a Scrum master.

7. You are your Agile team are currently discussing the variation and the causes of variation between the expected velocity and the observed velocity. Which Agile meeting is this?

A. Iteration planning

B. Iteration retrospective

C. Daily standups

D. Release planning

8. During an ESVP activity, each participant anonymously reports his or her attitude toward the retrospective as an Explorer, Shopper, Vacationer, or Prisoner. Who are the vacationers?

A. People who enjoy the proceeding of the retrospective.

B. People who are working part-time on the project.

C. People who aren't interested in the work of the retrospective.

D. People who want to lead the project.

9. You have just been awarded a new project. The goal of the project is to cut the indirect production cost of your manufacturing client by 15% with a focus on inventory management costs. You are confident that you can achieve this goal as you have recently helped several other organizations in the same industry to achieve a similar objective by introducing your proprietary inventory management and control framework. What is the problem with the project objective?

A. It is not time bound.

B. It is not measurable.

C. It is not specific.

D. It is not attainable.

10. A project has dynamic requirements. Project activities are required to be performed once for a given increment but each increment is supposed to produce deliveries for the customer. Further, the focus is on the speed of deliveries. Which of the following life cycles is most suitable in this scenario?

A. Incremental

B. Agile

C. Predictive

D. Iterative

11. When planning an iteration, don't:

A. Calculate estimate of expected velocity during the iteration.

B. Plan on using 100% of every team member's time.

C. Include buffers when multiple teams are involved.

D. Select stories based on their business value.

12. You are leading a retrospective and feel that things are not progressing as planned. There is a lot of negative energy in the room due to the drop of team velocity during the previous iteration. Which of the following Agile activities can help you provide a balance?

A. Brainstorming

B. Backlog grooming

C. Timeline

D. Locate Strengths

13. Which of the following is an organizational construct that focuses on the flow of value to customers through the delivery of specific products or services?

A. Kano Model

B. Business Canvas

C. Value Stream

D. Pareto Chart

14. A senior programmer on your Agile team is usually keen on trying and experimenting with new technologies and ideas. As a result of some of her successful spikes, some of the business requirements were delivered earlier than planned. Which ESVP role closely relates to this type of team members?

A. Experimenter

B. Shopper

C. Vacationer

D. Explorer

15. Agile methods and practices have both direct and indirect benefits. In Agile projects, which of the following Agile techniques also helps in managing quality of deliverables?

A. Backlog grooming

B. Rapid feature delivery

C. User story sizing

D. Team chartering

16. In iteration-based Agile, the product owner often works with the team to prepare some stories for the upcoming iteration, during one or more sessions in the middle of the iteration. The purpose of these meetings is to groom enough stories so the team understands what the stories are and how large the stories are in relation to each other. This is also known as:

A. Ground rules

B. Retrospectives

C. Backlog refinement

D. Group norms

17. Which of the following statements regarding a release burndown chart is incorrect?

A. A release burndown chart shows the number of story points remaining in the project.

B. The irregularity of the burndown chart comes from the change in team's velocity due to inaccurate estimates.

C. A release burndown chart can be used to accurately forecast the project completion.

D. A team's burndown is rarely perfectly smooth.

18. According to the Agile principles, which of the following enhances agility?

A. Continuous change requests.

B. Chain of command within an Agile team.

C. Time-boxed iterations and a fixed project scope.

D. Continuous attention to technical excellence.

19. An Agile team is currently playing planning poker. What does that mean?

A. Team is scheduling tasks.

B. Team is developing improvement strategies.

C. Team is estimating stories.

D. Team is on a well-earned holiday.

20. An Agile team wishes to subcontract some of the project work. Rather than formalizing an entire contracting relationship in a single contract, the team wishes to describe different aspects of the relationship in different documents. Mostly fixed items such was warranties and arbitration have been recommended to be locked in the master agreement. However, other items subject to change, series rates and product descriptions, for example, should be listed in a separate:

A. Project schedule

B. Memorandum of Understanding

C. Schedule of services

D. Contract

21. Which of the following is the correct sequence of agenda items in a typical retrospective?

A. Gather data -> Generate insights -> Decide what to do -> Set the stage -> Close retrospective.

B. Set the stage -> Gather data -> Generate insights -> Decide what to do -> Close retrospective.

C. Set the stage -> Generate insights -> Gather data -> Decide what to do -> Close retrospective.

D. Set the stage -> Generate insights -> Decide what to do -> Gather data -> Close retrospective.

22. An Agile team is working on a complex enterprise resource management system development project. The huge product backlog was prioritized based on their relative values. During each iteration, the team develops and successfully demonstrates the completed user stories. However, due to the prioritization of the user stories, user stories selected for a particular iteration may not be related with the user stories completed during the previous iteration. Which of the following activity will be a challenge in this situation?

A. Continuous integration.

B. Prototyping of the completed features.

C. User stories sizing.

D. Backlog refinement.

23. You have recently been hired to head the projects management office of a government organization. The projects management office is responsible for managing a wide range of improvement and transformation projects. Historically all past projects were managed using a traditional waterfall approach. You believe a hybrid of Agile and waterfall approaches is most suitable for most of the projects. How should you approach this transformation?

A. Plan a gradual transformation.

B. Switchover to a hybrid model immediately for all projects.

C. Continue with the waterfall approach for ongoing projects but use the hybrid approach for all new projects.

D. Stick to the waterfall approach as this method is best suited for governmental setups.

24. Which of the following actions will NOT reduce the lead time of a user story?

A. Reducing the response time by using new technology.

B. Scheduling the story sooner than later.

C. Including more stories in the iteration plan.

D. Increasing the velocity by adding new team members.

25. Which of the following is NOT considered a good Agile practice?

A. Forming a large Agile team proportional to the project size.

B. Restructuring large projects as multiple smaller projects.

C. Reducing the team down to its critical core members.

D. Trying a technology trial project first and then an implementation project.

26. You have been assigned to automate the core processes of an organization. Due to the size and the complexity of the project you would need multiple Agile teams working concurrently to achieve the project objectives. Which of the following approach is NOT recommended in this situation?

A. Scrum

B. Large Scale Scrum (LeSS)

C. Scrum of Scrum of Scrums

D. Scrum of Scrums

27. You are leading a five year long project. Your cost analyst reported that the accounting rate of return is 50% which can only be realized at the end of the project. You are not sure how meaningful that information is as the inflation rates haven't been factored in by the cost analyst. Which of the following financial measures will produce a more reliable estimate in this situation?

A. Discount rate

B. Net future value

C. Interest rate

D. Net present value

28. Agile teams rely on simplified cost calculations for each iteration rather than developing extensive project budgets during a planning phase at the start of the project. In Agile lexicon, this is also known as:

A. Run rate

B. Burn down

C. User stories

D. Epics

29. A dedicated Agile team is currently working on an ERP system customization and deployment project five days a week. Each iteration is time-boxed at three weeks. A total of 500 story points were estimated at the start of the project. The team has recently completed its 4th iteration on the project and have successfully delivered 30 story points during this iteration. So far, the team has delivered a total of 120 story points on the project. If no new stories have been added to the project since initiation, what was the response time (in weeks) for the 30 stories delivered during the last iteration?

A. 12

B. 2

C. 9

D. 0.5

30. If a project costing $125,000 produces a $139,000 return at the end of a year, what is the interest rate?

A. 0.112

B. 0.106

C. 0.114

D. 0.101

31. You have recently helped an organization transition to Agile. The new Agile teams have started to work in a cohesive and cooperative manner. You are expecting this transition to challenge some of the traditional HR policies in the company, because:

A. Individual incentives would make less sense and managers might struggle with the performance appraisals of the self-organizing teams.

B. Individual incentives would become more relevant and managers might conduct better performance appraisals of the self-organizing teams.

C. Individual incentives would become more relevant and managers might struggle with the performance appraisals of the self-organizing teams.

D. Individual incentives would make less sense and managers might conduct better performance appraisals of the self-organizing teams.

32. You are developing a financial application for a client with complex business requirements. After a cost/benefit analysis was performed for each requirement, you found that the requirements can be sorted based on their expected business value. Further these requirements are mutually exclusive and can be developed individually. Which of the following project life cycle would result in an earlier return on investment in this scenario?

A. Predictive life cycle; the traditional approach reduces uncertainty and results in lower costs.

B. Incremental life cycle; the team can only provide finished deliverables.

C. Agile life cycle; the team can deliver highest value work first.

D. Iterative life cycle; the team can obtain feedback on partially completed on unfinished work.

33. Which of the following is an Agile approach that was originally designed as a way to transition from Scrum to Kanban?

A. Lean

B. Scrumban

C. XP

D. Kaizan

34. Which of the following models can be used to categorize a product features based on organizational desirability?

A. PDCA model

B. Business operating model

C. Salience model

D. Kano model

35. Agile approaches emphasize early and frequent delivery. However, this accelerated delivery might not suit some organizations due to their ability to accommodate rapid deliveries. If an organization resists a project's outcome, which of the following risks becomes more likely to occur?

A. Project costs skyrocket.

B. Scope creep becomes unmanageable.

C. Story points get doubled for each item in the backlog.

D. Targeted return on investment is delayed.

36. Which of the following models can help in empowering Agile project teams?

A. Theory X

B. Root cause analysis

C. Rewards and penalties

D. Servant-leadership model

37. Which of the following refers to excess time arbitrarily added to an estimate?

A. Schedule buffering

B. Padding

C. Feature buffering

D. Adding lags

38. Which of the following is the correct formula for estimating the number of iterations remaining on the project?

A. Points remaining/velocity

B. Total story points/number of user stories) * velocity

C. Total story points/number of user stories

D. Number of user stories/total story points

39. How is the activity ROTI conducted?

A. At the end of retrospective, ask team members how do they plan on utilizing their non-working time.

B. At the start of retrospective, ask team members to give feedback on whether they spent their time well.

C. At the start of retrospective, ask team members how do they plan on utilizing their non-working time.

D. At the end of retrospective, ask team members to give feedback on whether they spent their time well.

40. You have analyzed all the themes of your project and have assigned each one of them to one of the four quadrants of a risk-value matrix that has a risk rating (high and low) on the y-axis, and a business value rating (high and low) on the x-axis. What is the recommend approach to be taken for the themes that fell under the "High Risk" and "High Value" quadrant?

A. Avoid

B. Do last

C. Do first

D. Do second

PMI-ACP Lite Mock Exam 6 Answer Key and Explanations

1. D - If a team has planned 50 story points to be completed in the upcoming project sprint, this implies that the expected velocity is 50 story points. The aspirational velocity should be higher than this and the actual velocity might be different at the end of the iteration. On Agile projects, there is no such thing as benchmark velocity. [Agile Practice Guide, 1st edition, Page 61] [Team Performance]

2. B - MoSCoW stands for must have, should have, could have, and won't have. DSDM refers to this sorting as the MoSCoW rules. Applying MoSCoW rules to project requirements ensure that the highest valued business requirements/features are developed first. [Cohn, M., 2006. Agile Estimating and Planning. 1st ed. Massachusetts: Pearson Education. Page 187] [Value-driven Delivery]

3. D - Task planning is not a recommended Agile approach. Agile plans cover three different levels–the release, the iteration, and the current day. The daily plan, as committed to by each participant in a team's daily meeting is the most precise. [Cohn, M., 2006. Agile Estimating and Planning. 1st ed. Massachusetts: Pearson Education. Page 245] [Adaptive Planning]

4. B - Since the team has successfully delivered 45 stories in three iterations, the velocity is 15 stories per iteration. There are 150 more story points to be delivered, which will require another 10 iterations (150/15). Since each iteration is fixed at three weeks, the expected completion time is 10 x 3 = 30 weeks. [Agile Practice Guide, 1st edition, Page 61] [Team Performance]

5. B - An Agile coach is usually responsible for helping the management of an organization to understand the advantages of Agile practices, tools and techniques. [Agile Practice Guide, 1st edition, Page 150] [Value-driven Delivery]

6. A - Knowing that a plan can be revised at the start of the next iteration shifts a team's focus from creating a perfect plan (an impossible goal) to creating a plan that is useful right now. [Cohn, M., 2006. Agile Estimating and Planning. 1st ed. Massachusetts: Pearson Education. Page 244] [Adaptive Planning]

7. B - During iteration retrospectives, Agile teams analyze their progress and share lessons learned. Retrospectives allow the teams to learn about, improve, and adopt their processes. [Agile Practice Guide, 1st edition, Page 50] [Continuous Improvement]

8. C - Vacationers aren't interested in the work of the retrospective, but are happy to be away from the daily grind. They may pay attention some of the time, but they are mostly glad to be out of the office. [Derby, E. and Larsen, D., 2006. Agile Retrospectives: Making Good Teams Great. 1st ed. Texas: Pragmatic Bookshelf, Page 45] [Continuous Improvement]

9. A - The objective is specific and measurable (cutting the indirect manufacturing cost by 15%), and also seems attainable (success with other clients). The problem with the project objective is that there is no time-frame defined to achieve the stated outcomes. [Derby, E. and Larsen, D., 2006.

Agile Retrospectives: Making Good Teams Great. 1st ed. Texas: Pragmatic Bookshelf, Page 107] [Agile Principles and Mindset]

10. A - An incremental life cycle is recommend in this case since the focus is on speed of deliveries which are made through a series of increments. [Agile Practice Guide, 1st edition, Page 18] [Agile Principles and Mindset]

11. B - When planning an iteration, do not plan on using 100% of every team member's time but leave some slack. Just as a highway experiences gridlock when filled to 100% capacity, so will a development team slow down when every person's time is planned to be 100% used. [Cohn, M., 2006. Agile Estimating and Planning. 1st ed. Massachusetts: Pearson Education. Page 250] [Adaptive Planning]

12. D - The objective of the "Locate Strengths" activity is to provide a balance when an iteration, release, or project hasn't gone well. [Derby, E. and Larsen, D., 2006. Agile Retrospectives: Making Good Teams Great. 1st ed. Texas: Pragmatic Bookshelf, Page 63] [Continuous Improvement]

13. C - Value Stream is an organizational construct that focuses on the flow of value to customers through the delivery of specific products or services. [Agile Practice Guide, 1st edition, Page 154] [Continuous Improvement]

14. D - Explorers are eager to discover new ideas and insights. They want to learn everything they can about the iteration/release/project. [Derby, E. and Larsen, D., 2006. Agile Retrospectives: Making Good Teams Great. 1st ed. Texas: Pragmatic Bookshelf, Page 45] [Continuous Improvement]

15. B - If the team does not pay attention to quality, it will soon become impossible to release anything rapidly. This is an indirect benefit of rapid feature delivery. [Agile Practice Guide, 1st edition, Page 56] [Value-driven Delivery]

16. C - Backlog grooming is also known as backlog refinement. In iteration-based Agile, the product owner often works with the team to prepare some stories for the upcoming iteration during one or more sessions in the middle of the iteration. The purpose of these meetings is to groom enough stories so the team understands what the stories are and how large the stories are in relation to each other. [Agile Practice Guide, 1st edition, Page 52] [Value-driven Delivery]

17. C - A release burndown chart shows the number of story points or ideal days remaining in the project as of the start of each iteration. A team's burndown is never perfectly smooth. It will vary because of inaccurate estimates, changed estimates, and changes in scope. A burndown chart can help in forecasting the project completion but the forecast is usually not very accurate. [Cohn, M., 2006. Agile Estimating and Planning. 1st ed. Massachusetts: Pearson Education. Page 218] [Team Performance]

18. D - According to the Agile principles, continuous attention to technical excellence and good design enhance agility. [Agile Practice Guide, 1st edition, Page 9] [Agile Principles and Mindset]

19. C - Planning poker is an Agile estimation technique. [Cohn, M., 2006. Agile Estimating and Planning. 1st ed. Massachusetts: Pearson Education. Page 56] [Adaptive Planning]

20. C - Listing these items in a separate contract or MOU doesn't make sense. Further, a project schedule has a specific objective which is not in line with the situation at hand. Items subject to change are recommended to be listed separately in a schedule of services. [Agile Practice Guide, 1st edition, Page 77] [Value-driven Delivery]

21. B - The recommended sequence is: Set the stage -> Gather data -> Generate insights -> Decide what to do -> Close retrospective. [Derby, E. and Larsen, D., 2006. Agile Retrospectives: Making Good Teams Great. 1st ed. Texas: Pragmatic Bookshelf, Page 4] [Continuous Improvement]

22. A - User stories sizing, backlog refinement and prototyping should be indifferent to the inter-relationship of features developed during different iterations. However, the team will find it challenging to continuously integrate new features to the previously developed features and test the system as a whole. [Agile Practice Guide, 1st edition, Page 56] [Value-driven Delivery]

23. A - Many teams are not able to make the switch to Agile ways of working overnight. The larger the organization, the more time is required for the transition. In such a setup, it makes sense to plan a gradual transition. [Agile Practice Guide, 1st edition, Page 30] [Problem Detection and Resolution]

24. C - The lead time is the total time it takes to deliver an item, measured from the time it is added to the board to the moment it is delivered. Cycle time is the time required to process an item. Lead time = response time + cycle time. The lead time can be reduced by either reducing the response time or the cycle time or both. Scheduling the story earlier reduces the response time, while increasing the velocity reduces the cycle time. However the number of stories in the iteration plan doesn't affect the lead time. [Agile Practice Guide, 1st edition, Page 64] [Problem Detection and Resolution]

25. A - Reducing the team down to its critical core members is recommended. Often too many people hinder a process, not help it. Consider restructuring a large project into multiple smaller projects or piloting complex projects before a full-scale implementation. [Agile Practice Guide, 1st edition, Page 121] [Agile Principles and Mindset]

26. A - The Scrum method is focused on a single small team. Scrum of Scrums (SoS), also known as "meta Scrum", is a technique used when two or more Scrum teams consisting of three to nine members each need to coordinate their work instead of one large Scrum team. Larger projects with several teams may result in conducting a Scrum of Scrum of Scrums, which follows the same pattern as SoS. Large Scale Scrum (LeSS) is a framework for organizing several development teams toward a common goal extending the Scrum method. [Agile Practice Guide, 1st edition, Pages 111, 113] [Value-driven Delivery]

27. D - Economists and financial analysts generally use alternative approaches to measure financial benefits such as IRR and NPV since the accounting rate of return measure doesn't factor in time value of money. [Cohn, M., 2006. Agile Estimating and Planning. 1st ed. Massachusetts: Pearson Education. Page 100] [Value-driven Delivery]

28. A - In Agile environments, project teams frequently determine and revise simplified cost calculations also known as the run rates. [Agile Practice Guide, 1st edition, Page 40] [Team Performance]

29. C - Response time is the time that an item waits until work starts. The 30 story points completed in the 4th iteration waited for three iterations, i.e., 3 x 3 = 9 weeks. [Agile Practice Guide, 1st edition, Page 64] [Team Performance]

30. A - Present Value (PV) = Future Value (FV) / (1 + interest rate) ^ periods. $125,000 = $139,000 / (1 + i)^1. Solving for i, we get the interest rate of 11.2%. [Cohn, M., 2006. Agile Estimating and Planning. 1st ed. Massachusetts: Pearson Education. Page 100] [Value-driven Delivery]

31. A - Human resources may notice individual incentives make less sense and managers may struggle with the performance appraisals of self-organizing employees. [Agile Practice Guide, 1st edition, Page 79] [Value-driven Delivery]

32. C - Agile life cycle leverages both the aspects of iterative and incremental characteristics. When teams use Agile approaches, they iterate over the product to create finished deliverables and get early feedback. Because the team can release earlier, the project may provide an earlier return on investment because the team delivers the highest value of work first. [Agile Practice Guide, 1st edition, Page 19] [Agile Principles and Mindset]

33. B - Scrumban is an Agile approach originally designed as a way to transition from Scrum to Kanban. As additional Agile frameworks and methodologies emerged, it became an evolving hybrid framework in and of itself where teams use Scrum as a framework and Kanban for process improvement. [Agile Practice Guide, 1st edition, Page 108] [Value-driven Delivery]

34. D - The Kano model is an approach that separates features into three categories: must-have features, linear features, and delighters. [Cohn, M., 2006. Agile Estimating and Planning. 1st ed. Massachusetts: Pearson Education. Page 110] [Adaptive Planning]

35. D - If an organization is resistant to the project's outcome, the targeted return on investment is delayed due to initial challenges related to the organizational change management. The rest of the risks are not directly related to the problem at hand. [Agile Practice Guide, 1st edition, Page 73] [Agile Principles and Mindset]

36. D - Theory X stresses the importance of strict supervision, external rewards, and penalties which negatively influence a team's performance. Rewards and penalties can influence an outcome but don't empower a team. Root cause analysis is irrelevant to the question; it's just a distractor. The correct response is a servant-leadership model. [Agile Practice Guide, 1st edition, Page 33] [Agile Principles and Mindset]

37. B - The term padding has the pejorative meaning of excess time arbitrarily added to an estimate. We pad an estimate when we think it will take three days to complete a task but declare a five day estimate, just in case. [Cohn, M., 2006. Agile Estimating and Planning. 1st ed. Massachusetts: Pearson Education. Page 197] [Adaptive Planning]

38. A - The simple way to predict the number of iterations remaining is to take the number of points remaining to be developed and divide this by the team's velocity and then round up to the next whole number. [Cohn, M., 2006. Agile Estimating and Planning. 1st ed. Massachusetts: Pearson Education. Page 232] [Team Performance]

39. D - ROTI stands for Return on Time Invested. This technique is used in the closing retrospective phase for iteration or release retrospectives. It helps generate feedback on the retrospective process and gauge the effectiveness of the session from the team members' perspectives. At the end of retrospective, the retrospective leader asks the team members to give feedback on whether they spent their time well. [Derby, E. and Larsen, D., 2006. Agile Retrospectives: Making Good Teams Great. 1st ed. Texas: Pragmatic Bookshelf, Page 124] [Team Performance]

40. C - "Do first" is recommended for themes that have been classified as "High Risk" and "High Value". [Cohn, M., 2006. Agile Estimating and Planning. 1st ed. Massachusetts: Pearson Education. Page 85] [Problem Detection and Resolution]

PMI-ACP Knowledge Area Quiz: Value-driven Delivery Practice Questions

Test Name: Knowledge Area Test: Agile Estimation
Total Questions: 15
Correct Answers Needed to Pass:
11 (73.33%)
Time Allowed: 25 Minutes

Test Description

This practice quiz specifically targets your knowledge of the Agile Estimation exam topic area.

Test Questions

1. Which of the following techniques involves the use of story cards, continuous integration, refactoring, automated testing, and test-driven development?

A. Lean

B. XP

C. Six Sigma

D. Scrum

2. You have been assigned to automate the core processes of an organization. Due to the size and the complexity of the project you would need multiple teams working concurrently to achieve the project objectives. Which of the following approaches is recommended in this situation?

A. AgileUP

B. Scrum of Scrums (SoS)

C. XP

D. Scrum

3. An Agile team is managing its work in progress on a Kanban board. Recently the WIP limits have been met and the team cannot pull further work from the "Ready" column into the "WIP" column. What is the question all team members need to address in the next daily stand-up?

A. Where do we go to celebrate today?

B. What do we do as a team to move work from the "WIP" column to the "Done" column?

C. Who is the weakest link on the team that has caused this issue?

D. How much increase in the WIP limit is required at this stage?

4. Traditional approaches govern vendor relationships by fixed milestones or phase gates focused on intermediate artifacts. On the other hand Agile approaches require:

A. Full deliverables of incremental business value.

B. Incomplete deliverables at the end of each iteration.

C. Partial but frequent deliveries.

D. One delivery at the end of the project.

5. IRR is defined as the interest rate at which the NPV of a cash flow stream is equal to:

A. Zero

B. Opportunity cost

C. Cost of capital

D. ROI

6. Which of the following Agile approaches is more suitable for a project that requires significant breadth of life cycle coverage and involves significant depth of guidance detail?

A. FDD

B. Kanban

C. Scrum

D. Disciplined Agile

7. You and your team are about to start a new project. In the past the team has faced issues with estimating user stories and provided inaccurate estimates. All of the following actions can help mitigate this risk from happing on this project EXCEPT:

A. Develop a team charter.

B. Reduce story size by splitting stories.

C. Use relative estimation.

D. Use Agile modeling or spiking.

8. Which of the following is not a best practice associated with Feature-Driven Development (FDD)?

A. Developing by feature

B. Domain object modeling

C. Configuration management

D. Change control boards

9. Which of the following financial metrics is generally considered best to compare different projects?

A. IRR

B. IRR and NPV used together

C. Payback period

D. NPV

10. When computing the net present value of a project, a reasonable discount rate is used in the calculation. What is this discount rate?

A. The opportunity cost

B. The interest rate on a savings account

C. The average inflation rate

D. The discounts allowed to the customer

11. An Agile team wants to outsource a chunk of project scope to a vendor. Instead of locking the entire procurement scope of work and budget into a single agreement, the team is considering decomposing the scope into fixed-price micro-deliverables. Which of the following can be used as micro-deliverables for the agreement?

A. WBS and WBS Dictionary

B. Kanban board

C. Team charter

D. User stories

12. Julia was assigned to program a feature in five days. Julia completed the expected work in four days and added a few bells and whistles to the feature on the last day. This additional work is commonly known as:

A. Value add

B. Scope creep

C. Gold plating

D. Laissez faire

13. You want to establish a mechanism to facilitate coordination between Agile teams by communicating between projects; a platform that will enable sharing items such as progress, issues, retrospective findings and improvement experiments. You need:

A. An Agile PMO

B. Command and control center

C. Collocation

D. External consultant

14. Which of the following statements regarding LeSS and Scrum is correct?

A. Scrum has one definition of "done" while LeSS has separate definitions of "done" for each team.

B. Scrum requires one potentially shippable product increment at the end of each sprint, while LeSS mandates a single final delivery.

C. Both approaches require a single product backlog.

D. Scrum has a product owner but this role is not recognized in LeSS.

15. Which of the following metrics can be used to determine the value of a feature?

A. CPI

B. ROI

C. TCPI

D. SPI

PMI-ACP Knowledge Area Quiz: Value-driven Delivery Answer Key and Explanations

1. B - XP-inspired engineering practices involve the use of story cards, continuous integration, refactoring, automated testing, and test-driven development. [Agile Practice Guide, 1st edition, Page 31] [Value-driven Delivery]

2. B - Scrum of Scrums (SoS), also known as "meta Scrum", is a technique used when two or more Scrum teams consisting of three to nine members each need to coordinate their work instead of one large Scrum team. [Agile Practice Guide, 1st edition, Page 111] [Value-driven Delivery]

3. B - When the team has met its WIP limits, the team cannot pull work from the left into the next column. The team works from the right-most full column and asks, "What do we do as a team to move this work into the next column?" [Agile Practice Guide, 1st edition, Page 66] [Value-driven Delivery]

4. A - Agile approaches prefer working products/features rather than partially developed products/features. Incomplete or partial deliveries are not required as they don't have business value. On the other extreme, one delivery at the end of the project is a waterfall approach. Agile teams focus on complete deliverables of incremental business value. [Agile Practice Guide, 1st edition, Page 77] [Value-driven Delivery]

5. A - IRR is defined as the interest rate at which the NPV of a cash flow stream is equal to 0. NPV of a project is generally compared with the minimum attractive rate of return (MARR) values set by the organization. Only projects with an IRR that exceeds the MARR are generally selected. [Cohn, M., 2006. Agile Estimating and Planning. 1st ed. Massachusetts: Pearson Education. Page 102] [Value-driven Delivery]

6. D - If a project requires significant breadth of life cycle coverage and involves significant depth of guidance detail, you should ideally be looking for a scaled Agile approach. From the given choices only Disciplined Agile is a scaled approach. [Agile Practice Guide, 1st edition, Page 100] [Value-driven Delivery]

7. A - Developing a team charter is a good practice but that cannot mitigate the risk at hand. The other choices are valid mitigation strategies. [Agile Practice Guide, 1st edition, Page 58] [Value-driven Delivery]

8. D - Feature-Driven Development activities are supported by a core set of software engineering best practices: Domain object modeling, developing by feature, individual class ownership, feature teams, inspections, configuration management, regular builds, and visibility of progress and results. Change control boards are recommended for traditional project management approaches. [Agile Practice Guide, 1st edition, Page 109] [Value-driven Delivery]

9. B - The payback period method doesn't consider the time-value of money and cannot be the ideal measure. Both NPV and IRR consider the time-value of money but each of these methods have their advantages and disadvantages. It is recommended using both measures together. [Cohn, M., 2006. Agile Estimating and Planning. 1st ed.

Massachusetts: Pearson Education. Pages 100 - 104] [Value-driven Delivery]

10. A - The rate by which organizations discount future money is known as their opportunity cost, and reflects the percentage return that is passed up in order to make this investment. [Cohn, M., 2006. Agile Estimating and Planning. 1st ed. Massachusetts: Pearson Education. Page 100] [Value-driven Delivery]

11. D - Rather than lock an entire project scope and budget into a single agreement, a team can decompose the scope into fixed-price micro-deliverables, such as user stories. Team charter and Kanban board are tools used by the team to manage the team's WIP. WBS and WBS dictionary are used in predictive approaches. [Agile Practice Guide, 1st edition, Page 77] [Value-driven Delivery]

12. C - This is known as gold plating. Gold plating refers to intentionally adding extra features or functions to the product which were not included in the product's scope. [Cohn, M., 2006. Agile Estimating and Planning. 1st ed. Massachusetts: Pearson Education. Page 13] [Value-driven Delivery]

13. A - An Agile PMO coordinates between Agile teams by communicating between projects. It facilitates sharing items such as progress, issues, retrospective findings and improvement experiments. An Agile PMO focuses on collaboration rather than establishing a command and control center. Collocation can help but usually is difficult to achieve for all Agile teams. [Agile Practice Guide, 1st edition, Page 82] [Value-driven Delivery]

14. C - Similarities of LeSS and Scrum include one single product backlog, one definition of done for all teams, one potentially shippable product increment at the end of each sprint, and one product owner. [Agile Practice Guide, 1st edition, Page 113] [Value-driven Delivery]

15. B - Agile projects increase ROIs by releasing higher value features before the lower value features. If somehow prioritized features can be released earlier than planned, this can further increase the ROI. [Agile Practice Guide, 1st edition, Page 61] [Value-driven Delivery]

PMI-ACP Lite Mock Exam 7 Practice Questions

Test Name: PMI-ACP Lite Mock Exam 7
Total Questions: 40
Correct Answers Needed to Pass:
30 (75.00%)
Time Allowed: 60 Minutes

Test Description

This is a cumulative PMI-ACP Mock Exam which can be used as a benchmark for your PMI-ACP aptitude. This practice test includes questions from all exam topic areas, including sections from Agile Tools and Techniques, and all three Agile Knowledge and Skills areas.

Test Questions

1. A project team trying Agile methods for the first time is considering Agile reporting methods. Historically the team has been reporting on project baselines and has used earned value management for status reporting. What should be the new approach?

   A. Continue using earned value management for project reporting.

   B. Consider ways to report project's ROI.

   C. Consider ways to report demonstrable value delivery to customers.

   D. Agile teams do not report project progress.

2. Which of the following is NOT a benefit of collocation?

   A. Ability to utilize usual tools.

   B. Increased velocity.

   C. Increased communication.

   D. Controlled changes.

3. During which of the following Agile approaches is project planning managed through weekly and quarterly cycles?

   A. XP

   B. Scrum

   C. Lean

   D. Kanban

4. Which of the following Agile terms means putting requirements in order based on what customers value most?

   A. Project scoping

   B. Backlog refinement

   C. Return on investment (ROI)

   D. Iteration planning

5. An Agile PMO is value-driven. What does that mean?

   A. All Agile projects are value-driven and as a result all Agile PMOs are value-driven.

   B. Agile projects should deliver the right value, to the right audience, at the right time. The Agile PMO's objective is to facilitate and enable this goal.

C. Agile PMOs deliver value to the organization by being the command and control center for all organizational projects.

D. Agile PMOs must ensure that all organizational projects deliver organizational value. The Agile PMOs ensure that by standardizing the project management approach.

6. Which of the following techniques requires frequent incorporation of work into the whole, no matter the product, and then retest to determine that the entire product still works as intended?

A. Continuous integration

B. Behavior Driven Development (BDD)

C. Spikes

D. Acceptance Test Driven Development (ATDD)

7. ABCon is an ERP consulting firm. For the past 15 years ABCon has been implementing ERP systems for it clients. So far, ABCon has followed traditional project management approaches and is now considering piloting Agile on a relatively small and less complex ERP upgrade project that requires a single small team and then trying it on a more complex green-field ERP implementation project for another client that requires multiple Agile teams. If the pilot is not successful, what must ABCon do?

A. Document lessons learned from the pilot project and try avoiding the mistakes made on the more complex project.

B. Shelf the Agile transformation program as this is not producing the desired results for the organization.

C. Do not try Agile on the more complex project. Instead, address the organizational impediments that prevented the pilot team from working in an Agile way.

D. Identify the weaker team members from the team piloting Agile and have them replace with stronger candidates.

8. For your upcoming project, you are currently looking for a balanced Agile framework that is neither too narrow in focus nor too prescriptive in detail. You are ideally looking for a process decision framework that integrates several Agile best practices into a comprehensive model. Which of the following Agile frameworks is recommended in this case?

A. Scrum

B. AgileUP

C. Disciplined Agile

D. Waterfall

9. If the customer wants to incorporate new ideas or features not originally planned into a not-to-exceed time and materials arrangement, which of the following approaches is recommended?

A. Converting the not-to-exceed time and material arrangement to a fixed-price arrangement.

B. Replacing original work with new work.

C. Issuing a new contract for the additional work.

D. Adding new work to the scope of work.

10. Which of the following is the best strategy for prioritizing features?

A. Sorting the desired features based on cycle time.

B. Sorting the desired features based on business value.

C. Sorting the desired features based on ideal days.

D. Sorting the desired features based on story points.

11. You are leading an Agile project. The team has proposed using a Kanban board to manage the team's work in progress and spot bottlenecks. Which of the following is the correct order of categories for the flow of work items on a Kanban board?

A. Ready -> Develop and Unit Test -> Dev-Done -> System Test -> Done

B. Ready -> Done -> Develop and Unit Test -> Dev-Done -> System Test

C. Develop and Unit Test -> Ready -> Dev-Done -> System Test -> Done

D. Ready -> Develop and Unit Test -> Dev-Done -> Done -> System Test

12. A dedicated Agile team is currently working on an ERP system customization and deployment project five days a week. Each iteration is time-boxed at three weeks. A total of 500 story points were estimated at the start of the project. The team has recently completed its 4th iteration on the project and have successfully delivered 30 story points during this iteration. So far, the team has delivered a total of 120 story points on the project. If no new stories have been added to the project since initiation, what was the lead time (in weeks) for the 30 stories delivered during the last iteration?

A. 12

B. 0.5

C. 2

D. 9

13. Which of the following contract types allows the supplier a higher hourly rate when the delivery is early but penalizes the supplier with a lower hourly rate when the delivery is late?

A. Not-to-exceed time and materials

B. Fixed price

C. Cost plus

D. Graduated time and materials

14. Without attention to the highest value for the customer, the Agile team may create features that are not appreciated, or otherwise insufficiently valuable. Which of the following roles is primarily responsible for creating a backlog of the features that are prioritized by value?

A. Servant-leader

B. Product owner

C. Agile team

D. Customer

15. You are currently conducting a culture assessment for an organization. As a first step, you want to identify areas where organizational emphasis is often applied. How should you start collecting this information?

A. Through conversations with stakeholders, team members, and senior management.

B. Through review of lessons learned from completed project.

C. Through review of enterprise environmental factors.

D. Through review of organizational policies and procedures.

16. You have recently completed a project iteration and prior to the commencement of the next iteration, a few defects have been found. Rather than fixing the defects, the project team is insisting on converting these into user stories and prioritizing with the rest of the stories. What is your view?

A. The project team is right.

B. The project team is wrong, the next iteration cannot commence until all defects have been fixed.

C. The project team is wrong, the defects need to be fixed immediately.

D. The project team is always right.

17. An Agile team estimated stories of a complex project in ideal days. During the first few iterations, it was observed that the team significantly underestimated all of the user stories. Can the team predict project completion date in this situation?

A. Yes, but the team first needs to re-estimate the entire project.

B. No, since the project team is incompetent in accurately estimating ideal days.

C. Yes, if all user stories' sizes are consistent and relatively correct.

D. No, Agile projects cannot predict completion dates.

18. Which of the following situations is a bad example of tailoring Agile practices?

A. Due to geographic distribution of team members, daily scrums were held through video conferencing.

B. Due to the project's complexity, the team decided to have more than one product owner.

C. Retrospectives were unpopular so the team decided to drop them.

D. Due to the project's complexity, the Kanban board was redesigned to include more categories.

19. Your organization has been awarded a contract to develop and implement a new resource management system for a client based in Asia. Your development team is distributed across Europe. You are also planned to relocate the implementation

team to the client location. What would be your biggest challenge in such a setup?

A. Documenting sprint retrospectives.

B. Controlling project costs.

C. Efficient and effective communication.

D. Monitoring project progress.

20. The practice of attempting to solve problems by just using specific predefined methods, without challenging the methods in light of experience is known as:

A. Traditional PDCA

B. Kaizan

C. Single loop learning

D. Lessons learned

21. Check-ins are an important section of an iteration retrospective as it helps people articulate what they want from the retrospective and helps them put aside other concerns and focus on the retrospective. Which of the following is NOT an appropriate question for the check-ins?

A. What is one thing that's on your mind?

B. What tasks you will be completing today?

C. What do you need for yourself from this session?

D. In one or two words, what is happening for you right now?

22. Most projects contain a tremendous amount of uncertainty. This uncertainty is reflected in the team estimates by the:

A. Number of change requests.

B. Width of the estimate ranges.

C. Total size of the project in story points.

D. Observed velocity.

23. An Agile team has recently completed the project release planning stage. What is the next step in the planning cycle?

A. Iteration plan

B. Product roadmap

C. Daily plan

D. Product vision

24. What does "Kanban" mean?

A. Bucket

B. Work

C. Visual sign

D. Placeholder

25. An Agile project's product backlog contains 25 user stories estimated at 10 story points each. The team estimates that 60% of the effort will be required to develop the stories, while 40% of the effort will be required to test and deliver the stories. During the first iteration, the team was able to develop five stories but was only able to complete three of them. What was the team's velocity?

A. 12 story points

B. 42 story points

C. 18 story points

D. 30 story points

26. How does Agile estimating and planning support the efficient exploration of new product development solution space?

A. Converging user stories into epics and themes for the ease of the users and the product owner.

B. Designing a fully functional prototype before starting the product development.

C. Developing an exhaustive list of user stories and grooming these stories throughout the project.

D. Frequently planning and progressively elaborating solution requirements.

27. You are managing a platform migration project. You have a team of experienced engineers and analysts and you are assigning project tasks to them. Which of the following principles will help you maximizing the team's time spent on value-adding tasks?

A. Assigning tasks in a way that each team member has two tasks at the most to perform at any given point in time.

B. Assigning tasks in a way that each team member has only one task to perform at any given point in time.

C. Assigning tasks in a way that each team member has two independent tasks to perform at any given point in time.

D. Assigning tasks in a way that each team member has multiple tasks to perform at any given point in time so that they always have something to do.

28. Which of the following can be classified as an Agile measurement?

A. Project's percent of completion.

B. Number of finished features.

C. Earned value measurements.

D. Project's RAG status.

29. Organizations usually prefer in-house Agile coaching instead of getting it from external coaches. This is due to:

A. Internal coaches have a wider breadth of cross-industry experience.

B. Internal coaches are more reliable.

C. Internal coaches have stronger relationships in their organizations.

D. Internal coaches cost less than external coaches.

30. Agile teams, along with the product owners, generally prioritize stories based on their business value. However, there are some situations where some of the lower value stories are selected to be developed first, for example:

A. Stories that are least expensive to develop.

B. Stories that involve tested technology.

C. Stories that can be developed very quickly.

D. Stories that help in eliminating some significant risk.

31. You need your team to generate new ideas. In the past, a couple of the team members were more vocal and dominated the entire discussion. This time, you want to ensure everybody gets a fair chance to voice their ideas and at the same time reduce the influence of dominating team members. What should you do?

A. Remove the dominating team members from the discussion.

B. Use "Triple Nickels".

C. Make it clear at the start that people who will try to dominate the group will be reported.

D. Do not conduct a face-to-face meeting and ask the team members to email their ideas.

32. Your project's next iteration retrospective is coming up. The last retrospective didn't go well and the team went off track. This time you want to help the team put aside other concerns and focus on the retrospective. What do you need to do this time?

A. Set the stage using check-ins

B. Keep the distractors out of the meeting.

C. Request the product owner to lead the session.

D. Conduct the retrospectives on a daily basis.

33. A good planning process supports all of the following except:

A. Risk reduction

B. Accurate upfront estimates

C. Communication

D. Better decision-making

34. Which of the following is the critical problem associated with change control policies used in traditional approaches to project management?

A. These focus on reviewing change and associated impact in detail before approving/rejecting them.

B. These do not help in controlling gold plating.

C. These do not help in controlling scope creep.

D. These constrain product changes, even highly valuable changes.

35. All of the following are data gathering activities EXCEPT:

A. Fishbone

B. Mad Sad Glad

C. Triple Nickels

D. Timeline

36. You want to use your project team to generate a large number of ideas and then prioritize them against a defined set of criteria. Which of the following activities can help the team generate a large list of divergent ideas?

A. Affinity diagrams

B. Multi-voting

C. Pareto Analysis

D. Brainstorming

37. You have recently joined an Agile team. The team is new to Agile approaches and occasionally struggles with some of the Agile tools and techniques. You have noticed that during each daily standup meeting the team discusses WIP statuses with a focus on where different items are during the development cycle. You think this is a waste and the team should rather focus on the objectives of the standups. Which of the following tools can help the team in this situation?

A. Fishbone diagram

B. Spikes

C. Kanban board

D. 5 Whys

38. Agile teams complete the features usually in the form of user stories. The teams periodically demonstrate the working product to the product owner who accepts or declines the stories. In iteration-based Agile, when are these demonstrations conducted?

A. At the end of the project.

B. During retrospectives.

C. At the end of the iteration.

D. When enough features have accumulated into a set that is coherent.

39. What is the role of the product owner in a planning poker meeting?

A. The product owner answers any questions that the estimators have.

B. The product owner can assume any role but the moderator of the planning poker meeting.

C. The product owner assumes the role of chief estimator.

D. The product owner estimates story sizes.

40. The linear trend of a burndown chart is usually:

A. Downward sloping

B. Upward sloping

C. Horizontal to the y-axis

D. Vertical to the y-axis

PMI-ACP Lite Mock Exam 7 Answer Key and Explanations

1. C - Agile favors empirical and value-based measurements instead of predictive measurements such as POC and earned value management techniques. Agile measures what the team delivers, not what the team predicts it will deliver. Agile is based on working products of demonstrable value to customers. [Agile Practice Guide, 1st edition, Page 61] [Team Performance]

2. D - Change is inevitable, regardless of if the team is collocated or not. The rest of the choices are the benefits that collocated teams realize. [Agile Practice Guide, 1st edition, Page 40] [Team Performance]

3. A - In XP projects, planning is carried out during weekly and quarterly cycles. [Agile Practice Guide, 1st edition, Page 102] [Value-driven Delivery]

4. B - Backlog grooming, also known as backlog refining, involves adding, removing, and prioritizing stories in the product backlog. The purpose of refinement is to help the team understand what the stories are and how large the stories are in relation to each other. [Agile Practice Guide, 1st edition, Page 52] [Adaptive Planning]

5. B - Agile projects should deliver the right value, to the right audience, at the right time. The Agile PMO's objective is to facilitate and enable this goal. [Agile Practice Guide, 1st edition, Page 81] [Value-driven Delivery]

6. A - Continuous integration requires frequent incorporation of work into the whole, no matter the product, and then retest to determine that the entire product still works as intended. [Agile Practice Guide, 1st edition, Page 56] [Value-driven Delivery]

7. C - Focusing on individual performances instead of team performance is against the Agile Manifesto. Shelfing the Agile transformation program would be a very drastic step. If using an Agile approach for a single team is not successful, it is recommending not to scale up to using Agile more broadly; instead, it is recommended to address the organizational impediments that prevented the team from working in an Agile way. [Agile Practice Guide, 1st edition, Page 80] [Problem Detection and Resolution]

8. C - Waterfall is not an Agile framework. Disciplined Agile (DA) is a process decision framework that integrates several best practices into a comprehensive model. DA was designed to offer a balance between those popular methods deemed to be either too narrow in focus (e.g. Scrum) or too prescriptive in detail (e.g. AgileUP). [Agile Practice Guide, 1st edition, Page 114] [Value-driven Delivery]

9. B - When customers want to incorporate new ideas in a not-to-exceed time and material arrangement, they will have to manage to a given capacity and replace original work with new work. [Agile Practice Guide, 1st edition, Page 78] [Problem Detection and Resolution]

10. B - The best strategy is to work on features in the order that optimizes the total value of the project. Story points, ideal days and cycle time are irrelevant to prioritization. [Cohn, M., 2006. Agile Estimating and Planning. 1st ed. Massachusetts: Pearson Education. Page 249] [Problem Detection and Resolution]

11. A - The correct sequence is Ready -> Develop and Unit Test -> Dev-Done -> System Test -> Done. "Ready" and "Done" are the two end points of the continuum of the work flow. [Agile Practice Guide, 1st edition, Page 65] [Value-driven Delivery]

12. A - Lead time is the total time it takes to deliver an item, measure from the time it is added to the board to the moment it is completed. The 30 stories were added at the start of the project but were completed at the end of the 4th iteration. The total lead time for the 30 stories completed in the 4th iteration was 4 x 3 weeks = 12 weeks. [Agile Practice Guide, 1st edition, Page 64] [Team Performance]

13. D - A graduated time and materials contract allows the supplier a higher hourly rate when the delivery is early but penalizes the supplier with a lower hourly rate when the delivery is late. [Agile Practice Guide, 1st edition, Page 78] [Value-driven Delivery]

14. B - In Agile, the product owners create the backlog for and with the team. The backlog helps the teams see how to deliver the highest value without creating waste. [Agile Practice Guide, 1st edition, Page 41] [Value-driven Delivery]

15. A - You should not limit your choices but as the first step initial information should be collected from stakeholders, team members and senior management. The preferred communication method is always face-to-face communication. [Agile Practice Guide, 1st edition, Page 76] [Agile Principles and Mindset]

16. A - We cannot generalize that the project team is always right but on this occasion it is. A defect found later (or not fixed during the iteration it was discovered) is treated the same as a user story. Fixing the defect will need to be prioritized into a subsequent iteration in the same way any other user story would be. [Cohn, M., 2006. Agile Estimating and Planning. 1st ed. Massachusetts: Pearson Education. Page 152] [Problem Detection and Resolution]

17. C - Yes, if all user stories' sizes are consistent and relatively correct. Velocity is a great equalizer. If the estimate for each story is made relative to each other, it does not matter if the estimates are correct, a little incorrect, or a lot incorrect. As long as the estimates are consistent, measuring velocity over the first few iterations will allow honing in on a reliable schedule. [Cohn, M., 2006. Agile Estimating and Planning. 1st ed. Massachusetts: Pearson Education. Pages 36, 63] [Problem Detection and Resolution]

18. C - The statement, "Retrospectives were unpopular so the team decided to drop them" indicates a more fundamental problem on the team that is unlikely to be addressed by tailoring the method. [Agile Practice Guide, 1st edition, Page 119] [Value-driven Delivery]

19. C - The most efficient and effective method of communication is face-to-face conversation. When a project has a virtual team, the biggest challenge is ensuring efficient and effective communications. None of the other choices are more significant than this. [Agile Practice Guide, 1st edition, Page 9] [Stakeholder Engagement]

20. C - Single loop learning is the practice of attempting to solve problems by just using specific predefined methods, without challenging the methods in light of

experience. [Agile Practice Guide, 1st edition, Page 154] [Problem Detection and Resolution]

21. B - Typically five to ten minutes are spent on check-ins. We use check-ins to set the stage in a retrospective. This helps people put aside other concerns and focus on the retrospective by helping them articulate what they want from the retrospective. Discussing daily progress is done during daily standups and not during retrospectives. [Derby, E. and Larsen, D., 2006. Agile Retrospectives: Making Good Teams Great. 1st ed. Texas: Pragmatic Bookshelf, Page 41] [Continuous Improvement]

22. B - This uncertainty is reflected in the team estimates by the width of the estimate ranges. Agile teams provide wider estimate ranges for stories that have a greater amount of uncertainty. [Cohn, M., 2006. Agile Estimating and Planning. 1st ed. Massachusetts: Pearson Education. Page 198] [Adaptive Planning]

23. A - The multiple levels of Agile planning are: Product Vision -> Product Roadmap -> Iteration Plan -> Daily Plan. [Cohn, M., 2006. Agile Estimating and Planning. 1st ed. Massachusetts: Pearson Education. Page 28] [Adaptive Planning]

24. C - The work Kanban is literally translated as "visual sign" or "card". [Agile Practice Guide, 1st edition, Page 103] [Stakeholder Engagement]

25. D - Points counted toward velocity are only for those stories or features that are complete at the end of the iteration. In this case three features were complete so the velocity was 3 x 10 = 30 story points. Incomplete stories are not counted toward velocity. [Cohn, M., 2006. Agile Estimating and Planning. 1st ed. Massachusetts: Pearson Education. Page 211] [Team Performance]

26. D - Agile estimating and planning support the efficient exploration of new product development solution space through frequently planning and progressively elaborating solution requirements. [Cohn, M., 2006. Agile Estimating and Planning. 1st ed. Massachusetts: Pearson Education. Page 243] [Adaptive Planning]

27. C - Multi-tasking exacts a horrible toll on productivity. Clark and Wheelwright (1993) studied the effect of multi-tasking and found that the time an individual spends on value-adding work drops rapidly when the individual is working on more than two tasks. With two value-adding tasks, if a team member becomes blocked on one task, he/she can switch to the other task. It is recommended that you assign tasks in a way that each team member has "two independent tasks" to perform at any given point in time. [Cohn, M., 2006. Agile Estimating and Planning. 1st ed. Massachusetts: Pearson Education. Page 15] [Team Performance]

28. B - Agile values empirical measurements such as finished features instead of predictive measurements such as percentage completion, RAG status and earned value measurements. [Agile Practice Guide, 1st edition, Page 60] [Team Performance]

29. C - Both external and internal coaches can be reliable. Internal coaches can be cheaper if they are 100% allocated to coaching, which is usually not the case. However, the benefit of internal coaches is their stronger

relationships which they can use to be more effective. [Agile Practice Guide, 1st edition, Page 41] [Problem Detection and Resolution]

30. D - Early termination of a significant risk can often justify developing a feature early. Similarly, if developing a particular feature early will allow the team to gain significant knowledge about the project or their effort to develop it, they should consider developing that feature early. [Cohn, M., 2006. Agile Estimating and Planning. 1st ed. Massachusetts: Pearson Education. Page 249] [Problem Detection and Resolution]

31. B - The purpose of the "Triple Nickels" activity is to generate ideas for actions or recommendations and uncover important topics about the project history. Triple Nickels allow team members time to think privately yet participate in a process that develops whole-team understanding. It also prevents the few people who are comfortable talking in a group from dominating the discussion. [Derby, E. and Larsen, D., 2006. Agile Retrospectives: Making Good Teams Great. 1st ed. Texas: Pragmatic Bookshelf, Page 57] [Continuous Improvement]

32. A - We use check-ins to set the stage in a retrospective. This helps people put aside other concerns and focus on the retrospective by helping them articulate what they want from the retrospective. [Derby, E. and Larsen, D., 2006. Agile Retrospectives: Making Good Teams Great. 1st ed. Texas: Pragmatic Bookshelf, Page 41] [Continuous Improvement]

33. B - Accurate estimates are typically impossible to get until late in a project. A good planning process helps in reducing risk, better decision-making and information communication. [Cohn, M., 2006. Agile Estimating and Planning. 1st ed. Massachusetts: Pearson Education. Pages 4, 5] [Adaptive Planning]

34. D - The main problem with change control on traditional projects is that change control policies constrain product changes, even highly valuable changes, as the hidden focus is to stick to the original plan. On the other hand, change control helps in controlling scope creep and gold plating. Analyzing change and associated impact is also done by Agile teams. [Cohn, M., 2006. Agile Estimating and Planning. 1st ed. Massachusetts: Pearson Education. Page 12] [Agile Principles and Mindset]

35. A - Fishbone is a root cause analysis technique and not a data gathering technique. The rest of the choices are all valid data gathering techniques. [Derby, E. and Larsen, D., 2006. Agile Retrospectives: Making Good Teams Great. 1st ed. Texas: Pragmatic Bookshelf, Page 78] [Continuous Improvement]

36. D - Brainstorming generates divergent ideas. The rest of the techniques help in converging the ideas. [Derby, E. and Larsen, D., 2006. Agile Retrospectives: Making Good Teams Great. 1st ed. Texas: Pragmatic Bookshelf, Page 78] [Continuous Improvement]

37. C - A Kanban board provides a means to visualize the flow of work, make impediments easily visible, and allow flow to be managed by adjusting the work in process limits. [Agile Practice Guide, 1st edition, Page 31] [Problem Detection and Resolution]

38. C - In iteration-based Agile, the team demonstrates all completed work items at the end of the iteration. [Agile Practice Guide, 1st edition, Page 55] [Value-driven Delivery]

39. A - The moderator is usually the product owner or an analyst and there is no special privilege associated with the role. The product owner answers any question that the estimators have but does not estimate. [Cohn, M., 2006. Agile Estimating and Planning. 1st ed. Massachusetts: Pearson Education. Page 56] [Adaptive Planning]

40. A - A burndown chart shows a team's progress by showing the number of story points remaining in the project. The vertical axis shows the number of story points remaining and the iterations are shown across the horizontal axis. The linear trend of a burndown chart is downward sloping. [Cohn, M., 2006. Agile Estimating and Planning. 1st ed. Massachusetts: Pearson Education. Page 213] [Team Performance]

PMI-ACP Lite Mock Exam 8 Practice Questions

Test Name: PMI-ACP Lite Mock Exam 8
Total Questions: 40
Correct Answers Needed to Pass: 30 (75.00%)
Time Allowed: 60 Minutes

Test Description

This is a cumulative PMI-ACP Mock Exam which can be used as a benchmark for your PMI-ACP aptitude. This practice test includes questions from all exam topic areas, including sections from Agile Tools and Techniques, and all three Agile Knowledge and Skills areas.

Test Questions

1. In an Agile team, who is responsible for resolving project bottlenecks?

A. Project team

B. Project manager

C. Agile coach

D. Servant-leader

2. Two projects are currently being analyzed. Project A will yield a net profit of $300,000 at the end of the second year. Project B will yield a net profit of $310,000 by the end of the fourth year. Assuming a 3% interest rate, which of the following is correct?

A. Project A has a PV that is $7,348 higher than Project B's PV.

B. Project B has a PV that is $7,348 higher than Project A's PV.

C. Project B is financially more attractive than Project A.

D. These projects are equal in net returns.

3. Which of the following statements regarding the Agile Manifesto is INCORRECT:

A. Working software is valued more than comprehensive documentation.

B. Customer collaboration is valued more than contract negotiation.

C. Processes and tools are valued more than individuals and interactions.

D. Responding to change is valued more than following a plan.

4. An Agile team wishes to subcontract some of the project work. Rather than formalizing an entire contracting relationship in a single contract, the team wishes to describe different aspects of the relationship in different documents. Which of the following documents should be used to define the mostly fixed items such as warranties, arbitration, etc.?

A. Key performance indicators

B. Service level agreements

C. Master agreement

D. Schedule of services

5. What is a team's velocity?

A. The rate of story points delivery.

B. The average of story points delivered in an iteration.

C. The median cycle time of user stories.

D. The rate of change of story points.

6. You are leading a workflow automation project. The project team wants to outsource some piece of work but is hesitant as they want to maintain highest Agile standards. What is your view about this?

A. The team shouldn't outsource as the vendor might not have dedicated teams.

B. The team shouldn't outsource as Agile teams value customer collaboration over contract negotiation.

C. The team should outsource as you can never fully conform to Agile standards.

D. The team should outsource work if that is in the best interest of the project.

7. A resource on your project has asked for a copy of the word processing software in use at your company so that they can install it at home and complete project work from there. What do you do?

A. Refer him to the IT group for assistance.

B. Show him where to download a copy on the Internet.

C. Loan him your personal copy.

D. Burn a copy of the software on CD.

8. Which of the following Agile tools help a team to micro-commit to each other, uncover problems, and ensure the work flows smoothly through the team on a continual basis?

A. Team charter

B. Backlog refinement

C. Retrospectives

D. Daily stand-ups

9. Many environments with emerging requirements find that there is often a gap between the real business requirements and the business requirements that were originally stated. How do Agile method identify the right business requirements?

A. Through user story size limits.

B. Through work breakdown structure management.

C. Through prototypes and feedback.

D. Through Kanban boards and throughput.

10. Which of following is not an Agile approach:

A. Crystal

B. XP

C. ScrumBan

D. Lean

11. Which of the following planning techniques allows detailed planning of only the work that needs to be accomplished in the near term, while the work in the future is kept at a higher level?

A. Rolling Wave Planning

B. Planning Poker

C. Hoshin Kanri

D. Kanban Planning

12. A team estimates that the development of a feature will take four days and the testing of the feature will take two days. In order to account for the uncertainty, the team provides a six day estimate for the development and adds a 2-day lag to the testing activity. What did the team do?

A. The team added feeding buffers to both the development and testing tasks.

B. The team padded the development estimate and added a feeding buffer between the two tasks.

C. The team padded both the development and testing tasks.

D. The team added a feeding buffer to the development task and added padding between the two tasks.

13. The Kanban Board is a work in process management tool originated from:

A. Toyota Production Systems

B. Six Sigma

C. ISO's Quality Management System

D. Total Quality Management

14. An Agile team has identified a number of epics on a project. Each epic consists of one or more related features. The epics were not decomposed into stories and rather loosely estimated, prioritized and put into the release plan. Due to this approach, which of the following issues is the team most likely to face in the near future?

A. The team is not likely to face any issues.

B. The number of total story points will significantly change after each iteration.

C. The team's velocity might not be consistent between the iterations.

D. The product themes cannot be identified.

15. By the end of the first iteration, an Agile team has got a number of incomplete stories. A number of actions can be taken at this stage to address this issue and avoid similar future situations, EXCEPT:

A. Re-estimating the stories if the original estimates are no longer accurate.

B. Calculating the percentage complete of the stories and using that toward calculating the velocity.

C. Moving the unfinished work to some future iteration.

D. Splitting the stories into smaller stories.

16. You are the project leader of a project executing work under a contract signed with a buyer organization. Just after the project has started, you notice that the buyer organization had made a mistake in the financial terms, and your organization stands to benefit considerably from this oversight. What should your stance be?

A. Bring the error to the notice of the buyer organization and have an amendment made to the contract since this was in good faith.

B. Do not take any action since a contract is a binding and legal document.

C. Informally check with your counterpart in the buyer organization to see whether he or she noticed this error.

D. Discuss with your management on how you could gain a bonus due to the increased revenue your company stands to gain.

17. You are managing a complex organizational redesign project. Reviewing project's statistics you determined that the team completes 75 story points on average per iteration. Reviewing the backlog, you determine that there are about another 750 points remaining. If each interval is time-boxed at two weeks, when you do expect to complete the project?

A. Agile teams cannot predict project completion.

B. In about 75 weeks from now.

C. In about 10 weeks from now.

D. In about 20 weeks from now.

18. What does an Agile team achieve by prioritizing project stories and features?

A. Stakeholder engagement

B. Risk reduction

C. Determine conditions of satisfactions

D. Optimize delivery of business value

19. You have just been assigned a new project. As an Agile project leader, which of the following should be your first focus?

A. How to conduct retrospectives and document lessons learned.

B. How quickly can you develop an exhaustive product backlog?

C. How you can create a team that is cross-functional and 100% dedicated.

D. Gather a reasonable number of high-priority user stories to kick start the project.

20. Many activities can be conducted to set the stage for an iteration retrospective. All of the following are such activities except:

A. Check-in

B. ESVP

C. Focus on/Focus off

D. Kaizen

21. Story points are the most widely used unit of measure for estimating Agile story sizes. How does an Agile team determine the size of a story?

A. By comparing the size of a story with already estimated stories.

B. By performing a bottom-up estimate.

C. By estimating the number of person hours required.

D. By estimating the time requirements.

22. If all features on a project have been classified by their risk and business value, which of the following group of themes would you recommend starting at the very last?

A. The features that have less impact on the total value and have low risk.

B. The features that have low value, especially those that are also high risk.

C. The features that deliver high value and eliminate the maximum risk from the project.

D. The features that deliver high value but are less risky.

23. A team is new to Agile approaches and is currently struggling with the new concepts, tools and techniques. How would you explain ideal time to them?

A. How long a story will take to complete without any interruptions.

B. The expected time required to deliver a story considering team assignments.

C. The shortest duration required to deliver a story.

D. The ideal time to include stories in an iteration plan.

24. Which of the following statements is an example of feature buffering on an Agile project?

A. Proactively removing roadblocks and facilitating feature development.

B. There are two sets of features in a product development plan; mandatory and optional.

C. Creating development buffers between the features to avoid schedule slippages.

D. Loading a few features on the Kanban board and buffering the rest in a ready state.

25. Organizations just beginning to use Agile approaches may find prototyping challenging due to the associated rework which can also be viewed negatively. Which of the following techniques should be used to address the hurdles of transitioning to the use of Agile approaches?

A. Scrum management

B. Change management

C. Scope management

D. Risk management

26. Who determines the "Conditions of Satisfaction" for the user stories?

A. Scrum Master

B. Agile Team

C. Agile Coach

D. Product Owner

27. You have been hired by an organization as the Agile Consultant. The organization has recently embarked upon the Agile journey. Which of the following is not a change-friendly characteristic for organizations beginning to use Agile approaches?

A. Focus on short-term budgeting and metrics versus long-term goals.

B. Executive management's commitment.

C. Existence of departmental silos.

D. Talent management maturity and capabilities.

28. A team is using the Five Whys technique to uncover the underlying root cause of a problem. However, after the fifth iteration the team thinks that the real root cause hasn't been discovered. You may proceed in a number of directions from this point EXCEPT:

A. Using the cause identified in the fourth iteration.

B. Include some subject matter experts during the activity.

C. Use a fishbone chart to see if other areas are also explored.

D. Do a couple of rounds to see if the root cause is found.

29. Geographically distributed team need virtual workspaces. Which of the following are the techniques generally considered for managing communication in a dispersed team?

A. Fishbowl windows and remote pairing

B. Video conference and collocation

C. Fishbone diagrams and pair programming

D. Kanban boards and burndown charts

30. You are helping an organization transform to Agile practices. You are currently developing guidelines regarding forming Agile teams. All of the following would be your recommendations EXCEPT:

A. Most or all team members should be "T-shaped".

B. Teams should be small.

C. Most or all team members should be "I-shaped".

D. Teams should be collocated.

31. During an ESVP activity, each participant anonymously reports his or her attitude toward the retrospective as an Explorer, Shopper, Vacationer, or Prisoner. Who are the explorers?

A. People who want to lead the team.

B. People who have recently successfully implemented a new idea.

C. People who are eager to discover new ideas and insights.

D. People who want to explore other opportunities outside of the project.

32. Two of the senior subject matter experts have different opinions on the use of management tools on a project. The use of Kanban and Agile approaches are being proposed by these experts. In case you decide to use both of the approaches on your project, which of the following can be a valid justification for such a decision?

A. Senior subject matter experts cannot be turned down.

B. Project teams sometime blend various methods to achieve project objectives.

C. Management approaches are irrelevant as long as majority of the stakeholders are happy.

D. Kanban is a part of the Agile Manifesto; the debate was irrelevant.

33. Which of the following is bad feature prioritization criteria?

A. Features considered valuable by the customer.

B. Features considered valuable by the self-organizing team.

C. High risk features.

D. Features considered valuable by the product owner.

34. In projects following Scrum framework, who is responsible for maximizing the value of the product?

A. Scrum master

B. Development team

C. Testing team

D. Product owner

35. Team members in successful Agile teams work to collaborate in various ways. Which of the following is not a valid example of these ways?

A. Swarming

B. Mobbing

C. Pairing

D. Multi-tasking

36. Agile task estimates during iteration planning are expressed in:

A. Story points

B. Cycle time

C. Spikes

D. Ideal time

37. Agile teams measure WIP during the beginning of the project and determine the available options for rapid product delivery. Which of the following is the recommended approach when comparing different delivery options?

A. Deliver detailed designs at least halfway through the project.

B. Deliver upfront designs instead of value.

C. Deliver value instead of upfront designs.

D. Deliver detailed designs as early as possible.

38. You have called in key stakeholders for a brainstorming session. The main agenda item is to identify suitable project life cycles for a number of new initiatives launched by the organization. Two of the stakeholders are proposing exclusive use of predictive and Agile life cycles respectively. What should be your response?

A. Exclusive use of Predictive life cycle is recommended as this is a tried and tested method.

B. Exclusive use of Agile life cycle is recommended as this is new way to manage projects.

C. Exclusive use of a life cycle on all projects is not recommended.

D. A blended life cycle needs to be designed which can then be exclusively used on all projects.

39. You are leading an Agile team responsible for developing an ERP system for an organization. The enterprise PMO has asked to develop a detailed schedule Gantt chart and report Red/Amber/Green status against each project task on a weekly basis. What's your opinion about the enterprise PMO?

A. Enterprise PMO hasn't transitioned to Agile practices.

B. Enterprise PMO cannot exist in an Agile organization.

C. Enterprise PMO has the right to demand project status reports in the format they deem fit.

D. Enterprise PMO should also focus on project risk and issues and not primarily on the project schedule.

40. During which Agile planning event does an Agile team first consider user stories?

A. Daily planning

B. Demonstration planning

C. Iteration planning

D. Release planning

PMI-ACP Lite Mock Exam 8 Answer Key and Explanations

1. A - In an Agile environment, the servant-leader, the Agile coach, or the project manager helps to expose and communicate bottlenecks inside and between teams. Then the teams resolve those bottlenecks. [Agile Practice Guide, 1st edition, Page 35] [Agile Principles and Mindset]

2. A - Project A's PV is $282,779 while the Project B's PV is $275,431. Project A's PV is $7,348 higher than Project B's PV making it more attractive. The formula for Present Value is: PV = FV / (1+r)^n. [Cohn, M., 2006. Agile Estimating and Planning. 1st ed. Massachusetts: Pearson Education. Page 100] [Value-driven Delivery]

3. C - According to the Agile Manifesto: Individuals and interactions are valued more than processes and tools, working software is valued more than comprehensive documentation, customer collaboration is valued more than contract negotiation, and responding to change is valued more than following a plan. [Agile Practice Guide, 1st edition, Page 8] [Agile Principles and Mindset]

4. C - A majority of fixed items such as warranties and arbitration are locked in a master agreement. [Agile Practice Guide, 1st edition, Page 77] [Value-driven Delivery]

5. A - Agile teams monitor its progress by its velocity that is expressed as the number of story points (or ideal days) completed per iteration. [Cohn, M., 2006. Agile Estimating and Planning. 1st ed. Massachusetts: Pearson Education. Page 211] [Team Performance]

6. D - Although according to the Agile Manifesto, customer collaboration is valued over contract negotiation, that doesn't mean Agile teams do not negotiate contracts. If it is in the best interest of the project to outsource some work, that should be done. [Agile Practice Guide, 1st edition, Page 77] [Agile Principles and Mindset]

7. A - Refer the resource to the IT group for assistance. Agile practitioners are required to protect others' intellectual property—including copyrighted information such as software—in accordance with all applicable policies, laws, and regulations. [PMI Code of Ethics and Professional Conduct] [Stakeholder Engagement]

8. D - Teams use stand-ups to micro-commit to each other, uncover problems, and ensure the work flows smoothly through the team on a continual basis. Retrospectives, on the other hand, are held at discrete time intervals. [Agile Practice Guide, 1st edition, Page 53] [Adaptive Planning]

9. C - Agile methods purposefully build and review prototypes and release versions in order to refine business requirements. [Agile Practice Guide, 1st edition, Page 91] [Agile Principles and Mindset]

10. D - Agile is a subset of Lean. While some of the Lean approaches are part of Agile, some are not, e.g., SMED and Hoshin Kanri, etc. [Agile Practice Guide, 1st edition, Page 11] [Agile Principles and Mindset]

11. A - Rolling Wave Planning is an iterative planning technique in which the work to be accomplished in the near term is planned in detail, while the work in the future is planned

at a higher level. [Agile Practice Guide, 1st edition, Page 153] [Adaptive Planning]

12. B - Padding an estimated means extending the estimate. For example if a task that is expected to take five days, is estimated to take seven days, we would say that the estimate has been padded. On the other hand, feeding buffers are placed between the tasks to handle the uncertainty but the tasks' estimates are not increased. [Cohn, M., 2006. Agile Estimating and Planning. 1st ed. Massachusetts: Pearson Education. Page 204] [Adaptive Planning]

13. A - The Kanban Board is a work in process management tool originated from Toyota Production Systems (TPS). [Agile Practice Guide, 1st edition, Page 103] [Stakeholder Engagement]

14. C - Although Agile approaches do not promote detailed upfront planning, insufficient planning can bring surprises. In this scenario the epics were not decomposed into stories and not estimated to a reasonable degree of confidence. As a result, the assigned story points to the epics might not be an accurate indicator of the required effort and this would eventually show up in the variability of the team's velocity. [Cohn, M., 2006. Agile Estimating and Planning. 1st ed. Massachusetts: Pearson Education. Page 246] [Team Performance]

15. B - Points counted toward velocity are only for those stories or features that are complete at the end of the iteration. Incomplete stories are not counted toward velocity. The rest of the choices are acceptable available options. [Cohn, M., 2006. Agile Estimating and Planning. 1st ed. Massachusetts: Pearson Education. Pages 211, 212] [Problem Detection and Resolution]

16. A - The ethical thing to do would be to bring this to the notice of the buyer organization and have an amendment made to the contract. [PMI Code of Ethics and Professional Conduct] [Stakeholder Engagement]

17. D - If the team averages 75 story points per iteration, and the team estimates there are about another 750 points remaining, it is safe to estimate that another 10 iterations would be required to complete the project. Each iteration is two weeks and the project completion will be about 20 weeks from now. [Agile Practice Guide, 1st edition, Page 61] [Team Performance]

18. D - Agile teams focus on business priorities. The objective of prioritization of stories and features is to optimize value delivery to the business. [Cohn, M., 2006. Agile Estimating and Planning. 1st ed. Massachusetts: Pearson Education. Page 25] [Value-driven Delivery]

19. C - As an Agile project leader, first focus on how you can create a team that is cross-functional and 100% dedicated to one team. Even if it means just getting key team members to work and communicate together on a daily basis, that is a step in the right direction toward agility. [Agile Practice Guide, 1st edition, Page 47] [Agile Principles and Mindset]

20. D - Kaizen means improvement through small incremental steps. This is a process improvement technique which is not suitable for setting the stage for retrospectives. The rest of the choices are valid Agile approaches. [Derby, E. and Larsen, D., 2006. Agile Retrospectives: Making Good Teams Great. 1st ed. Texas: Pragmatic Bookshelf, Pages 41-45] [Continuous Improvement]

21. A - Story points are a unit of measure for expressing the overall size of a user story. When we estimate with story points we assign a point value to each item. The raw value we assign is unimportant. What matters are the relative values. Once the first story is estimated, the remaining stories are estimated by comparing them to the already estimated stories. [Cohn, M., 2006. Agile Estimating and Planning. 1st ed. Massachusetts: Pearson Education. Page 36] [Adaptive Planning]

22. A - The low value, low risk features are recommend to be attempted at the very last. These are sequenced after the "High Risk/High Value" and the "Low Risk/High Value" features because they will have less impact on the total value of the product if they are dropped and because they are low risk. [Cohn, M., 2006. Agile Estimating and Planning. 1st ed. Massachusetts: Pearson Education. Page 85] [Adaptive Planning]

23. A - Ideal time is the amount of time that something takes when stripped of all peripheral activities. [Cohn, M., 2006. Agile Estimating and Planning. 1st ed. Massachusetts: Pearson Education. Page 43] [Value-driven Delivery]

24. B - Buffering a project with features means we tell our customers, "We'll get you all the functionality in this pile and hopefully some of the functionality in that pile." Project buffering requires classifying features as mandatory and optional. [Cohn, M., 2006. Agile Estimating and Planning. 1st ed. Massachusetts: Pearson Education. Page 186] [Adaptive Planning]

25. B - Leaders should consider change management techniques to address the hurdles of transitioning to the use of Agile approaches. [Agile Practice Guide, 1st edition, Page 73] [Agile Principles and Mindset]

26. D - Conditions of Satisfaction is the criteria that is used to gauge the success of a deliverable. Since the product owner has the ultimate responsibility of the project, the product owner provides the Conditions of Satisfaction. [Cohn, M., 2006. Agile Estimating and Planning. 1st ed. Massachusetts: Pearson Education. Page 30] [Value-driven Delivery]

27. C - If the organization is decomposed into departmental silos, that prevents accelerated delivery and doesn't encourage forming cross-functional teams. The rest of the choices are desirable attributes. [Agile Practice Guide, 1st edition, Pages 73, 74] [Agile Principles and Mindset]

28. A - You can proceed in multiple directions from here. However, compromising on the fourth answer, given that the team wasn't comfortable with the fifth answer, doesn't look like a rational choice. [Derby, E. and Larsen, D., 2006. Agile Retrospectives: Making Good Teams Great. 1st ed. Texas: Pragmatic Bookshelf, Pages 85, 87] [Continuous Improvement]

29. A - Fishbowl windows and remote pairing are communication management techniques used with dispersed teams. [Agile Practice Guide, 1st edition, Page 46] [Team Performance]

30. C - Agile teams should be small, collocated, and mostly consist of "T-Shaped" people where possible. [Agile Practice Guide, 1st edition, Pages 39, 42] [Value-driven Delivery]

31. C - Explorers are eager to discover new ideas and insights. They want to learn everything they can about the iteration/release/project. [Derby, E. and Larsen, D., 2006. Agile Retrospectives: Making Good Teams Great. 1st ed. Texas: Pragmatic Bookshelf, Page 45] [Continuous Improvement]

32. B - Although Kanban and Agile approaches can slightly differ, both focus on delivering value, respect for people, minimizing waste, adapting to change, and continuous improvement. Project teams sometime blend various methods to achieve project objectives. [Agile Practice Guide, 1st edition, Page 12] [Agile Principles and Mindset]

33. B - Features should not be prioritized based on a team's assessment of value. This assessment should come from product owners or customers. However, a team may prioritize high risk features. [Cohn, M., 2006. Agile Estimating and Planning. 1st ed. Massachusetts: Pearson Education. Page 80] [Adaptive Planning]

34. D - The product owner is responsible for maximizing the value of the product. The product owner owns the product backlog and is responsible for its refinement. [Agile Practice Guide, 1st edition, Page 101] [Value-driven Delivery]

35. D - Pairing, swarming, mobbing are valid WIP management and collaboration techniques. Multi-tasking is considered a waste in Agile environments. [Agile Practice Guide, 1st edition, Page 39] [Value-driven Delivery]

36. D - Agile task estimates during iteration planning are expressed in ideal time, such as ideal days or ideal hours. [Cohn, M., 2006. Agile Estimating and Planning. 1st ed. Massachusetts: Pearson Education. Page 155] [Adaptive Planning]

37. C - Upfront designing is waterfall. When selecting delivery options, Agile teams choose value over upfront designs. This is the fundamental difference between Agile and traditional approaches. [Agile Practice Guide, 1st edition, Page 59] [Value-driven Delivery]

38. C - No life cycle can be perfect for all projects. Instead, each project finds a spot on the continuum that provides an optimum balance of characteristics of its context. [Agile Practice Guide, 1st edition, Page 19] [Agile Principles and Mindset]

39. A - Agile approaches do not include detailed schedules and task status reporting; these are traditional approaches. If the PMO is still using these tools, it implies that it hasn't successfully transitioned to Agile approaches. [Cohn, M., 2006. Agile Estimating and Planning. 1st ed. Massachusetts: Pearson Education. Page 51] [Value-driven Delivery]

40. D - Release planning considers the user stories or themes that will be developed for a new release of a product or system. Once the release plan is developed, the Agile team moves on to the iteration planning and subsequently daily planning during the iteration. [Cohn, M., 2006. Agile Estimating and Planning. 1st ed. Massachusetts:

Pearson Education. Page 28] [Adaptive Planning]

PMI-ACP Knowledge Area Quiz: Stakeholder Engagement Practice Questions

Test Name: Knowledge Area Test: Agile Analysis and Design
Total Questions: 15
Correct Answers Needed to Pass: 11 (73.33%)
Time Allowed: 25 Minutes

Test Description

This practice quiz specifically targets your knowledge of the Agile Analysis and Design exam topic area.

Test Questions

1. You have recently joined a new company as a project lead. While reviewing the procurement arrangements for a project you will be taking over, you see that the company is considering using one of the most expensive manufacturers to provide certain equipment required for the project. At your previous employer, you had used a different supplier for the same equipment and had paid significantly less. Without telling your boss, you now call that supplier for a quote. Have you violated the rule of keeping proprietary information confidential?

   A. No. There is no harm in sharing the information with your current employer, because you are no longer working for your old employer.

   B. You have not violated any rule.

   C. Yes. The supply source is proprietary information, and you should not contact the supplier.

   D. Maybe. You need to talk to your boss first.

2. An Agile team wants to setup an information radiator that will be utilized to manage the product and sprints backlog and show the flow of work and its bottlenecks. Which Agile tool would you recommend to achieve this objective?

   A. Scrum Board

   B. Daily Standup

   C. Kaizen Events

   D. War Room

3. You have just completed planning the first sprint of your project. What should be your next step?

   A. Communicate the plan to relevant stakeholders.

   B. Groom the product backlog.

   C. Estimate the user stories.

   D. Prioritize the user stories.

4. The product owner has asked you how many story points the team would like to include in the next sprint. What should you do next?

   A. Calculate the average velocity.

   B. Determine the number of story points available on the backlog.

C. Quote the least velocity on the last five sprints.

D. Quote the number of story points available divided by number of stories.

5. You are assisting Benjamin, another project lead, to interview candidates for a resource position on his project. While reviewing your interview notes together, you notice that he sorts the candidate‘s resumes into two piles: One pile for further interviews, the other for candidates that did not meet the requirements for the position. You also notice that he has placed several of the highly qualified candidates in the second pile, stating that those interviewees "did not fit the corporate profile." Upon further review, you discover that all these candidates are of the same ethnic group. What do you do?

A. Report this to the appropriate management.

B. Excuse yourself from the interviewing process.

C. File a complaint with PMI.

D. Do nothing.

6. You are an electrical engineer with extensive experience in managing transmission projects but limited experience with electronic design projects. However, in a stretch assignment, you were recently transferred to another department in your company that focuses on electronic design. Furthermore, you were asked to lead the technical team of a highly important project involving both transmission and electronic design. In preparation for a meeting with your manager to discuss this opportunity, you review the initial project design brief. Due to your limited background in electronic design, a number of items in this document seem unclear to you. When you arrive at your meeting, your manager asks if you will be leading the technical team. How do you respond?

A. Decline the project, citing your lack of experience in electronic design.

B. Accept the project, but do not discuss your qualifications or lack thereof.

C. Accept the project and tell your manager that your expertise in transmission makes you an ideal technical lead on this project.

D. State that you would like to lead the technical team, but you must disclose that your primary domain of expertise is transmission, and that you may need supplementary training in electronics design.

7. You are developing an online complaint management system. Recently the product owner has requested you to drop a feature from the current iteration plan that was earlier requested by the compliance department. What should you do?

A. Drop the feature from the iteration plan and notify compliance.

B. Reject the change request as feature was requested by compliance.

C. Arrange a meeting between the product owner and compliance.

D. Drop the feature from the release plan.

8. Which of the following statements regarding the "Cone of Uncertainty" is correct?

   A. It flattens over time.

   B. It widens over time.

   C. It narrows over time.

   D. It drops over time.

9. Which of the following Agile methods is openly credited as the first Agile method that contains a specific component no other methods have: the focus on delivering multiple measurable value requirements to stakeholders?

   A. Extreme Programming

   B. Continuous Integration

   C. Evolutionary Value Delivery (EVO)

   D. Disciplined Agile (DA)

10. Which of the following organizational improvement models consist of five phases: initiating, diagnosing, establishing, acting and learning?

    A. IDEAL

    B. PMBOK

    C. Malcom Baldrige

    D. CMMI

11. Which of the following is NOT a prime benefit of prototyping project features?

    A. Clarifying user requirements

    B. Keeping the customer engaged

    C. Obtaining customer feedback

    D. Developing accurate estimates

12. On Agile projects, who is primarily responsible for developing product roadmaps?

    A. Agile coach

    B. Agile team

    C. Servant-leader

    D. Product owner

13. When is a good time for soliciting feedback on project deliverables, processes and methods?

    A. During demonstrations.

    B. During daily standups.

    C. Throughout the life of the project.

    D. During retrospectives.

14. You have to resolve a conflict. Your programmer has developed a new feature. The product owner is not happy as he wasn't involved in this decision. What should you do?

    A. Ask both parties to amicably resolve the issue.

    B. Agree with the product owner and ask him how he wants to resolve the issue.

C. Support your team member as the project team can make business decisions.

D. Remove the feature from the next release.

15. You will soon be leading a complex project. Project communication is critical to the success of the project; specifically all team members need to be kept updated on project progress. Which of the following approaches will produce the best results?

A. Discuss progress during sprint planning events.

B. Use a Kanban board.

C. Discuss progress during retrospectives.

D. Discuss progress during daily standups.

PMI-ACP Knowledge Area Quiz: Stakeholder Engagement Answer Key and Explanations

1. B - No rule has been violated as you have not disclosed any proprietary or confidential information. [PMI Code of Ethics and Professional Conduct] [Stakeholder Engagement]

2. A - A Scrum Board is an information radiator that is utilized to manage the product and sprint backlogs and show the flow of work and its bottlenecks. [Agile Practice Guide, 1st edition, Page 154] [Stakeholder Engagement]

3. A - Grooming, prioritizing and estimating the stories are all part of planning activities. Since you have completed all of the planning activities for your upcoming sprint, the next thing to do is to communicate the plan to the stakeholders. [Cohn, M., 2006. Agile Estimating and Planning. 1st ed. Massachusetts: Pearson Education. Page 7] [Stakeholder Engagement]

4. A - Quoting the least velocity on the last five sprints will be too pessimistic. You need to quote the average team velocity which is your best estimate for the work that can be complete during the next sprint. [Agile Practice Guide, 1st edition, Page 61] [Stakeholder Engagement]

5. A - Report this to the appropriate management immediately. Discrimination based on nationality is prohibited by the PMI Code of Ethics and may also be illegal, depending on local laws. PMI requires Agile practitioners to report discriminatory behavior to the appropriate management; not doing so is a violation of the Code of Ethics. [PMI Code of Ethics and Professional Conduct] [Stakeholder Engagement]

6. D - State that you would like to lead the technical team, but disclose that your expertise is in transmission, not electronic design. PMI's Code of Ethics and Professional Conduct mandates that Agile practitioners accept only those projects for which they have appropriate qualifications and experience. However, if project stakeholders are fully informed of the areas where you may be lacking skills or knowledge, and they still wish you to lead the technical team, this is not a violation of the code. [PMI Code of Ethics and Professional Conduct] [Stakeholder Engagement]

7. A - The product owner is ultimately responsible and accountable for the product being developed. If the product owner has request to drop a feature from the current iteration plan, that decision needs to be honored. To manage the stakeholder expectation at compliance, notifying compliance of the change is a good idea. [Agile Practice Guide, 1st edition, Page 41] [Stakeholder Engagement]

8. C - The "Cone of Uncertainty" narrows as the project progresses. [Cohn, M., 2006. Agile Estimating and Planning. 1st ed. Massachusetts: Pearson Education. Page 4] [Stakeholder Engagement]

9. C - Evolutionary Value Delivery (EVO) is openly credited as the first Agile method that contains a specific component no other methods have: the focus on delivering multiple measurable value requirements to

stakeholders. [Agile Practice Guide, 1st edition, Page 151] [Stakeholder Engagement]

10. A - IDEAL is an organizational improvement model that is named for the five phases it describes: initiating, diagnosing, establishing, acting, and learning. [Agile Practice Guide, 1st edition, Page 152] [Stakeholder Engagement]

11. D - A prototype encourages feedback and a better understanding of the requirements that can be incorporated into each deliverable. This also helps in keeping the customer engaged with the project. Since most estimates are made prior to any development work, prototyping doesn't help directly in estimating. [Agile Practice Guide, 1st edition, Page 22] [Stakeholder Engagement]

12. D - A product roadmap shows the anticipated sequence of deliverables over time. Product owners are primarily responsible for developing product roadmaps. [Agile Practice Guide, 1st edition, Page 52] [Stakeholder Engagement]

13. C - Feedback and adjustments are the backbone of Agile projects. The feedback should be solicited and acted upon throughout the life of the project. [Agile Practice Guide, 1st edition, Page 15] [Stakeholder Engagement]

14. B - Here the product owner is correct. The new feature shouldn't have been developed without their consent. Now the best course of action is to ask the product owner if they would like to retain the feature or have it removed from the next release. [Agile Practice Guide, 1st edition, Page 41] [Stakeholder Engagement]

15. B - The most effective method would be to use a Kanban board as that would provide a continuous means to visually communicate project status to the team. [Agile Practice Guide, 1st edition, Page 65] [Stakeholder Engagement]

PMI-ACP Lite Mock Exam 9 Practice Questions

Test Name: PMI-ACP Lite Mock Exam 9
Total Questions: 40
Correct Answers Needed to Pass:
30 (75.00%)
Time Allowed: 60 Minutes

Test Description

This is a cumulative PMI-ACP Mock Exam which can be used as a benchmark for your PMI-ACP aptitude. This practice test includes questions from all exam topic areas, including sections from Agile Tools and Techniques, and all three Agile Knowledge and Skills areas.

Test Questions

1. When developing project timelines, which of the following adds the LEAST value to the timeline?

A. Color coding functions

B. Color coding feelings

C. Color coding events

D. Color coding user stories

2. A team is developing an online appraisals management system using an incremental project life cycle. The customer is complaining about the number of bugs that are detected by the customer which should have been detected by the project team. Which of the following techniques encourage a mistake-proofing discipline?

A. Cost of quality

B. Team penalties

C. Individual penalties

D. Test-driven development

3. An Agile team is working on a SCM project. At the end of the 3rd iteration, the team had successfully delivered 81 story points. The team was able to successfully address some improvement opportunities and during the 4th iteration the team was able to deliver 39 story points. What is the team's current velocity?

A. 120 story points per iteration.

B. 39 story points per iteration.

C. 27 story points per iteration.

D. 30 story points per iteration.

4. What is the difference between an Epic and a Theme?

A. An epic is a large user story while a theme is a collection of user stories.

B. A theme is a large user story while an epic is a collection of user stories.

C. A theme is a subset of a user story while an epic is a superset of user stories.

D. An epic is a subset of a user story while a theme is a superset of user stories.

5. The project sponsor took over the leadership of your Agile project while you were away on a holiday. In your absence, the sponsor asked for a detailed project schedule and the team developed a detailed task-level, resource loaded Gantt chart. What should be your next step now?

A. Revoke the detailed schedule and explain your reasons to the sponsor.

B. Create feeding buffers and pad the schedule.

C. Continue tracking the project against the recently developed schedule.

D. Retain the schedule but drop the resource assignments.

6. Many traditional plans are created with the assumption that all identified project requirements will be completed and so the work is typically prioritized and sequenced for the convenience of the project team. What is the main disadvantage with this sort of requirements prioritization?

A. Lower value requirements might get delivered earlier than higher value requirements.

B. Requirements might get changed during the course of the project.

C. Once requirements have been prioritized, they become a baseline for progress measurement.

D. Formal change control procedures influence all change requests.

7. You are leading a project that was initiated as a result of your organization's Blue Ocean Strategy. The product of the project will have features that have never been developed by anyone. These features are supposed to serve the unknown needs of the customers. According to the Kano model, these features are known as:

A. Delighters

B. Linear

C. Must-have

D. Threshold

8. Which of the following attributes of an Agile team facilitate better communication and improve team dynamics?

A. Collocation

B. Stable work environment

C. Cross-functional team members

D. Dedicated people

9. You have just been assigned as the project manager for a new project. The goal of the project is to cut the production cost of raw materials in the next six months so that the company can lower the price of goods and obtain a competitive advantage. According to the feasibility report there a couple of feasible approaches that have been analyzed that can result in reasonable cost savings. What is the problem with this objective?

A. It is not time bound.

B. It is not attainable.

C. It is not specific.

D. It is not measurable.

10. Your project has a big number of features that you now wish to classify according to

the Kano model. Which of the following approach will yield the best results?

A. Use questionnaires and survey users to accurately classify features.

B. The Agile team, facilitated by the servant-leader, classifies the features.

C. Ask the product owner to classify the features.

D. Estimate story points and categorize the features based on their sizes.

11. You are leading a critical organizational project and want to setup a visible, physical display that provides information to the rest of the organization enabling up-to-the-minute knowledge sharing without having to disturb the team. What should you setup?

A. Project charter

B. Information radiator

C. Fishbone diagram

D. PDCA loop

12. The practice of leading through service to the team, by focusing on understanding and addressing the needs and development of team members in order to enable the highest possible team performance, is known as:

A. Transactional leadership

B. Laissez-faire

C. Servant-leadership

D. Bureaucratic leadership

13. You are leading an Agile project. The team has proposed using a Kanban board to manage the team's work in progress and spot bottlenecks. The following work flow has been agreed on for the Kanban board: Ready -> Develop and Unit Test -> Dev-Done -> System Test -> Done. According to this Kanban board, the response time of an item is the:

A. The time it enters the "Ready" bin till the time it exits the "Develop and Unit Test" bin.

B. The time it enters the "Ready" bin till the time it enters the "Develop and Unit Test" bin.

C. The time it enters the "Ready" bin till the time it enters the "Dev-Done" bin.

D. The time it enters the "Ready" bin till the time it exits the "Dev-Done" bin.

14. Which of the following events doesn't warrant adding a burnup to a release burndown chart?

A. New scope of work is added to project.

B. A team realizes that the remaining work was underestimated.

C. Product owner wants to add new features to the project.

D. A team wishes to extend the project deadline.

15. Which of the following activities can be used to close a retrospective?

A. Five Whys

B. Fishbone

C. Brainstorming

D. Appreciations

16. You overhead your colleague saying that he isn't interested in attending the upcoming retrospective but happy that he would get a break from his daily routine job. Which ESVP role closely relates to this attitude?

A. Prisoners

B. Vacationers

C. Distractors

D. Pests

17. You are conducting a workshop on Agile methods, tools and techniques. Most of the participants have a background in traditional project management which pivots around managing project baselines. How does Agile view project baselines?

A. Agile teams focus primarily on scope baseline and disregard cost and schedule baselines.

B. Project baselines are promises that Agile team strive to meet.

C. All project baselines are consolidated into a single product backlog.

D. Baselines are often an artifact of attempted prediction.

18. A team is planning its first iteration on a project. The team is considering using historical values to forecast the team's velocity on this project. Which of the following is irrelevant to this consideration?

A. Is the project charter the same?

B. Is the working environment the same?

C. Is the domain the same?

D. Is the technology the same?

19. Which of the following is a characteristic of servant-leadership?

A. Controlling team members.

B. Promoting self-awareness.

C. Rewarding the best.

D. Micromanagement.

20. You have been recently hired in an organization as an Agile Coach. The organization has recently recognized the benefits of the Agile approach to project management and have also successfully piloted a couple of projects using the approach. You have overheard Rupesh, a project manager at the organization, claiming that an Agile project doesn't need to be planned and the project team should always be ready to accommodate all sort of changes. What is your view about this?

A. Rupesh is wrong, while responding to change is valued more than following a plan, that doesn't mean Agile projects do not require any planning effort.

B. Rupesh is always wrong, further he's is not PMI certified.

C. Rupesh is correct, the Agile Manifesto mandates responding to change over following a plan.

D. Rupesh is correct; he has recently completed a couple of Agile projects.

21. Which of the following two tasks need to be completed prior to starting the next iteration of the project?

A. Demonstration and retrospective.

B. Backlog grooming and iteration planning.

C. Release planning and iteration planning.

D. Iteration planning and retrospective.

22. Agile teams start a project iteration with loosely defined stories and turn these into functioning software by the end of the iteration. One exception to starting with loosely defined stories rather than putting more thought into the user stories prior to the start of the iteration is:

A. When the performing organization is rooted in traditional practices.

B. When the project consists of multiple Agile teams.

C. When the project duration is greater than one year.

D. When the product owner is not fluent with Agile practices.

23. An Agile team is halfway through the iteration when it feels that it needs detailed feedback on some of the features. What should be done?

A. Compromise and use some other feedback gathering technique, such as questionnaires.

B. Wait for the current iteration to be finished and then arrange a demonstration.

C. Terminate the current iteration and arrange a demonstration.

D. Arrange a demonstration during the iteration.

24. Your organization has recently acquired an HR management system that cost $100,000. The system would need a major upgrade after 10 years which will cost approximately $150,000. If the organization can earn 8% interest on an investment bond, how much money does the organization need to put in the bond now to have $150,000 when the upgrade is required?

A. 100000

B. 69479

C. 833334

D. 150000

25. You are helping an organization transition to Agile approaches, tools and techniques. You have noticed that historically the organization has followed traditional project management approaches and has highly valued the accuracy of the estimation effort. What is your view on estimating?

A. Agile teams highly value getting the estimates right.

B. Agile teams do not estimate or plan.

C. Agile teams do not strive for accurate estimation.

D. Estimation is time consuming activity, hence considered a waste.

26. Who can provide best estimates for a given piece of work on an Agile project?

A. Those who will do the work.

B. Scrum master

C. Product owner

D. Customer

27. Which project artifact first documents the "definition of done" for the project?

A. Product backlog

B. Sprint backlog

C. Project charter

D. Product roadmap

28. Earned value in Agile is:

A. Based on finished features.

B. Similar to the traditional earned value management.

C. Not a valid technique.

D. A measure of project's ROI.

29. An Agile team can only finish one story at a time. To complete a large feature that contains several stories, the team may not complete that entire feature until several more time periods have passed. Which of the following tools can help the team show its completed value?

A. Fishbone diagram

B. Product backlog burnup chart

C. Scatter chart

D. Pareto chart

30. One of the 12 Agile principles states that, "The most efficient and effective method of conveying information to and within a development team is face-to-face conversation". Which of the following Agile techniques help achieve this?

A. Backlog preparation

B. Backlog refinement

C. Team composition

D. Daily standups

31. You are examining your project's statistics. For the iterations one to six the team's velocity has been 40, 50, 43, 47, 46, and 44 story points respectively. What is the most reasonable velocity estimate for the next sprint?

A. Future velocity cannot be predicted.

B. 40 story points.

C. 50 story points.

D. 45 story points.

32. Some organizations resist starting projects without having any idea how long those projects will take. You are not comfortable in sharing any estimates until the first few iterations are completed. What should you do?

A. Determine the management's risk tolerance and estimate accordingly.

B. Forecast values based on historic data on past projects.

C. Stress that you desire to run a few iterations to provide reliable estimates.

D. Revert back to traditional project management approaches as the organization is not ready for Agile.

33. You have been made responsible to quickly deploy a new supply chain management system in an organization. You have been given authority to select any organizational resources to deliver the project and you have also been promised that the selected resources will remain dedicated to the project. However, you have also been asked to deliver features in increments so that necessary changes can be made as early as possible. You have also been asked to select team members in a way that the project team can perform independently. How should you select your team?

A. Select 3 to 9 team members.

B. Select team members with Agile certifications.

C. Select cross-functional team members.

D. Select team members that can be available 100% of their time.

34. When should an Agile team reflect on how to become more effective and tune its behavior accordingly?

A. Daily

B. At the start and end of the project.

C. At regular intervals.

D. At the end of each iteration.

35. Like traditional teams, Agile teams also track their progress. Which of the following measures is generally used by Agile teams to monitor its progress rate?

A. Cycle time

B. Velocity

C. Ideal time

D. Story points

36. You are leading the deployment of an inventory management system for a multinational client. The project team is geographically distributed and many time zones apart. Conducting daily standups is a major problem. How should this problem be tackled?

A. Ask the team members to record their updates and upload on the project site.

B. Encourage smaller group meetings (two or three people at a time) instead of whole-project daily standups.

C. Schedule standups on a round-robin basis so that each project team member gets at least one standup during his/her working time.

D. Schedule standups at a time that falls during the working hours of most of the team members.

37. Which of the following arrangements allows least flexibility to the buyer to alter the contracted scope of works?

A. Not-to-exceed time and materials arrangement.

B. Dynamic scope option.

C. Early cancellation option.

D. Fixed-price arrangements.

38. Which of the following Agile methods focus on the activities of a single, small, usually collocated, cross-functional team rather than for initiative that requires collaboration of multiple Agile teams in a program or portfolio?

A. Disciplined Agile

B. Scaled Agile Framework

C. Large Scale Scrum

D. eXtreme Programming

39. During a planning poker meeting, the team was not able to converge on a single estimate for a particular story after the third round. What needs to be done next?

A. Park the user story on the parking lot.

B. Take the average of the estimates at the end of the third round.

C. Remove the user story from the estimating process.

D. Continue to repeat the process.

40. Which of the following is an artefact that an Agile team must produce by the end of each retrospective?

A. Work breakdown structure

B. Product acceptance criteria.

C. Risk register.

D. List of improvement actions.

PMI-ACP Lite Mock Exam 9 Answer Key and Explanations

1. D - Due the number and size of user stories, color coding user stories is not recommended. If the team desires to classify by product functionality, color coding by themes would be a more appropriate approach. The rest of the choices are all acceptable. [Derby, E. and Larsen, D., 2006. Agile Retrospectives: Making Good Teams Great. 1st ed. Texas: Pragmatic Bookshelf, Page 53] [Continuous Improvement]

2. D - Penalties and fear cannot encourage a mistake-proofing discipline. The team should consider using various test-driven development practices. This mistake-proofing discipline makes it difficult for defects to remain undetected. [Agile Practice Guide, 1st edition, Page 32] [Problem Detection and Resolution]

3. D - Velocity = average story points per iteration. Since the team had delivered 120 story points in 4 iterations, the velocity is 120/4 = 30 story points per iteration (on average). [Agile Practice Guide, 1st edition, Page 61] [Team Performance]

4. A - An epic is a large user story while a theme is a collection of user stories. [Cohn, M., 2006. Agile Estimating and Planning. 1st ed. Massachusetts: Pearson Education. Page 53] [Adaptive Planning]

5. A - Agile projects are not plan driven and do not follow detailed plans as this compromises the team agility in responding to changes. You need to revoke the detailed schedule and explain the reason to the project sponsor. [Agile Practice Guide, 1st edition, Page 17] [Problem Detection and Resolution]

6. A - The question is asking to identify the weakness in the "prioritization" process and not with the traditional approaches to requirements management. The main problem in the scenario is that the requirements are not prioritized by the value to the user and customer. Since there is no attempt to work on features in a customer-value-based priority order, there is a risk that lower value requirements might get delivered earlier than higher value requirements. [Cohn, M., 2006. Agile Estimating and Planning. 1st ed. Massachusetts: Pearson Education. Page 16] [Adaptive Planning]

7. A - Delighters are those features that provide great satisfaction, often adding a price premium to a product. However, the lack of an exciter or delighter will not decrease customer satisfaction below neutral as in the case of "must-have" features, also known as the threshold features. In fact, exciters and delighters are often called unknown needs because customers or users do not know they need these features until they see them. [Cohn, M., 2006. Agile Estimating and Planning. 1st ed. Massachusetts: Pearson Education. Page 110] [Adaptive Planning]

8. A - Collocation facilitates better team communication and improves team dynamics. [Agile Practice Guide, 1st edition, Page 40] [Team Performance]

9. D - Although the objective is specific (reduction of the cost of raw materials) the problem with the objective that it is not measurable. Say if the project results in 10% cost savings, will this be called a success or a

failure? [Derby, E. and Larsen, D., 2006. Agile Retrospectives: Making Good Teams Great. 1st ed. Texas: Pragmatic Bookshelf, Page 107] [Agile Principles and Mindset]

10. A - The Kano model gives us an approach to separate features into three categories: must-have features, linear features, and delighters. Users are the ideal people to approach when assessing the features on the Kano model. [Cohn, M., 2006. Agile Estimating and Planning. 1st ed. Massachusetts: Pearson Education. Page 112] [Adaptive Planning]

11. B - An information radiator is a physical display that provides information to the rest of the organization enabling up-to-the-minute knowledge sharing without having to disturb the team. [Agile Practice Guide, 1st edition, Page 152] [Stakeholder Engagement]

12. C - Servant-leadership is the practice of leading through service to the team, by focusing on understanding and addressing the needs and development of team members in order to enable the highest possible team performance. [Agile Practice Guide, 1st edition, Page 154] [Value-driven Delivery]

13. B - Response time is the time that an item waits until work starts. On the Kanban board, this is the time an item enters the "Ready" bin till the time it enters the "Develop and Unit Test" bin (or exits the "Ready" bin). [Agile Practice Guide, 1st edition, Pages 64, 65] [Value-driven Delivery]

14. D - Adding new features means additional scope. This would increase the total remaining story points and add a burnup. If re-estimating remaining work increases the total story points, this will also add a burnup. However, adding a burnup just to secure a deadline extension is not acceptable. [Cohn, M., 2006. Agile Estimating and Planning. 1st ed. Massachusetts: Pearson Education. Page 219] [Team Performance]

15. D - Brainstorming, Five Whys, and Fishbone diagrams are analysis techniques used during the retrospectives and not as a closing activity. Appreciations is one of the recommended closing activities. [Derby, E. and Larsen, D., 2006. Agile Retrospectives: Making Good Teams Great. 1st ed. Texas: Pragmatic Bookshelf, Page 117] [Continuous Improvement]

16. B - Vacationers aren't interested in the work of the retrospective, but are happy to be away from the daily grind. They may pay attention some of the time, but they are mostly glad to be out of the office. [Derby, E. and Larsen, D., 2006. Agile Retrospectives: Making Good Teams Great. 1st ed. Texas: Pragmatic Bookshelf, Page 45] [Continuous Improvement]

17. D - Unlike traditional methods, Agile methods do not pivot around project baselines. Agile teams view baselines as artifacts of attempted prediction, which usually are not accurate representations of reality. [Agile Practice Guide, 1st edition, Page 61] [Team Performance]

18. A - This is a tricky question. Since each project is unique, project charters for both projects will be different. But this is irrelevant to estimating the team's velocity. The rest of the choice give valid considerations. [Cohn, M., 2006. Agile Estimating and Planning. 1st ed. Massachusetts: Pearson Education. Page 176] [Adaptive Planning]

19. B - Servant leadership prefers coaching vs. controlling. Micromanagement and rewarding the best doesn't create an Agile environment. Promoting self-awareness is one of the key requirements of a servant-leadership environment. [Agile Practice Guide, 1st edition, Page 34] [Agile Principles and Mindset]

20. A - Rupesh is not correct, but the statement that he is always wrong is just too harsh. We don't have enough information to claim that. Although according to the Agile Manifesto, responding to change is valued more than following a plan, that doesn't mean that Agile projects do not require any planning effort. [Agile Practice Guide, 1st edition, Page 8] [Agile Principles and Mindset]

21. A - An iteration cannot be completed until the completed features are demonstrated to the product owner. Further, a retrospective is a part of the iteration and happens at the end of the iteration. [Agile Practice Guide, 1st edition, Page 51] [Continuous Improvement]

22. B - Ideally, an Agile team begins an iteration with vaguely defined requirements and turns those vague requirements into functioning, tested software by the end of the iteration. Going from vague requirements to working software in one iteration is usually easier on a single team than it is when there are multiple teams. On a multiple team project it is often appropriate and necessary to put more though into the user stories prior to the start of the iteration. [Cohn, M., 2006. Agile Estimating and Planning. 1st ed. Massachusetts: Pearson Education. Page 201] [Adaptive Planning]

23. D - There is no reason for the team to compromise on some secondary technique. If a product demonstration is required, that should be immediately arranged. [Agile Practice Guide, 1st edition, Page 55] [Stakeholder Engagement]

24. B - To solve this question, you need to determine the present value of $150,000 (money required at the end of ten years) at 8% interest rate. The formula is Present Value (PV) = Future Value (FV) / (1 + interest rate) ^ periods. So to calculate, PV = $150,000 / (1+8%)^10 = $69,479. [Cohn, M., 2006. Agile Estimating and Planning. 1st ed. Massachusetts: Pearson Education. Page 100] [Value-driven Delivery]

25. C - Agile teams do estimate and plan but the focus is not on developing accurate estimates and plans, instead the focus is on delivering value to the customer as soon as possible. [Cohn, M., 2006. Agile Estimating and Planning. 1st ed. Massachusetts: Pearson Education. Page 4] [Value-driven Delivery]

26. A - It is well-known that the best estimates are given by those who will do the work. [Cohn, M., 2006. Agile Estimating and Planning. 1st ed. Massachusetts: Pearson Education. Page 59] [Adaptive Planning]

27. C - The project charter documents the "definition of done" for the project. The project charter is usually the first project artifact. [Agile Practice Guide, 1st edition, Page 49] [Value-driven Delivery]

28. A - Earned value in Agile is based on finished features. This is shown through a product backlog burnup chart that shows completed work compared to total expected

work at interval milestones or iterations. [Agile Practice Guide, 1st edition, Page 67] [Team Performance]

29. B - The team can show its completed value with a product backlog burnup chart. The rest of the choices are quality management tools. [Agile Practice Guide, 1st edition, Page 68] [Team Performance]

30. D - Daily standups require collocated team members to meet face-to-face, share progress and make team commitments. [Agile Practice Guide, 1st edition, Page 98] [Agile Principles and Mindset]

31. D - The velocity is moving around 45 story points and the variation is showing a declining trend. It is most likely that the variation will further reduce and the team's velocity will stable around 45 story points. [Agile Practice Guide, 1st edition, Page 61] [Team Performance]

32. C - Reverting back to traditional project management approaches would be an extreme step. In this situation, it is important to stress that your desire to run a few iterations first stems not from a desire to avoid making an estimate but to avoid making an estimate without adequate foundation. [Cohn, M., 2006. Agile Estimating and Planning. 1st ed. Massachusetts: Pearson Education. Page 179] [Problem Detection and Resolution]

33. C - Agile certifications can be helpful but cannot be a prime selection criteria. If team members lack exposure to Agile approaches, they can be coached. The management has already promised 100% availability of selected resources. Team size of three to nine members is recommended for any team. Since the objective is to form an independent team, cross-functional team members need to be selected so that team has all the necessary expertise it requires to deliver the project. [Agile Practice Guide, 1st edition, Page 40] [Value-driven Delivery]

34. C - According to the Agile principles, the team reflects on how to become more effective (through retrospectives) at regular intervals. Conducting daily retrospectives will not be an efficient approach. [Agile Practice Guide, 1st edition, Page 9] [Agile Principles and Mindset]

35. B - Story points and ideal times are story sizing measures. Cycle time measures the time consumed to deliver stories. Agile teams monitor their progress by velocity that is expressed as the number of story points (or ideal days) completed per iteration. [Cohn, M., 2006. Agile Estimating and Planning. 1st ed. Massachusetts: Pearson Education. Page 211] [Team Performance]

36. B - Recording updates is a bad idea that takes away the required interaction between the team members. When team members are many time zones apart, consider using whole-project interactions less frequently, while encouraging more frequent personal meetings (two or three people at a time). [Agile Practice Guide, 1st edition, Page 122] [Problem Detection and Resolution]

37. D - A not-to-exceed time and materials allows replacing original scope with new scope. The dynamic scope option allows scope adjustments at specified points in the project. The early cancellation option allows termination halfway through the project. The fixed-price arrangement is the least flexible option. [Agile Practice Guide, 1st edition, Page 78] [Value-driven Delivery]

38. D - eXtreme programming focuses on the activities of a single, small, usually collocated, cross-functional team. The rest of the choices provide guidance for initiatives that require collaboration of multiple Agile teams in a program or portfolio. [Agile Practice Guide, 1st edition, Page 80] [Agile Principles and Mindset]

39. D - In many cases, the estimates will already converge by the second round. But if they have not, continue to repeat the process. The goal is for the estimators to converge on a single estimate that can be used for the story. It rarely takes more than three rounds but continue the process as long as the estimates are moving closer together. [Cohn, M., 2006. Agile Estimating and Planning. 1st ed. Massachusetts: Pearson Education. Page 57] [Problem Detection and Resolution]

40. D - Retrospectives allow Agile teams to learn about, improve, and adapt their processes. The prime retrospective artefact is a list of agreed improvement actions. [Agile Practice Guide, 1st edition, Page 50] [Continuous Improvement]

PMI-ACP Lite Mock Exam 10 Practice Questions

Test Name: PMI-ACP Lite Mock Exam 10
Total Questions: 40
Correct Answers Needed to Pass: 30 (75.00%)
Time Allowed: 60 Minutes

Test Description

This is a cumulative PMI-ACP Mock Exam which can be used as a benchmark for your PMI-ACP aptitude. This practice test includes questions from all exam topic areas, including sections from Agile Tools and Techniques, and all three Agile Knowledge and Skills areas.

Test Questions

1. An organization has recently begun its Agile transformation. Which of the following can help motivate more frequent handoffs across departments, and thus more frequent interactions and a faster flow of value across the organization?

   A. Size of project deliverables.

   B. Highly functionalized structures.

   C. Agile PMO.

   D. Geographically distributed project sites.

2. Your organization needs to select one of the following two projects: Project A: IRR = 8%, NPV = $25,500, duration = 3 years; Project B: IRR = 12%, NPV = $18,700, duration = 6 years. What is the opportunity cost of project A?

   A. 25500

   B. 6800

   C. 18700

   D. -6800

3. An Agile team collected all the requirements for a particular project iteration. These requirements were translated to the design specifications followed by the development work. During the acceptance testing, the team realized that some of the design assumptions were not valid and most of the features requires rework. What went wrong?

   A. The team fell into the trap of mini-waterfall.

   B. The team didn't document the assumptions in the design specifications.

   C. Nothing went wrong, Agile teams welcome rework.

   D. The requirements collection process was probably flawed.

4. How many clarifying principles flowed from the Agile Manifesto?

   A. 8

   B. 6

   C. 12

   D. 4

5. You are about to start the third iteration on your project. The team believes that some of the high priority items on the backlog are

high risk items. What should you do to manage this risk?

A. Increase the duration of the iteration.

B. Schedule the risky items at the very end of the project.

C. Include fewer story points in the current iteration.

D. Call a retrospective meeting.

6. In Agile projects with evolving requirements, high risk, or significant uncertainty, the scope is often not understood at the beginning of the project or it evolves during the project. How do Agile projects handle project scope in such circumstances?

A. Developing a preliminary product backlog at the start of the project and prioritizing the backlog during the course of the project.

B. Spending more time in defining and agreeing on scope and spending less time in establishing the process of its ongoing discovery.

C. Developing an exhaustive product backlog at the start of the project and prioritizing the backlog during the course of the project.

D. Spending less time in defining and agreeing on scope and spending more time in establishing the process of its ongoing discovery.

7. You will be leading a complex organizational restructure project in the near future. The goal of the project is to optimize organizational workflows and reduce costs by at least 20%. Since, everybody will be affected by this project, you need to consider a big number of stakeholders. During the project, you would need some timely business decisions to be taken. Who makes business decisions on Agile projects?

A. Servant-leader

B. End customer

C. Functional managers

D. Product owner

8. You are leading a complex Agile project and have added a 10% schedule buffer to mitigate the schedule risk on the project. How should you communicate this to the product owner?

A. Task padding was carried out in line with the Agile Manifesto.

B. Don't communicate this information and expand the task durations to include the padding.

C. The project tasks have been padded to manage the scheduling risk.

D. The buffer is intended to provide a schedule everyone can be confident in.

9. Which of the following two projects should be selected if the goal of the company is to maximize the return on investment? Project A: NPV = $25,081, IRR = 15%; Project B: NPV = $40,318, IRR = 13%.

A. Project B because the NPV $40,318.

B. Project A because the IRR is 15%.

C. Project B because the IRR is 13%.

D. Project A because the NPV is $25,081.

10. Agile teams strive for rapid product delivery. A set of features goes through a series of development and testing stages until the release. Which of the following is considered the first delivery stage?

A. Storyboarding

B. Regression testing

C. User acceptance testing

D. Demonstration

11. When you divide the team into small groups and keep the people who worked closely with each other together, you are creating:

A. ESVP groups

B. Affinity groups

C. Lean groups

D. Pareto groups

12. Chris will be conducting an introduction to Agile workshop in the next few days. On one of the slides, he put a number of areas that Agile teams highly value. The list included customer collaboration, working software, responding to change and attention to detail. What mistake did Chris make?

A. Showed "Responding to change" as a value instead of showing "Change management".

B. Showed "Attention to detail" as a value instead of showing "Individuals and Interactions".

C. Showed "Customer collaboration" as a value instead of showing "Contract negotiation".

D. Showed "Working software" as a value instead of showing "Individuals and Interactions".

13. Which of the following statements regarding Agile environments is incorrect?

A. Many Agile frameworks and approaches do not address the role of the project manager.

B. Pragmatic Agile practitioners realize that project managers can add significant value in many situations.

C. Agile teams are self-organizing and self-managing.

D. The role of the project manager has been clearly articulated in many Agile frameworks.

14. Forecasting velocity based on the observed velocity on a project generally produces reliable estimates. If the project team has completed its first three iterations and the observed velocity was 20 story points per iteration (on average), what would be a reasonable estimate of velocity for the fourth iteration?

A. 12 to 32 story points per iteration.

B. 17 to 23 story points per iteration.

C. 16 to 25 story points per iteration.

D. 18 to 22 story points per iteration.

15. You are leading an Agile project. The team has proposed using a Kanban board to manage the team's work in progress and spot bottlenecks. The following work flow has been agreed on for the Kanban board: Ready -> Develop and Unit Test -> Dev-Done -> System Test -> Done. If the team wants to limit its WIP, where are these limits shown on the board?

A. The WIP limits are shown in the "Ready" column.

B. The WIP limits are shown in the "Done" column.

C. The WIP limits are shown against each work item.

D. The WIP limits are shown at the top of each column.

16. You and your Agile team are developing a new workflow management system for your organization. According to the ICT Systems & Tools Development Policy, you are required to produce detailed software documentation. What should you do?

A. Use traditional project management practices to manage this project.

B. Develop the required documentation as part of the project.

C. Reject the policy as it is against the Agile Manifesto.

D. Educate the higher management on why you will not be developing detailed documentation on this project.

17. You are leading an ERP development project and currently developing a release plan. Which of the following are the general steps involved during a release plan?

A. Conditions of satisfaction -> estimating user stories -> prioritizing user stories -> selecting release date.

B. Estimating user stories -> prioritizing user stories -> conditions of satisfaction -> selecting release date.

C. Estimating user stories -> conditions of satisfaction -> selecting release date > prioritizing user stories.

D. Selecting release date -> conditions of satisfaction -> estimating user stories -> prioritizing user stories.

18. How can an Agile team ensure that the features an Agile team is developing and releasing delivers the maximum value to the business?

A. Team collaborates with the feature users/customers.

B. Team collaborates with the product owner.

C. Servant-leader collaborates with the team.

D. Product owner collaborates with feature users/customers.

19. In Agile software development, what does the term "technical debt" means?

A. The estimated cost of opportunity lost by not selecting a more lucrative project.

B. The pro-rated cost of external technical experts hired by the project.

C. The accrued cost of debt taken by the technical team members.

D. The deferred cost of work not done at an earlier point in the product life cycle.

20. You are leading a project that involves some safety-critical products that will require additional documentation and conformance checks beyond what Agile processes suggest. What should you do?

A. Have appropriate additional layers of conformance review, documentation, and certification that is required by the project.

B. Complete the project using Agile approaches and then develop the required documentation using traditional approaches.

C. Arrange Agile training sessions for the customer in hopes that they relax the documentation and conformance requirements.

D. Switch to traditional project management approaches as Agile approaches will not be effective in this environment.

21. During a retrospective event, you want to identify which project events created a positive or negative team atmosphere. Which of the following activities can be used in conjunction with a project timeline to obtain and analyze this information?

A. Histograms

B. Sampling

C. Round Robin

D. Color Code Dots

22. An Agile team's average velocity for the first couple of iterations is 20 story points per iteration. Since the team wanted to increase the velocity, it decided to increase the iteration duration from 3 week to 4 weeks. What is your view on this?

A. Increasing the duration doesn't increase the velocity.

B. Increasing the duration can actually decrease the velocity.

C. Increasing the duration might increase the velocity but this doesn't increase the performance.

D. Velocity doesn't depend on iteration duration.

23. A project team has recently adopted Agile approaches to project management. However, the team is still not proficient in these methods as it has only recently adopted these approaches. Which of the following questions should the team address to ensure it has successfully adopted an Agile Mindset?

A. How can the team deliver quickly and obtain early feedback to benefit the next delivery cycle?

B. How to ensure all contractual obligations are fulfilled?

C. How can project management processes be tailored to suit each project?

D. How to handle confidential information during the project?

24. An Agile coach has to wear multiple hats from time to time. All of the following are such roles except:

A. Release manager

B. Problem solver

C. Facilitator

D. Advisor

25. A fast food retailer has recently hired a team to develop a bespoke inventory management system. The team has never worked with each other in the past. Further, the team requires coaching on Agile approaches. If the firm does not have in-house Agile coaches, what should be done?

A. Nothing needs to be done; an Agile team is self-managed.

B. Select the senior-most team member to provide the required coaching.

C. Product owner should provide the required coaching.

D. Invite external Agile coaches to help the team.

26. Most projects with multiple teams benefit from establishing a common estimating baseline at the start of the project. However, the only time separate teams may consider estimating in different units without a common baseline is:

A. When some features are better estimated in ideal days while the rest are better estimated in story points.

B. When the products being built are truly separate.

C. When the product owner is indifferent to the estimation approach.

D. When there are three or more Agile teams on a project.

27. Which of the following is a lean enterprise technique used to document, analyze, and improve the flow of information or materials required to produce a product or service for a customer?

A. One Piece Flow

B. Theory of Constraints

C. Value Stream Mapping

D. A3 Reporting

28. You have recently taken charge of a team managing a complex project that heavily relies on knowledge work. Your team is currently spending four hours per week in refining user stories. What is the probable cause behind this?

A. The product owner could be over-preparing or the team may be lacking some critical skills.

B. The product owner is not available for the team.

C. The previous project manager was following a hybrid development approach.

D. The scrum master is not available for the team.

29. Which of the following regarding AgileUP and Unified Process (UP) is correct?

A. AgileUP features more accelerated cycles and less heavyweight processes than Unified Process.

B. AgileUP features less accelerated cycles and more heavyweight processes than Unified Process.

C. AgileUP features less accelerated cycles and less heavyweight processes than Unified Process.

D. AgileUP features more accelerated cycles and more heavyweight processes than Unified Process.

30. When conducting a Triple Nickels activity with six team members, which of the following is NOT recommended:

A. Dividing the group into smaller teams.

B. Ask the participants to write their ideas on a piece of paper and pass on every five minutes.

C. Passing the ideas paper only five times.

D. The retrospective leader should facilitate the activity.

31. Which of the following is an effective and light-weight iteration or release retrospective closing technique that helps the retrospective leader get feedback to improve skills and processes?

A. Helped, Hindered, Hypothesis

B. Inputs, Process, Outputs, Feedback loop

C. Current State, Future State, Gap Analysis

D. Supplier, Input, Process, Output, Customer

32. Although the payback period is very commonly used to financially compare two or more projects, the primary disadvantage to the payback period is that:

A. It fails to take into account the time value of money.

B. It fails to take into account the future cash flows beyond the breakeven period.

C. It calculates the breakeven point based on the estimated cash flows.

D. It discounts the cash flows based on market interest rate.

33. When conducting a release planning meeting, what should be the prime goal of the Agile team?

A. Deliver smallest increment that provides the highest value to the customer.

B. Develop a minimum viable product.

C. Deliver all captured requirements in the smallest possible time.

D. Deliver the product in the least possible cost budget.

34. You are currently forming a team for a project that will be developed on Agile principles and practices. You requested a full-time accountant on the team but got a part-time accountant. What should you do first?

A. Negotiate with the functional manager for a full-time resource.

B. Ask the part-time resource to maintain daily time-sheets.

C. Escalate the issue to the product owner.

D. Plan enough work in each iteration so that the part-time resources do not get overloaded.

35. The burndown charts are rarely straight lines. There are many reasons why a straight line cannot always be achieved. Which of the following events doesn't affect the burndown chart?

A. Addition of scope of work.

B. Merging related stories into themes.

C. Inconsistent team velocity.

D. Incomplete stories by the end of the iteration.

36. A higher than expected velocity would most probably result in:

A. Increased costs for the project.

B. Reduced number of expected iterations.

C. Reduced costs for the project.

D. Increased number of expected iterations.

37. You are responsible for deploying a new supply chain management system for a client organization. You need to analyze the client organization's current processes and procedures, design future-state processes in consultation with the subject matter experts at the client organization, and customize the supply chain system to suit these processes. According to the contract, all prototypes presented to the client must accompany user instruction sets. Your team is objecting to this documentation requirements and insist in developing a user manual only at the very end of the project. What should you do?

A. Let the team know that producing the user instruction set with the released prototype is a contractual requirement.

B. Negotiate with the client organization and convince them to drop the documentation requirement.

C. Negotiate with the team and convince them to develop comprehensive documentation before releasing any prototypes.

D. Accept the team's demand; Agile Manifesto values working software over comprehensive documentation.

38. Which of the following statements is correct regarding the Kanban method?

A. The Kanban method is less prescriptive than some Agile approaches and less disruptive.

B. The Kanban method is relatively difficult to implement.

C. The Kanban method prescribes the use of timeboxed iterations.

D. The Kanban method is based on the principle of pushing items through the process.

39. You are managing a complex, high-change project. Although the project doesn't have a completion deadline, there is a general expectation that the project should complete in nine to twelve months. The project team is currently struggling to collaborate to expedite work across the board. Which of the following actions might help the situation and facilitate collaboration?

A. Adopting traditional project management approaches.

B. Crashing the project by increasing the work in progress.

C. Limiting the work in progress.

D. Increasing the team size and shortening the delivery iterations.

40. During a retrospective meeting, team members work in pairs to brainstorm all the tasks necessary to complete an improvement idea. After brainstorming, team members eliminate redundant tasks and fill in gaps. The tasks are then arranged in order, and team members sign up for tasks they will complete. What Agile activity is this?

A. Retrospective planning game.

B. Developing a release plan.

C. Planning poker.

D. Developing an iteration plan.

PMI-ACP Lite Mock Exam 10 Answer Key and Explanations

1. A - Highly functionalized structures and geographically distributed project sites create impediments to Agile approaches. An Agile PMO can help but the frequency of the deliverables is directly related to the size of the deliverables. Reducing the size of a project deliverable will motivate more frequent handoffs across departments, and thus more frequent interactions and a faster flow of value across the organization. [Agile Practice Guide, 1st edition, Page 83] [Agile Principles and Mindset]

2. C - Opportunity cost is the foregone benefit of the alternative. If project A is selected instead of project B, the opportunity cost will be the value of project B, $18,700. The given IRR and duration data is extraneous. [Cohn, M., 2006. Agile Estimating and Planning. 1st ed. Massachusetts: Pearson Education. Page 100] [Value-driven Delivery]

3. A - Mini-waterfalls occur when the team manages project iterations in a waterfall style. Although Agile teams welcome change, the rework in this scenario could have been avoided by delivering smaller finished features to the customer and obtaining feedback. [Agile Practice Guide, 1st edition, Page 39] [Problem Detection and Resolution]

4. C - Twelve clarifying principles flowed from the four Agile manifesto values. [Agile Practice Guide, 1st edition, Page 9] [Agile Principles and Mindset]

5. C - Calling a retrospective is not going to help as retrospectives look in the past in order to identify improvement opportunities. Increasing the iteration duration is not a recommended Agile practice. The risk can be managed by including fewer story points (scope) in the next iteration. [Cohn, M., 2006. Agile Estimating and Planning. 1st ed. Massachusetts: Pearson Education. Page 28] [Problem Detection and Resolution]

6. D - The product backlog is prioritized by the product owner and not the team. Agile teams manage project scope by spending less time in defining and agreeing on scope at the start of the project and spending more time in establishing the process of its ongoing discovery. [Agile Practice Guide, 1st edition, Page 91] [Value-driven Delivery]

7. D - Product owners make decisions on behalf of business stakeholders on Agile projects. [Agile Practice Guide, 1st edition, Page 41] [Value-driven Delivery]

8. D - Individuals add padding to an estimate if they expect to be beaten up if they are wrong. A schedule buffer is different. A schedule buffer is a necessary margin of safety added to the sum of estimates from which local safety has been removed. Tell the product owner that the buffer is intended to provide a schedule everyone can be confident in. [Cohn, M., 2006. Agile Estimating and Planning. 1st ed. Massachusetts: Pearson Education. Page 197] [Stakeholder Engagement]

9. B - When the goal is to maximize the return on investment, the project with higher IRR is selected. [Cohn, M., 2006. Agile Estimating and Planning. 1st ed. Massachusetts: Pearson Education. Page 102] [Value-driven Delivery]

10. D - The first part of the delivery is a demonstration. Demonstrations or reviews are a necessary part of the Agile project flow. [Agile Practice Guide, 1st edition, Page 57] [Value-driven Delivery]

11. B - When you divide the team into small groups and keep the people who worked closely with each other together, you are creating affinity groups. [Derby, E. and Larsen, D., 2006. Agile Retrospectives: Making Good Teams Great. 1st ed. Texas: Pragmatic Bookshelf, Page 51] [Continuous Improvement]

12. B - "Attention to detail" is not a value of the Agile Manifesto. Chris has incorrectly showed "Attention to detail" as a value instead of showing "Individuals and Interactions". [Agile Practice Guide, 1st edition, Page 8] [Continuous Improvement]

13. D - Although pragmatic Agile practitioners realize that project managers can add significant value in many situations, the role of the project manager has not been clearly articulated in many Agile frameworks. Many Agile frameworks and approaches do not address the role of the project manager. [Agile Practice Guide, 1st edition, Page 37] [Agile Principles and Mindset]

14. B - The cone of uncertainty can be used to calculate the ranges of the estimates. If the team has completed the first iteration, the multipliers are 0.6 and 1.6. If the team has completed two iterations, the multipliers are 0.8 and 1.25. If the team has completed three iterations, the multipliers are 0.85 and 1.15. [Cohn, M., 2006. Agile Estimating and Planning. 1st ed. Massachusetts: Pearson Education. Page 178] [Team Performance]

15. D - On a Kanban board, the work in progress (WIP) limits are shown at the top of each column. [Agile Practice Guide, 1st edition, Page 66] [Value-driven Delivery]

16. B - Although according to the Agile Manifesto working software is valued over comprehensive documentation, this doesn't mean that Agile teams do not produce detailed documentation. If documentation is required of the project, the team must develop it. [Agile Practice Guide, 1st edition, Page 8] [Problem Detection and Resolution]

17. A - The correct sequence is: Conditions of satisfaction -> estimating user stories -> prioritizing user stories -> selecting release date. [Cohn, M., 2006. Agile Estimating and Planning. 1st ed. Massachusetts: Pearson Education. Page 133] [Adaptive Planning]

18. D - The product owner represents the customer on an Agile team; the Agile team doesn't directly collaborate with the customer. Only customers/end users can determine the value of a required (or already developed) feature. [Agile Practice Guide, 1st edition, Page 41] [Value-driven Delivery]

19. D - The "technical debt" is the deferred cost of work not done at an earlier point in the product life cycle. This term is usually used in the context of degraded quality of code. [Agile Practice Guide, 1st edition, Pages 58, 154] [Value-driven Delivery]

20. A - Agile approaches can still be used in this environment, but they need to have the appropriate additional layers of conformance reviews, documentation, and certification that is required by the project. Agile approaches are not set in the stone and can be tailored according to the needs of the

project. [Agile Practice Guide, 1st edition, Page 122] [Problem Detection and Resolution]

21. D - A "Color Code Dots" activity is used in conjunction with a timeline to gather data about feelings in a longer iteration, release, or project retrospective. This activity is used to show how people experienced events on the timeline. [Derby, E. and Larsen, D., 2006. Agile Retrospectives: Making Good Teams Great. 1st ed. Texas: Pragmatic Bookshelf, Page 59] [Continuous Improvement]

22. C - Velocity is the number of story points completed per iteration. If the iteration size is increased, the team should be able to deliver more story points, which will increase the velocity. But the increase in velocity through this approach will just be a wash as this approach doesn't increase the team's performance. [Agile Practice Guide, 1st edition, Page 61] [Problem Detection and Resolution]

23. A - Tailoring project management processes, handling confidential information, and compliance to contractual obligations are considerations of all project teams regardless of the chosen project management approach. However, Agile approaches stress on the need to deliver quickly and obtain early feedback to benefit the next delivery cycle. [Agile Practice Guide, 1st edition, Page 33] [Value-driven Delivery]

24. A - Agile coaches do not manage the product release. The self-organizing Agile team manages the release. [Agile Practice Guide, 1st edition, Page 150] [Value-driven Delivery]

25. D - Initially, many organizations invite external Agile coaches to help them when their internal coaching capability is not fully developed. Product owners might have a different skillset and are not necessarily Agile coaches. [Agile Practice Guide, 1st edition, Page 41] [Problem Detection and Resolution]

26. B - The only time separate team may consider estimating in different units without a common baseline is when the products being built are truly separate and there is absolutely no opportunity for developers from one team to move onto another. Even then, it is recommended to establish a common baseline, if possible, as it facilitates communicating about the project. [Cohn, M., 2006. Agile Estimating and Planning. 1st ed. Massachusetts: Pearson Education. Page 200] [Adaptive Planning]

27. C - Value Stream Mapping is a lean enterprise technique used to document, analyze, and improve the flow of information or materials required to produce a product or service for a customer. [Agile Practice Guide, 1st edition, Page 154] [Continuous Improvement]

28. A - The scenario doesn't give enough context to determine the unviability of the product owner or the scrum master. Further, it doesn't give any context behind the use of development methodology. This leaves only one choice. Generally speaking, if the team needs to spend more than an hour per week refining stories, the product owner could be over-preparing, or the team may be lacking some critical skills needed to evaluate and refine the work. [Agile Practice Guide, 1st edition, Page 53] [Problem Detection and Resolution]

29. A - The Agile Unified Process (AgileUP) is an offshoot of the Unified Process (UP) for software projects. AgileUP features more accelerated cycles and less heavyweight processes than Unified Process. [Agile Practice Guide, 1st edition, Page 111] [Value-driven Delivery]

30. A - The purpose of the "Triple Nickels" activity is to generate ideas for actions or recommendations and uncover important topics about the project history. If there are seven or fewer people in the group, it is recommended not to divide into small groups and instead do the activity as whole group and pass the paper only five times. [Derby, E. and Larsen, D., 2006. Agile Retrospectives: Making Good Teams Great. 1st ed. Texas: Pragmatic Bookshelf, Page 57] [Continuous Improvement]

31. A - "Helped, Hindered, Hypothesis" is an effective and light-weight iteration or release retrospective closing technique that helps the retrospective leader get feedback to improve skills and processes. The rest of the choices are in-depth process analysis models. [Derby, E. and Larsen, D., 2006. Agile Retrospectives: Making Good Teams Great. 1st ed. Texas: Pragmatic Bookshelf, Page 122] [Continuous Improvement]

32. A - Unlike financial measures such as IRR and NPV, the primary disadvantage to the payback period is that it fails to take into account the time value of money. Money received in the future is valued the same as the money paid out today. [Cohn, M., 2006. Agile Estimating and Planning. 1st ed. Massachusetts: Pearson Education. Page 104] [Value-driven Delivery]

33. A - Part of planning a release is determining how much can be accomplished by what date. By prioritizing requirements, Agile teams thrive to deliver maximum value in the shortest possible time. [Cohn, M., 2006. Agile Estimating and Planning. 1st ed. Massachusetts: Pearson Education. Page 132] [Value-driven Delivery]

34. A - The first thing you should do is negotiate with the functional manager for a full-time resource. You must educate the functional manager that Agile teams require dedicated resources. [Agile Practice Guide, 1st edition, Page 44] [Stakeholder Engagement]

35. B - Addition of scope of work will show up as a burnup. Incomplete stories will move the burndown line above the linear trendline. Inconsistent velocity will show a random walk by the burndown line. However, merging stories into themes will not have any effect on the burndown chart as this doesn't add or remove any story points from the project's scope. [Cohn, M., 2006. Agile Estimating and Planning. 1st ed. Massachusetts: Pearson Education. Page 213] [Team Performance]

36. B - A higher than expected team velocity would generally result in reduced number of expected iterations. [Agile Practice Guide, 1st edition, Page 61] [Team Performance]

37. A - Although according to the Agile Manifesto a working software is preferred over comprehensive documentation, that doesn't not mean Agile approaches do not allow documentation. It is the project manager's duty to conform to all contractual requirements and that needs to be communicated to the team. [Agile Practice

Guide, 1st edition, Page 8] [Problem Detection and Resolution]

38. A - The Kanban method is based on the principle of pulling work and does not prescribe the use of timeboxed iterations. The Kanban method is less prescriptive than some Agile approaches and less disruptive to being implemented. Organizations can begin applying the Kanban method with relative ease. [Agile Practice Guide, 1st edition, Page 103] [Value-driven Delivery]

39. C - Traditional project management approaches are not recommended for complex and high-change projects. Crashing the project and increasing the team size doesn't help in increasing the team's agility. However, by limiting the work in progress, it is more likely that team members can collaborate to expedite work across the board. [Agile Practice Guide, 1st edition, Page 39] [Problem Detection and Resolution]

40. A - This is a trick question. It must be noted that the team is currently in a retrospective meeting. Planning poker and developing release and iteration plans are not in the scope of retrospective meetings. The activity the team is conducting is a Retrospective Planning Game. [Derby, E. and Larsen, D., 2006. Agile Retrospectives: Making Good Teams Great. 1st ed. Texas: Pragmatic Bookshelf, Page 103] [Continuous Improvement]

PMI-ACP Knowledge Area Quiz: Problem Detection and Resolution Practice Questions

Test Name: Knowledge Area Test: Interpersonal Skills
Total Questions: 15
Correct Answers Needed to Pass: 11 (73.33%)
Time Allowed: 25 Minutes

Test Description

This practice test specifically targets your knowledge of the Interpersonal Skills knowledge area.

Test Questions

1. You have analyzed all the themes of your project and have assigned each one of them to one of the four quadrants of a risk-value matrix that has a risk rating (high and low) on the y-axis, and a business value rating (high and low) on the x-axis. What is the recommend approach to be taken for the themes that fell under the "Low Risk" and "Low Value" quadrant?

A. Avoid

B. Do second

C. Do last

D. Do first

2. You are currently troubleshooting a pain point on your project. You ask the team to start using Kanban boards to see the flow of work and work in progress limits to understand the impact of the demand on the team or product. Which of the following is most probably your pain point?

A. Lack of project charter.

B. Lack of team charter.

C. Unexpected or unforeseen delays.

D. Inefficiently ordered product backlog.

3. Without attention to the highest value for the customer, the Agile team may create features that are not appreciated, or otherwise insufficiently valuable, therefore wasting effort. How does an Agile team mitigate this risk?

A. By creating the detailed project management plan with the help of the project manager.

B. By creating the detailed project management plan with the help of the product owner.

C. By creating the product backlog with the help of the product owner.

D. By creating the product backlog with the help of the project manager.

4. You are leading an Agile team responsible for developing an ERP system for an organization that has recently transitioned to Agile approaches. The enterprise PMO has asked to develop a detailed schedule Gantt chart and report Red/Amber/Green status against each project task on a weekly basis. What should you do?

A. Educate and help enterprise PMO transition to Agile approaches.

B. Educate senior leadership and make enterprise PMO redundant.

C. Negotiate with the enterprise PMO to only oversee projects following traditional lifecycles.

D. Provide the required reports but continue using Agile practices.

5. An Agile team wants to contract out part of the project's scope of work. A fixed-price contract hedges their financial risk but doesn't provide the required agility in the relationship. A time and material contract provides the required agility but doesn't hedge the financial risk. Due to the complexity of the project, agility is required but the team wants some degree of control over the costs. What do you recommend?

A. Cost reimbursable arrangement.

B. Contracting is not recommended in this complex situation.

C. Firm fixed-price arrangement.

D. Not-to-exceed time and materials arrangement.

6. Which of the following terms refers to the deferred cost of work not done at an earlier point in the product life cycle?

A. Technical debt

B. Sunk cost

C. Opportunity cost

D. Net present value

7. The product owner has requested some major changes that will have a significant impact on the project and require reprioritizing the remaining backlog items. What should you do?

A. Complete the started stories but do not bring any more "Ready" stories into "WIP".

B. Terminate the current sprint and reprioritize the entire project.

C. Complete the current iteration, reprioritize the backlog and adapt the new plan for the next iteration.

D. Cancel the current sprint and immediately call a retrospective.

8. Jane is responsible for migrating critical applications used in the organization over to a cloud platform. The non-critical applications that are currently integrated with these critical applications will be moved to the cloud once the current migration project is successful. Which of the following is the best approach for Jane given the high uncertainties associated with the project?

A. Break the interconnections and migrate one application at a time.

B. Migrate the critical and non-critical applications at the same time.

C. Tackle the project via strict waterfall approach.

D. Tackle the project via small increments of work.

9. You have been assigned to lead a massive enterprise process reengineering and

automation project. Due to the size and complexity of the project a very large team has been formed. How should you approach estimating user stories?

A. Estimate the stories yourself with the help of the product owner.

B. Gather the entire team in a hall and ask them to estimate all stories.

C. Split the larger team into smaller teams and let each team estimate a subset of stories.

D. Form a smaller expert group and ask them to estimate all stories.

10. Your project is halfway through the third iteration. One of the key stakeholders emails a change request that would make one of the backlog items unwanted by the business. How should you respond to this change request?

A. Reject any change requests unless they come through the product owner.

B. Work with the product owner to have this item removed from the backlog.

C. Trigger the integrated change control process.

D. Ask the team to remove the item from the backlog.

11. You have recently been hired by a pharmaceutical company to design and build an ERP system for the company. The system is supposed to cover the end-to-end operations of the business. Due to the complexity and size of the project, you cannot have a single product owner. If you want to deliver this project using Agile methodologies, how should you approach this problem?

A. Create a product owner's team headed by the servant-leader.

B. Select the most senior product owner.

C. Hire an external resource.

D. Create a product owner's team headed by the product manager.

12. An Agile team is struggling with coordinating work in progress. This is causing unnecessary conflicts and delays on the project. Which of the following two techniques can help this situation?

A. Agile modeling and spiking.

B. Kanban boards and daily stand-ups.

C. Prototyping and backlog grooming.

D. Story boards and retrospectives.

13. Halfway through the iteration, a major issue with the product has surfaced. This would require immediate attention from the team. However, the time required to fix the issue is expected to be more than the time left on the sprint. What should be done now?

A. Product owner adds an item to the product backlog.

B. Team owner adds an item to the sprint backlog.

C. Product owner adds an item to the sprint backlog.

D. Team owner adds an item to the product backlog.

14. You are leading an Agile team currently developing a mission-critical system. The product is complex as some of the critical requirements haven't been clearly defined. You and the team understand that this project will involve a high degree of change and uncertainty. How should be the product complexity by tackled in this case?

A. Select complicated and clearer requirements to be prototyped and developed first.

B. Select the most complicated and ambiguous requirements to be prototyped and developed first.

C. Select a subset of the requirements randomly and develop them through prototyping.

D. Select simpler and clearer but valuable requirements to be prototyped and developed first.

15. You are leading are enterprise process mapping project. Your team consists of process analysts and modelers. Process analyst are responsible for gathering process knowledge from organizational SMEs and passing it on to the modelers to map the process. Halfway during the first iteration you noticed that work is getting accumulated in the "Work in Process" and few of these items are being moved to the "Completed" section of your Kanban board. Upon a detailed inspection, you found out that the analysts' throughput is greater than the modelers' throughput, and as a result fewer processes get drafted than what get started. What should you do first?

A. Hire more analysts.

B. Remove some analysts from the team to create a balance.

C. Hire more modelers.

D. Ask the analyst to help the modelers complete the processes.

PMI-ACP Knowledge Area Quiz: Problem Detection and Resolution Answer Key and Explanations

1. C - "Do last" is recommended for themes that have been classified as "Low Risk" and "Low Value". [Cohn, M., 2006. Agile Estimating and Planning. 1st ed. Massachusetts: Pearson Education. Page 85] [Problem Detection and Resolution]

2. C - Kanban boards are visual management tools that help manage the flow of the project work. Recommending Kanban boards means there is something wrong with the flow of work. Based on this logic, the project charter and team charter choices can easily be eliminated. Inefficiently ordered product backlog will affect the release value and not the flow of work during the iteration. The best answer to this question is, "unexpected or unforeseen delays". [Agile Practice Guide, 1st edition, Page 59] [Problem Detection and Resolution]

3. C - Agile teams do not create detailed project management plans. In Agile, the product owners create the product backlog for and with the team. The backlog helps the team see how to deliver highest value without creating waste. [Agile Practice Guide, 1st edition, Page 41] [Problem Detection and Resolution]

4. A - Agile approaches do not include detailed schedules and task status reporting; these are traditional approaches. If the PMO is still using these tools, it implies that it hasn't successfully transitioned to Agile approaches. As an Agile practitioner, you need to educate and help enterprise PMO transition to Agile approaches. [Cohn, M., 2006. Agile Estimating and Planning. 1st ed. Massachusetts: Pearson Education. Page 51] [Problem Detection and Resolution]

5. D - Customers incur unwanted risk from a traditional time and material or cost reimbursable arrangement. On the other hand, suppliers incur unwanted risk from a fixed-price arrangement. One alternative is to limit the overall budget to a fixed amount using a not-to-exceed time and materials contract. [Agile Practice Guide, 1st edition, Page 78] [Problem Detection and Resolution]

6. A - Technical debt refers to the deferred cost of work not done at an earlier point in the product life cycle. [Agile Practice Guide, 1st edition, Page 154] [Problem Detection and Resolution]

7. C - Agile teams typically don't adjust their long term plan during a sprint unless all of the items being developed are dropped from the backlog. It is recommended to complete the current sprint and then re-plan and adjust accordingly. [Agile Practice Guide, 1st edition, Page 25] [Problem Detection and Resolution]

8. D - Migrating the non-critical applications is not in the scope. Breaking the interconnections might render the critical applications inoperative. Waterfall approach is not recommended in this scenario as the project has high uncertainties. Tackling the project via small increments of work sounds like the most reasonable approach among the given options. [Agile Practice Guide, 1st edition, Page 13] [Problem Detection and Resolution]

9. C - Gathering the entire team in a hall and asking them to estimate all the stories would not only be a challenge but it would be very inefficient. It is possible to play planning poker with a subset of the team, rather than involving everyone. This isn't ideal but may be a reasonable option. The best way to do this is to split the larger team into multiple smaller teams and let each team estimate a subset of stories. [Cohn, M., 2006. Agile Estimating and Planning. 1st ed. Massachusetts: Pearson Education. Page 57] [Problem Detection and Resolution]

10. B - Since the product owner is ultimately responsible for the product, you need to work with them to have the item removed from the backlog. [Agile Practice Guide, 1st edition, Page 41] [Problem Detection and Resolution]

11. D - The product owner needs to be an internal resource; an external resource cannot prioritize business requirements. Selecting the senior-most is not the solution as no single person has domain expertise across the organization. In this situation a team of product owners, headed by a product manager is recommended. [Agile Practice Guide, 1st edition, Page 52] [Problem Detection and Resolution]

12. B - Help the team learn that they self-manage their work. Consider Kanban boards to see the flow of work. Consider a daily stand-up to walk the board and see what work is where. [Agile Practice Guide, 1st edition, Page 58] [Problem Detection and Resolution]

13. C - The team doesn't add items to the backlogs, only the product owner is authorized to do that. If the issue requires immediate attention, then the item needs to be added to the iteration backlog. [Agile Practice Guide, 1st edition, Page 41] [Problem Detection and Resolution]

14. D - When product complexity is high, the team should be encouraged to determine simple solutions that would work and apply the Agile principle of "Simplicity – the art of minimizing the amount of work that needs to get done". This helps reduce complexity. [Agile Practice Guide, 1st edition, Page 59] [Problem Detection and Resolution]

15. D - Agile teams work as a unit. In order to control the work flow, items in "work in process" has to be limited. If the bottleneck is with the modeling work, analysts should be encouraged to help the modelers complete the processes before new work is taken on. Hiring more modelers seems a lucrative option but that should not be your first course of action. Further, prior to taking such a step, some further analysis would be required. [Agile Practice Guide, 1st edition, Page 66] [Problem Detection and Resolution]

PMI-ACP Lite Mock Exam 11 Practice Questions

Test Name: PMI-ACP Lite Mock Exam 11
Total Questions: 40
Correct Answers Needed to Pass:
30 (75.00%)
Time Allowed: 60 Minutes

Test Description

This is a cumulative PMI-ACP Mock Exam which can be used as a benchmark for your PMI-ACP aptitude. This practice test includes questions from all exam topic areas, including sections from Agile Tools and Techniques, and all three Agile Knowledge and Skills areas.

Test Questions

1. What's the maximum allowed build cycle on XP projects?

A. 120 minutes

B. 10 minutes

C. 30 minutes

D. 60 minutes

2. Which of the following tools can help Agile teams in measuring earned value?

A. Product backlog burnup chart

B. Cost baseline

C. S-Curve

D. Box plot

3. Which of the following Crystal methods would you consider if the project has a low criticality rating and has a small Agile team assigned?

A. Crystal Red

B. Crystal Yellow

C. Crystal Orange

D. Crystal Clear

4. Which of the following conditions is of topmost priority for a feature-driven project?

A. Delivering the highest value features by the agreed deadline.

B. Delivering maximum features by the agreed deadline.

C. Delivering the agreed set of features as soon as possible.

D. Delivering the agreed set of features by the agreed deadline.

5. Which of the following Agile techniques is a process decision framework that enables simplified process decisions around incremental and iterative solution delivery?

A. Design of Experiments

B. Design for Six Sigma

C. Disciplined Agile

D. Balanced Scorecard

6. Some organizations choose to implement projects primarily through vendors. The major issue with this approach is the loss of project knowledge once vendors complete their obligations and leave the engagement. Which of the following can help mitigate this issue?

A. Conducting retrospectives and following up on possible improvement areas when the vendor is still engaged.

B. The risk is inherent in contracting and can only be mitigated through conducting make or buy analysis.

C. Including a three-year product support requirement in the contract.

D. Mandating the vendors to document daily progress and submitting the documentation with the final deliverable.

7. Which of the following types of features do NOT necessarily call for early development in an Agile project?

A. Features that need the least cost and time to develop.

B. Features that have high business value.

C. Features that help in eliminating significant risk from the project.

D. Features that allow the team to gain significant knowledge about the product.

8. Which of the following is the correct approach for a servant-leader in regards to management and control processes?

A. Shift focus on management processes and tools from individuals and interactions.

B. Abolish management processes and focus on team interactions.

C. Analyze and streamline management processes.

D. Select management processes that focus on exhaustive documentation.

9. The feature buffering process helps in mitigating the risk of schedule slippages on projects applying the Dynamic Systems Development Method. According to the MoSCoW rules, what is the recommended size of the feature buffer in comparison to the project duration?

A. 0.5

B. 0.4

C. 0.6

D. 0.3

10. You have recently been hired in a company to lead the central PMO of the organization. You have recently found out that project teams usually generate a big number of improvement ideas during retrospectives but fail to implement these during the iterations. Which of the following recommendations can help the teams in the current situation?

A. Capture all improvement ideas as lessons learned and only implement them on a new project.

B. Capturing improvement ideas during an on-going project is not recommended.

C. Capture all improvement ideas into some log and assign the servant-leader to track progress during daily stand-ups.

D. Capture no more than three items to improve at each retrospective.

11. You are leading an Agile project. Some of the team members are complaining that a couple of functional managers are constantly interrupting the project work and pulling out resources to compete routine business work. What should you do?

A. Authorize the team to ignore any external requests.

B. Note down the issue and discuss during the next retrospective.

C. Escalate the issue to the product owner.

D. Approach the functional managers and negotiate alternatives.

12. During an iteration demonstration, the product owner and the developer are having a conflict: a completed feature is not being accepted by the product owner. How could this problem have been avoided?

A. Establishing a quality control process.

B. Agreement on definition of done for each story at the start of the sprint.

C. Establishing working agreements.

D. Keeping the product owner out of the demonstration.

13. You have recently been hired by a construction company to help transform a traditional PMO into an Agile PMO. You have scheduled daily stand-ups so that the team starts to get the exposure to Agile methods. During these stand-ups the team is reporting problems and attempting to solve them. What's wrong with this?

A. Reported issues should be parked.

B. Resolved issues should be documented.

C. Issues should not be reported.

D. Resolved issues should be parked.

14. Which of the following is a "pure" measure of size?

A. Both story points and ideal days

B. Story points

C. Neither story points nor ideal days

D. Ideal days

15. Conducting frequent product demonstrations can help an Agile team avoid which of the following project risks?

A. Ungroomed user stories.

B. Shorter sprint size.

C. Scope creep.

D. Project team heading in a wrong direction.

16. Which of the following is the most effective and Agile quality assurance approach?

A. Establishing a highly detailed quality management plan.

B. Correctly prioritizing backlog items.

C. Creating highly detailed user stories.

D. Frequent inspection, review and demonstration sessions.

17. You are leading a complex project and are exploring various technologies to be used on the project. Such a complex project is typically expected to span five years. The team is new to Agile and currently struggling to estimate in story points. The team might come up to speed with estimating in ideal days fairly quickly due to the very intuitive feel associated with ideal days. However, you are worried that ideal days estimates will soon decay as the teams gets more experienced and proficient with the involved technologies and the project scope becomes clearer. Which of the following approaches is recommended in this scenario?

A. Estimate in ideal days as this is a valid Agile estimating measure.

B. Estimate in story points; the team will eventually get it.

C. Revert back to a traditional project management approach if the team is struggling with Agile concepts, tools and methods.

D. Start with estimating in ideal days but then help the team transition to story points.

18. The process of moving future amounts back into their present value, taking the time value of money into account, is generally known as:

A. Extrapolating

B. Reversing

C. Discounting

D. Back tracking

19. In addition to the total number of story points on a product backlog, which of the following information is required to predict a project completion date?

A. Velocity and iteration duration.

B. Velocity and team size.

C. Number of user stories and team size.

D. Number of user stories and iteration duration.

20. Which of the following is not a recognized Agile tool or technique?

A. Daily standups

B. Burndown charts

C. Regression analysis

D. Velocity measurement

21. Which of the following frameworks is known best for its emphasis on constraint-driven delivery (The framework will set cost, quality, and time at the outset, and then use formalized prioritization of scope to meet those constraints)?

A. Dynamic Systems Development Method

B. Scrum of Scrums

C. Constraint-Driven Development

D. Feature-Driven Development

22. An Agile project team is currently struggling with meeting customer's expectations regarding rapid feature delivery while maintaining required quality standards. Upon further analysis, it was revealed that the throughput of the testers was significantly less than the throughput of the developers. In this scenario, which of the following cannot help the situation?

A. Increasing the number of developers.

B. Optimizing processes.

C. Optimizing the batch size.

D. Increasing the number of testers.

23. You have recently taken over a project. Upon the inspection of the release burndown chart you see that although the linear trend is downward sloping, the burndown line is constantly moving up and down the trendline. Which of the following correctly explains this?

A. The team's velocity is not constant.

B. The cycle time for each story is different.

C. The story sizes were not accurately estimated.

D. The team is not completing some stories by the end of each iteration.

24. Why do Agile approaches recommend keeping estimates of size and duration separate?

A. Size estimates are easier to obtain than duration estimates.

B. To avoid confusion and maintain a clear distinction between the two.

C. Size estimates are a measure of business value while duration estimates are not.

D. Size is not correlated with duration.

25. You have recently been hired as a consultant to help define project management methodology for an airport operator. You realize that each project may require a slightly tailored set of policies, practices and processes in order to meet the project's unique characteristics. For example, replacing a document management system requires a different approach than constructing an aircraft hangar. Which of the following Agile frameworks can help you develop project management methodologies based on project criticality and number of people involved?

A. Scrum

B. XP

C. Crystal methods

D. Lean

26. Which of the following statements provides sufficient information to make a project selection decision in favor of the project?

A. Project's IRR is lower than the organization's MARR.

B. The organization's cost of capital is higher than project's IRR.

C. Project's NPV is greater than 0.

D. Project's IRR is higher than the organization's MARR.

27. How do Kanban boards help in increasing productivity and quality?

A. By allowing the team to work on the highest priority items.

B. By limiting work in progress.

C. The Kanban board helps in managing the team's WIP but does not have any effect on productivity and quality.

D. By pushing work from "Ready" to "Done".

28. Which of the following is the ideal way to estimate a team's velocity?

A. Making a random forecast.

B. Running an iteration or two.

C. Using historical values.

D. Conducting Monte Carlo analysis.

29. In Agile, scope management includes:

A. Scope statement

B. Work breakdown structure

C. High-level requirements

D. Comprehensive documentation

30. A user story on your travel reservation system development project states that, "As a user, I want to be able to cancel a reservation." In discussing this story with the product owner, the developers discover the following conditions associated with the story: a user who cancels more than 24 hours in advance gets a complete refund; a user who cancels less than 24 hours in advance is refunded all but a $25 cancellation fee. What are these conditions called?

A. Conditions of satisfaction

B. Story Points

C. Terms and conditions

D. Story Plot

31. During which of the following Agile events does an Agile team meet to discuss the ongoing work plan and make any adjustment to the work plan as required and address any impediments to work?

A. Planning poker

B. Retrospectives

C. Spikes

D. Daily Scrum

32. Your friend went to a conference where he heard the term "follow-the-sun" development process. What does that mean?

A. Teamwork only during working hours and no overtime is allowed.

B. Teams are dedicated to the project 365 days a year.

C. Team begins the work slowly in the morning and reaches a peak point by the noon.

D. Work is handed off at the end of every day from one site to the next.

33. Which of the following factors is LEAST recommended to be considered while prioritizing themes or user stories for a project?

A. Expertise of the Agile team.

B. The financial value of having the features.

C. The cost of developing the features.

D. The amount of risk removed by developing the features.

34. What is the purpose of the "Circle of Questions" activity used during a retrospective meeting?

A. Set up information radiators.

B. Help teams document working agreements.

C. Help the team conduct daily standups.

D. Help teams choose an experiment or action steps for the next iteration.

35. You are the servant-Leader of an Agile team. You should be careful not to?

A. Resolve team issues.

B. Facilitate communication.

C. Estimate user stories.

D. Facilitate retrospectives.

36. You have recently been hired by a major airport operator to head its project management office. The PMO has been following a waterfall-based project management approach consistently across all projects. You want to pilot Agile approaches on a couple of new projects and see how these approaches can benefit the organization. However, the team members are not experienced in the use of Agile approaches. What should you do first?

A. Train the team members in effectively using the XP approach.

B. Train the team members in effectively using the Scrum methodology.

C. Train the team members in effectively using the Kanban approach.

D. Train the team members in the fundamentals of the Agile Mindset and principles.

37. You are leading an Agile project. The team has proposed using a Kanban board to manage the team's work in progress and spot bottlenecks. The following work flow has been agreed on for the Kanban board: Ready -> Develop and Unit Test -> Dev-Done -> System Test -> Done. According to this Kanban board, the cycle time of an item is the:

A. The time an item enters the "Develop and Unit Test" bin till the time it exits the "Done" bin.

B. The time an item enters the "Ready" bin till the time it exits the "Done" bin.

C. The time an item enters the "Ready" bin till the time it enters the "Done" bin.

D. The time an item enters the "Develop and Unit Test" bin till the time it enters the "Done" bin.

38. Team A is responsible for developing a feature, while team B is responsible for testing the feature. If the testing activity is planned to start two days after the completion of the development of the feature, this is known as:

A. Adding a feeding buffer

B. Adding a feature buffer

C. Project delays

D. Resource optimization

39. An Agile team is developing a production control system. Which of the following should be selected as a primary measure to monitor the team's progress?

A. Velocity

B. Working software

C. Burndown chart

D. Percentage of completion

40. What is the difference between padding activities duration estimates and adding feeding buffers?

A. There is not difference since both extend the project duration.

B. Padding is an acceptable Agile practice while feeding buffers are not.

C. Feeding buffers increase the duration estimates while padding doesn't.

D. Padding increases the duration estimates while feeding buffers do not.

PMI-ACP Lite Mock Exam 11 Answer Key and Explanations

1. B - On XP projects, builds should be run many times a day, initiated by a schedule or in response to some asynchronous event such as checking source code into the repository. XP requires investing in continuous improvement and code optimization to maintain a ten-minute build cycle; any longer than ten minutes and the build won't be used as often and won't provide as much feedback. [Agile Practice Guide, 1st edition, Page 102] [Value-driven Delivery]

2. A - Cost baseline and S-Curves are used in traditional approaches to earned value management. Agile teams can use a product backlog burnup chart to measure earned value. Box plot is a statistical tool. [Agile Practice Guide, 1st edition, Page 68] [Team Performance]

3. D - Crystal Clear is the simplest method in the Crystal Family of methods. This method is advisable for projects with a low criticality rating and smaller Agile teams. [Agile Practice Guide, 1st edition, Page 106] [Value-driven Delivery]

4. C - Many project are either date-driven or feature-driven. A date-driven project is one that must be released by a certain date but for which the feature set is negotiable. A feature-driven is one where the release date is as soon as possible but the completion of a set of features is more important. [Cohn, M., 2006. Agile Estimating and Planning. 1st ed. Massachusetts: Pearson Education. Page 133] [Adaptive Planning]

5. C - Disciplined Agile is a process decision framework that enables simplified process decisions around incremental and iterative solution delivery. [Agile Practice Guide, 1st edition, Page 151] [Value-driven Delivery]

6. A - Agile techniques such as retrospectives and follow up on possible improvement areas when the vendor is still engaged can help mitigate loss of product knowledge. Make or buy analysis helps in the contracting decisions and this doesn't mitigate the risk of loss of product knowledge. The rest of the choices are not collaborative techniques. [Agile Practice Guide, 1st edition, Page 83] [Problem Detection and Resolution]

7. A - Apart from prioritizing features based on their business value, early termination of a significant risk can often justify developing a feature early. Similarly, if developing a particular feature early will allow the team to gain significant knowledge about the project or their effort to develop it, they should consider developing that feature early. Cost and time requirements alone are not used to prioritize features. [Cohn, M., 2006. Agile Estimating and Planning. 1st ed. Massachusetts: Pearson Education. Page 249] [Value-driven Delivery]

8. C - The first value of the Agile Manifesto is individuals and interactions over processes and tools. However, that does not mean management and control processes need to be abolished all together. The servant-leader is responsible for taking a hard look at processes that are impeding a team's agility and work to streamline them. Selecting management processes that focus on exhaustive documentation will impede the team's agility. [Agile Practice Guide, 1st edition, Page 35] [Agile Principles and Mindset]

9. D - DSDM projects create a feature buffer equivalent to 30% of the duration of the project. [Cohn, M., 2006. Agile Estimating and Planning. 1st ed. Massachusetts: Pearson Education. Page 187] [Value-driven Delivery]

10. D - When there is slow or no improvement in the teamwork process, it is recommended to capture no more than three items to improve at each retrospective. Ask the servant-leader to help the team learn how to integrate those items, however daily stand-ups are not status reporting meetings. [Agile Practice Guide, 1st edition, Page 59] [Continuous Improvement]

11. D - Delaying the resolution until next retrospective is not recommended. The best thing to do is to collaborate with the functional managers and negotiate other workable solutions. Escalating to the product owner or barring the team to entertain the functional managers are not the solutions to this problem. [Agile Practice Guide, 1st edition, Page 33] [Stakeholder Engagement]

12. B - You cannot keep the product owner out of the demonstration. The product owner "owns" the product and has the authority to accept or reject the features. The problem could have been avoided if the definition of done for this feature would have been agreed upon at the start of the iteration. [Agile Practice Guide, 1st edition, Page 151] [Problem Detection and Resolution]

13. A - An anti-pattern typically seen in stand-ups is that the team begins to solve problems as they become apparent. Stand-ups are for realizing there are problems – not for solving them. Add the issues to a parking lot, and then create another meeting, which might be right after the stand-up, and solve problems there. [Agile Practice Guide, 1st edition, Page 54] [Problem Detection and Resolution]

14. B - Story points are a pure measure of size. Ideal days are not. Ideal days may be used as a measure of size, but with some deficiencies; an estimate in ideal days will change as the team's proficiency changes. [Cohn, M., 2006. Agile Estimating and Planning. 1st ed. Massachusetts: Pearson Education. Page 71] [Adaptive Planning]

15. D - Product demonstrations do not mitigate any risk arising from selected sprint size or the selected technique for user stories grooming. Scope creep means uncontrolled scope changes which is irrelevant to product demonstrations. Frequent demonstrations allow frequent feedback that prevents the team from heading in a wrong direction. [Agile Practice Guide, 1st edition, Page 55] [Value-driven Delivery]

16. D - Correct prioritization of backlog items will enable the team to deliver value faster. Detailed quality management plans are not developed in Agile projects. The correct response is: frequent inspection, review and demonstration sessions. [Agile Practice Guide, 1st edition, Page 55] [Stakeholder Engagement]

17. D - Since story points are a pure measure of size, the preference is always for story points. However, if the team is struggling with the concept of estimating pure size, it is recommended to start them estimating in ideal days but then convert them to story points. The problem with estimating in ideal days, especially with such a complex project,

is that the estimates decay over time as the team become more proficient in executing project tasks. [Cohn, M., 2006. Agile Estimating and Planning. 1st ed. Massachusetts: Pearson Education. Pages 74, 75] [Problem Detection and Resolution]

18. C - The process of moving future amounts back into their present value, taking the time value of money into account, is generally known as discounting. [Cohn, M., 2006. Agile Estimating and Planning. 1st ed. Massachusetts: Pearson Education. Page 100] [Value-driven Delivery]

19. A - In addition to total story points, you would need to know the velocity and the iteration duration to predict the completion date. For example, a team estimates a project to include 200 points of work. If the velocity is 20 points per iteration that means the team needs 10 iterations to complete the project. Now if the iteration duration is known, the project completion date can be predicted. [Cohn, M., 2006. Agile Estimating and Planning. 1st ed. Massachusetts: Pearson Education. Page 39] [Team Performance]

20. C - Regression analysis is an advanced statistical technique that can be utilized on some Agile projects but is not necessarily an Agile tool or technique. [Cohn, M., 2006. Agile Estimating and Planning. 1st ed. Massachusetts: Pearson Education. Page 28] [Value-driven Delivery]

21. A - Dynamic Systems Development Method (DSDM) is an Agile project delivery framework initially designed to add more rigor to existing iterative methods popular in the 1990s. DSDM is known best for its emphasis on constraint-driven delivery. The framework will set cost, quality, and time at the outset, and then use formalized prioritization of scope to meet those constraints. [Agile Practice Guide, 1st edition, Page 110] [Value-driven Delivery]

22. A - The problem at hand is the mismatch of the productivity of the different team members. Increasing the number of developers will further aggravate the situation by increasing the development throughput even further. The rest of the choices need to be further analyzed and the best option should be selected. [Agile Practice Guide, 1st edition, Page 42] [Problem Detection and Resolution]

23. A - The situation above can be a result of poor story estimation or incomplete stories by the end of each iteration. However, the scenario doesn't provide enough evidence to support either of these conditions. The random walk of the burndown chart means that (due to any reason) the team's velocity hasn't been constant. [Cohn, M., 2006. Agile Estimating and Planning. 1st ed. Massachusetts: Pearson Education. Page 213] [Team Performance]

24. B - Agile approaches recommend maintaining a clear distinction between an estimate of size and one of duration through using separate units that cannot be confused. Estimating size in story points and translating size into duration using velocity is an excellent way of doing this. [Cohn, M., 2006. Agile Estimating and Planning. 1st ed. Massachusetts: Pearson Education. Page 248] [Adaptive Planning]

25. C - Crystal is a family of methodologies. Crystal methodologies are designed to scale, and provide a selection of methodology rigor based on project size (number of people involved in the project) and the criticality of the project. [Agile Practice

Guide, 1st edition, Page 106] [Value-driven Delivery]

26. D - The project will not be selected if the IRR is lower than the cost of capital or MARR. If the project's NPV is positive, this is a good sign, but without the knowledge of the initial investment, the financial value of the decision cannot be determined. Many organizations will specify a minimum attractive rate of return (MARR) for all projects. If a project's IRR is higher than the organization's MARR, this is sufficient to make a decision in the favor of the project. [Cohn, M., 2006. Agile Estimating and Planning. 1st ed. Massachusetts: Pearson Education. Page 102] [Value-driven Delivery]

27. B - By allowing the team to work on the highest priority items, Kanban boards allow the team to do minimal work to deliver highest possible value. Kanban boards also help in increasing productivity and quality by limiting work in progress. [Agile Practice Guide, 1st edition, Page 103] [Team Performance]

28. B - The ideal way to forecast velocity is to run an iteration or two and then estimate velocity from the observed velocity during these iterations. [Cohn, M., 2006. Agile Estimating and Planning. 1st ed. Massachusetts: Pearson Education. Page 177] [Team Performance]

29. C - Agile scope management involves high-level requirements. The other choices relate to predictive project management approaches. [Cohn, M., 2006. Agile Estimating and Planning. 1st ed. Massachusetts: Pearson Education. Page 11] [Value-driven Delivery]

30. A - Conditions of satisfaction is the criteria that is used to gauge the success of a deliverable. [Cohn, M., 2006. Agile Estimating and Planning. 1st ed. Massachusetts: Pearson Education. Page 30] [Adaptive Planning]

31. D - Daily Scrums are brief, daily collaboration meetings in which the team reviews progress from the previous day, declares intentions for the current day, and highlights any obstacles encountered or anticipated. Also known as daily standups. [Agile Practice Guide, 1st edition, Page 151] [Adaptive Planning]

32. D - A follow-the-sun development process is one where work is handed off at the end of every day from one site to the next, many time zones away in order to speed up product development. [Agile Practice Guide, 1st edition, Page 44] [Value-driven Delivery]

33. A - Themes should be prioritized by business value. The Agile team's expertise does not help measure business value of the feature being developed. The rest of the choices do help measure the business value. [Cohn, M., 2006. Agile Estimating and Planning. 1st ed. Massachusetts: Pearson Education. Page 80] [Adaptive Planning]

34. D - The purpose of the "Circle of Questions" activity is to help teams choose an experiment or action steps for the next iteration, particularly when team members need to listen to one another. [Derby, E. and Larsen, D., 2006. Agile Retrospectives: Making Good Teams Great. 1st ed. Texas: Pragmatic Bookshelf, Page 107] [Continuous Improvement]

35. C - Agile teams estimate user stories, the servant-leader is not involved in estimating. However, the servant-leader might facilitate the estimation event. [Agile Practice Guide, 1st edition, Page 34] [Team Performance]

36. D - Consider starting by training team members in the fundamentals of the Agile Mindset and principles. If the team decides to use a specific approach such as Scrum or Kanban, provide a workshop on that approach so that team members can learn how to use it. [Agile Practice Guide, 1st edition, Page 32] [Agile Principles and Mindset]

37. D - Cycle time is from the time you start a task until you complete it. This is represented by the time an item enters "Develop and Unit Test" bin till the time it enters the "Done" bin. Time required for the customer delivery is not included in the cycle time. [Agile Practice Guide, 1st edition, Page 65] [Value-driven Delivery]

38. A - A feeding buffer, like the schedule buffer, protects the on-time delivery of a set of new capabilities. This is a somewhat complicated way of saying that if your team needs something from my team tomorrow morning, my team shouldn't plan on finishing it the day before. [Cohn, M., 2006. Agile Estimating and Planning. 1st ed. Massachusetts: Pearson Education. Page 204] [Adaptive Planning]

39. B - Although Agile teams are free to use any KPI to monitor their progress, "working software" is the primary measure of progress. [Agile Practice Guide, 1st edition, Page 9] [Stakeholder Engagement]

40. D - Padding an estimate means extending the estimate. For example if a task that is expected to take five days is estimated to take seven days, we would say that the estimate has been padded. On the other hand, feeding buffers are placed between the tasks to handle the uncertainty but the tasks' estimates are not increased. [Cohn, M., 2006. Agile Estimating and Planning. 1st ed. Massachusetts: Pearson Education. Page 204] [Adaptive Planning]

PMI-ACP Lite Mock Exam 12 Practice Questions

Test Name: PMI-ACP Lite Mock Exam 12
Total Questions: 40
Correct Answers Needed to Pass:
30 (75.00%)
Time Allowed: 60 Minutes

Test Description

This is a cumulative PMI-ACP Mock Exam which can be used as a benchmark for your PMI-ACP aptitude. This practice test includes questions from all exam topic areas, including sections from Agile Tools and Techniques, and all three Agile Knowledge and Skills areas.

Test Questions

1. What is "velocity"?

A. Average story points per iteration.

B. The total time it takes to deliver including the waiting time.

C. The time that an item waits until the work starts.

D. The time required to process an item.

2. Which of the following requires the bulk of planning activities to be conducted upfront and then executing the project in a single pass?

A. Iterative life cycle

B. Predictive life cycle

C. Incremental life cycle

D. Agile life cycle

3. Which of the following is a critical success factor for teams transitioning to Agile approaches?

A. Preferring XP over any other method.

B. Taking the Agile Manifesto and principles as gospel.

C. Starting with Scrum before adopting any other Agile methods.

D. Adopting an Agile Mindset

4. Which of the following methods provides guidance on the use of a product backlog, sprint planning, daily scrum, sprint review and sprint retrospective sessions?

A. Sprint

B. Kanban

C. XP

D. Scrum

5. A user story describes the user, the requirement, and the:

A. Test case

B. Condition of satisfaction

C. Approach

D. Value

6. Which of the following Agile measures help in translating a size estimate into a duration estimate?

   A. Gantt charts

   B. Backlog grooming

   C. Cycle time

   D. Velocity

7. What are the two axes in a release burndown chart?

   A. Ideal days and velocity

   B. Cycle time and velocity

   C. Stories and iterations

   D. Story points and iterations

8. A release burndown bar chart is more expressive than the traditional burndown chart. This type of burndown chart uses bars rather than lines to help distinguish the regions above and below the horizontal axis at 0. The bottom is moved up whenever work is removed from an iteration. If the bottom is below the horizontal axis at 0, it means overall work has been added to the release. During which of the following situations should you NOT use this type of chart?

   A. If the organization is not mature enough to understand why work has been plotted below the 0-line.

   B. If you strictly want to stick to Agile practices.

   C. The team's velocity is not accurately being reflected by a burndown line-type chart.

   D. New scope of work is constantly being added to the project.

9. Functionality that will be added in the near future (within the next few iterations) should be:

   A. Planned in a way that they all get delivered at the same time.

   B. Started at the same time.

   C. Decomposed into relatively small user stories.

   D. Aggregated into epics for release planning.

10. What is the first value of the Agile Manifesto?

   A. Customer collaboration over contract negotiation

   B. Responding to change over following a plan

   C. Working software over comprehensive documentation

   D. Individuals and interactions over processes and tools

11. ABCon is a projectized company that performs all of its projects using the Scrum method. You have been recently hired by ABCon to deploy the Scrum method on a holistic organizational level. The aim is to use Agile approaches beyond project execution by enabling disruptive innovation.

Which of the following Agile approaches you should consider?

A. Scrum of Scrum of Scrums

B. Agile Unified Process

C. Scrum of Scrums

D. Enterprise Scrum

12. On an Agile project, who is authorized to make decisions necessary to complete the project work?

A. Agile team

B. Project sponsor

C. Product owner

D. Scrum master

13. Which of the following scenarios will produce the most accurate result when a team is forecasting its velocity?

A. When the team has just finished a similar project.

B. When the team is moving onto a new release of a product they just worked on.

C. When the team has access to industry standards.

D. When the team has completed multiple Agile projects.

14. Your project team is geographically distributed and rely on virtual workspaces. You are considering a number of collaboration tools to boost the team's throughput. Which of the following is one such tool you may consider?

A. Discount window

B. House of quality

C. Fishbowl window

D. Fishbone diagram

15. All of the following are insight generation activities EXCEPT:

A. Five Whys

B. Triple Nickels

C. Brainstorming

D. Fishbone

16. In Agile projects, time-boxed research or experiments are known as:

A. Behavior Driven Development (BDD)

B. Continuous integration

C. Spikes

D. Acceptance Test Driven Development (ATDD)

17. You have recently taken over the leadership of a huge Agile project consisting of multiple Agile teams. You want to predict how much longer is needed to complete a set of user stories but are finding it difficult as some of the stories have been estimated in ideal days and some have been estimated in story points. What is the root cause of this problem?

A. A common basis for estimates was not established at the start of the project.

B. The product owner hasn't groomed the user stories.

C. The project is not compliant with the Agile Manifesto.

D. There is a lack of communication between different teams working on the project.

18. You are an Agile practitioner working on experimental work. The goal of this activity is to try a new technology in a test environment and determine its feasibility. Which Agile activity are you conducting?

A. Acceptance testing

B. Spike

C. Feasibility study

D. Load testing

19. All of the following are attributes of a predictive life cycle EXCEPT:

A. Serial

B. Plan-driven

C. Non-Agile approach

D. Iterative life cycle

20. Kanban in lean manufacturing is a system for:

A. Eliminate the seven wastes from the process.

B. Placing just-in-time procurement orders.

C. Scheduling inventory control and replenishment.

D. Moving incomplete car parts from one floor to another.

21. For complex and high-change Agile projects, a cross-functional and dedicated team is highly recommended. A mixed team of generalists and specialists is recommended because:

A. Generalists provide discipline while specialists provide agility.

B. Generalists provide dedicated expertise while the specialists provide flexibility.

C. Specialists provide agility while generalists provide discipline.

D. Specialists provide dedicated expertise while the generalists provide flexibility.

22. In cases where there is significant uncertainty associated with a release schedule, which of the following risk management strategies can help mitigate the risk?

A. Reducing the product backlog.

B. Decreasing the number of tasks on the iteration plan.

C. Increasing the iteration size.

D. Including buffers.

23. During the start of the iteration, you worked with the product owner to define and groom the user stories. However, during the user acceptance testing, some new requirements got discovered. These new requirements are related to product performance and ease of use. What should you do?

A. Issue a change request and follow the change control procedure.

B. Create new stories and add to the product backlog for prioritization.

C. Update the product configuration and add the new stories to the next iteration.

D. Call a retrospective and discuss why these performance issues were not identified earlier.

24. You are leading an Agile team tasked to develop an ERP system. The system will be iteratively developed and each iteration is time boxed (three week iterations). What is your opinion about release frequency on such a project?

A. There needs to be a mid-iteration release and a final release for each iteration.

B. Each iteration must produce a release.

C. Every second iteration should produce a release.

D. Releases may occur at varying intervals.

25. What is "Automated Code Quality Analysis"?

A. Conducting analysis of the test plan.

B. Developing software test management and control plan.

C. Analyzing customer testing requirements.

D. The scripted testing of code base for bugs and vulnerabilities.

26. Which of the following usually maximizes an Agile team's throughput?

A. Individual throughputs of team members.

B. Multi-tasking team members.

C. 100% dedicated team members.

D. Teams with more than 25 team members.

27. Agile teams use which of the following Agile events to collaboratively size user stories based on the effort required for their development?

A. Planning poker

B. Backlog refinement

C. Five whys analysis

D. Kanban board

28. "Individuals and interactions over processes and tools" is one of the key Agile Manifesto values. Which of the following Agile approaches helps in achieving this value?

A. Agile measurements

B. Daily standups

C. Backlog preparation

D. Demonstration and review

29. As you examine a list of job candidates for your project, you find that your cousin is one of the three shortlisted candidates. You know that they were desperately looking for a job. After reviewing the three resumes, you will send them to the electronics engineer for a technical interview. From your review of these resumes, you see that all three shortlisted candidates have similar qualifications and experience. What should you do?

A. Call your cousin and conduct an informal interview yourself before forwarding the resumes.

B. Consult your boss before forwarding the resumes for interview.

C. Forward all three resumes.

D. To avoid conflict of interest, ignore your cousin's resume but forward the other two resumes.

30. You are demonstrating the results of your first iterations and discover that some of the stakeholders are not happy with the user interface of the features you have developed. What should you have done to prevent this situation?

A. Collected detailed user interface specifications.

B. Hired qualified developers for this project.

C. Used prototypes.

D. Create a contingency reserve for this risk.

31. Your project team has recently completed the 3rd iteration on the project. So far 45 story points have been successfully delivered to the customer. For this project, the iteration size is fixed at three weeks. The team (six team members) is dedicated to working five days per week. Looking at the backlog, you have 150 story points remaining to be delivered. What is the project's cycle time?

A. 30

B. 15

C. 1

D. 10

32. Which of the following tools is generally used by Agile teams to monitor the progress against the release plan?

A. Burndown charts

B. Release critical path

C. Gantt charts

D. Flowcharts

33. Agile teams use which of the following Agile events to collaboratively prioritize user stories based on their respective value to the project's customer?

A. Kanban board

B. Planning poker

C. Backlog refinement

D. Rapid application development

34. You are using a project retrospective to assess the magnitude of deviation from the original project estimates. Once the degree of variation is known, what step is performed next?

A. Establish new project controls.

B. Audit the project team.

C. Perform root cause analysis of the variance.

D. Re-estimate the entire project.

35. Which of the following methods is most commonly used by Agile teams to report performance and share information?

A. Iteration retrospectives

B. Daily stand-ups

C. A3 reports

D. Spikes

36. A team is currently developing a bespoke enterprise resource planning (ERP) system for a manufacturing plant. At the start of the project that backlog was estimated to have 10,000 story points and the order of magnitude cost estimate for the project was $1M. The team has just finished the 15th iteration and has provided the following project statistics: Completed features value = $450,000; Actual costs to date = $600,000; Completed story points = 550; Planned story points = 700. What is the project's CPI?

A. 0.75

B. 1.33

C. 0.79

D. 1.27

37. In a software development project, the project team completed development of a charter and identification of key stakeholders. The team has collected proprietary information from vendors during the project initiation. What should the team do when a functional manager from the same organization wants to see this information?

A. Deny the request to protect the confidentiality of the information.

B. Deny the request as the manager is not part of the project.

C. Accept the request as the manager belongs to the same organization.

D. Accept the request but caution the manager to maintain confidentiality.

38. Why do Agile teams conduct the "Short Subjects" activity during retrospective meetings?

A. Quickly wrap up the retrospective.

B. Escalate project issues to the stakeholders.

C. Help discover differing perspectives on how the team is doing.

D. Determine the top priority features of the product.

39. In your organization the Service Request Manager role is responsible for ordering service requests to maximize value in a continuous flow or Kanban environment. This role is equivalent to which Agile role?

A. Scrum master

B. Servant-leader

C. Project manager

D. Product owner

40. As a general rule of thumb, how much productivity is lost when task switching?

A. 30% to 50%

B. 40% to 60%

C. 20% to 40%

D. 10% to 30%

PMI-ACP Lite Mock Exam 12 Answer Key and Explanations

1. A - Velocity = average story points per iteration. [Agile Practice Guide, 1st edition, Pages 61] [Team Performance]

2. B - Predictive life cycle, also known as the traditional approach, requires the bulk of the planning to happen upfront and then executing the project in a single pass. [Agile Practice Guide, 1st edition, Page 17] [Adaptive Planning]

3. D - Taking Agile Manifesto and principle as gospel is perhaps an extreme measure as for a number of projects a hybrid approach is more suitable than either strictly following Agile or waterfall approaches. However, when transitioning from waterfall approaches to Agile approaches, the first critical step is to adopt an Agile Mindset. This can help compare the benefit of both approaches and tailor the most suitable approach for the project. [Agile Practice Guide, 1st edition, Page 33] [Agile Principles and Mindset]

4. D - The scrum method provides guidance on the use of a product backlog, a product owner, scrum master, and a cross-functional development team, including sprint planning, daily scrum, sprint review and sprint retrospective sessions. [Agile Practice Guide, 1st edition, Page 31] [Agile Principles and Mindset]

5. D - A user story describes the user, the requirement, and the associated value. [Cohn, M., 2006. Agile Estimating and Planning. 1st ed. Massachusetts: Pearson Education. Page 25] [Value-driven Delivery]

6. D - Agile approaches recommend maintaining a clear distinction between an estimate of size and one of duration through using separate units that cannot be confused. Estimating size in story points and translating size into duration using velocity is an excellent way of doing this. [Cohn, M., 2006. Agile Estimating and Planning. 1st ed. Massachusetts: Pearson Education. Page 248] [Adaptive Planning]

7. D - A release burndown chart shows a team's progress by showing the number of story points remaining in the project. The vertical axis shows the number of story points remaining and the iterations are shown across the horizontal axis. [Cohn, M., 2006. Agile Estimating and Planning. 1st ed. Massachusetts: Pearson Education. Page 212] [Team Performance]

8. A - A burndown bar chart is a well-accepted Agile tool. This type of chart is recommended if the scope of work is constantly being significantly altered and when the team's true velocity is not being reflected by a traditional line-type burndown chart. However, the burndown bar chart is only for use in organizations mature enough not to argue about whether something belongs above the line or below the line. [Cohn, M., 2006. Agile Estimating and Planning. 1st ed. Massachusetts: Pearson Education. Page 217] [Team Performance]

9. C - Functionality that will be added in the near future (within the next few iteration) should be decomposed into relatively small user stories, typically items that will take from one to two days up to no more than 10 days. [Cohn, M., 2006. Agile Estimating and Planning. 1st ed. Massachusetts: Pearson Education. Page 249] [Value-driven Delivery]

10. D - The first value of the Agile Manifesto is "Individuals and interactions over processes and tools". [Agile Practice Guide, 1st edition, Page 8] [Agile Principles and Mindset]

11. D - Enterprise Scrum is a framework designed to apply the Scrum method on a more holistic organizational level rather than a single product development effort. The intent is to use Agile approaches beyond project execution by enabling disruptive innovation. [Agile Practice Guide, 1st edition, Page 114] [Value-driven Delivery]

12. A - On an Agile project, the Agile team is authorized to take decisions necessary to complete the project work. [Agile Practice Guide, 1st edition, Page 39] [Agile Principles and Mindset]

13. B - Historical values are of the greatest value when very little has changed between the old project and team and the new project and team. When the team is moving onto a new release of a product they just worked on, using the historical values is entirely appropriate. [Cohn, M., 2006. Agile Estimating and Planning. 1st ed. Massachusetts: Pearson Education. Page 176] [Team Performance]

14. C - House of quality and fishbone diagrams are quality management tools. A discount window is a monetary policy instrument which is totally irrelevant to the question. A Fishbowl window is a long-lived video conferencing link between various locations. [Agile Practice Guide, 1st edition, Page 46] [Team Performance]

15. B - Triple Nickels is a data gathering activity and not an insight generation activity. The rest of the choices are all activities used to generate insights. [Derby, E. and Larsen, D., 2006. Agile Retrospectives: Making Good Teams Great. 1st ed. Texas: Pragmatic Bookshelf, Page 56] [Continuous Improvement]

16. C - In Agile projects, time-boxed research or experiments are known as spikes. [Agile Practice Guide, 1st edition, Page 56] [Continuous Improvement]

17. A - Although it would be nice to let each individual sub-team choose whether to estimate in story points or ideal days, most projects with multiple teams will benefit from estimating in a common unit and establishing a baseline meaning for that unit. In this scenario it is obvious that this was not established at the start of the project. [Cohn, M., 2006. Agile Estimating and Planning. 1st ed. Massachusetts: Pearson Education. Page 200] [Adaptive Planning]

18. B - You are conducting a spike event. Spikes are time-boxed research experiments and are useful for learning and may be used in circumstances such as estimation, acceptance criteria definition, and understanding the flow of a user's action through the product. [Agile Practice Guide, 1st edition, Page 56] [Continuous Improvement]

19. D - Predictive approach is also known as plan-driven, serial or traditional approach. This is in contrast to the Agile approach which is both incremental and iterative. [Agile Practice Guide, 1st edition, Page 17] [Agile Principles and Mindset]

20. C - Kanban in lean manufacturing is a system for scheduling inventory control and

replenishment. [Agile Practice Guide, 1st edition, Page 103] [Team Performance]

21. D - A mixed team of generalists and specialists is recommended because specialists provide dedicated expertise while the generalists provide flexibility of who does what. [Agile Practice Guide, 1st edition, Page 40] [Value-driven Delivery]

22. D - In case there is either greater uncertainty or greater implication to being wrong about a release schedule, it is useful to include a buffer in the determination of the schedule. A buffer is a margin for error around an estimate. [Cohn, M., 2006. Agile Estimating and Planning. 1st ed. Massachusetts: Pearson Education. Page 179] [Problem Detection and Resolution]

23. B - New requirements are added to the product backlog where they get prioritized along with other pending backlog items. In some cases, these might get assigned to the next iteration but automatic assignment to the next iteration is not recommended. [Cohn, M., 2006. Agile Estimating and Planning. 1st ed. Massachusetts: Pearson Education. Page 66] [Problem Detection and Resolution]

24. D - Releases may occur at varying intervals. The first release may take six months to be developed, while the second release may take three months, and so on. [Cohn, M., 2006. Agile Estimating and Planning. 1st ed. Massachusetts: Pearson Education. Page 25] [Value-driven Delivery]

25. D - Automated Code Quality Analysis involves scripted testing of code base for bugs and vulnerabilities. . [Agile Practice Guide, 1st edition, Page 150] [Problem Detection and Resolution]

26. C - When team members are 100% dedicated to the project, the team has the fastest possible throughput. The rest of the choices are incorrect: The difference in individual throughputs can be a pain-point and create bottlenecks. Recommended Agile team size is less than 9 members. Multi-tasking is considered a waste. [Agile Practice Guide, 1st edition, Page 44] [Team Performance]

27. A - Planning poker is generally recognized as the best Agile estimating technique. Planning poker combines expert opinion, analogy, and disaggregation into an enjoyable approach to estimating that results in a quick but reliable estimate. [Cohn, M., 2006. Agile Estimating and Planning. 1st ed. Massachusetts: Pearson Education. Page 56] [Adaptive Planning]

28. B - Instead of developing a formal communication management plan, Agile teams rely on daily standups for team communication. Daily standups are used to make team commitments. [Agile Practice Guide, 1st edition, Page 97] [Agile Principles and Mindset]

29. C - Send all three candidates' resumes. Since all the candidates have similar profiles, all three deserve a full chance of evaluation. Because you have not shortlisted the resumes nor will you be the interviewer or make the final decision, there is no question of discrimination, partiality or conflict of interest. [PMI Code of Ethics and Professional Conduct] [Stakeholder Engagement]

30. C - If the stakeholders are not happy with the user interface during the demonstration, this means they haven't been involved during the development of these features. This problem could have been avoided through successive prototypes or proofs of concept. [Agile Practice Guide, 1st edition, Page 21] [Value-driven Delivery]

31. C - Cycle time = number of days per delivered story. Since the team has successfully delivered 45 stories in 3 iterations, the velocity is 15 stories per iteration. Each iteration is 3 weeks; the team delivers on average five stories per week or one story per day (team works five days per week). [Agile Practice Guide, 1st edition, Page 61] [Team Performance]

32. A - Burndown charts are the primary way of tracking and communicating the team's progress against the release plan. [Cohn, M., 2006. Agile Estimating and Planning. 1st ed. Massachusetts: Pearson Education. Page 232] [Team Performance]

33. C - Backlog grooming, also known as backlog refining, involves adding, removing, and prioritizing stories in the product backlog. The purpose of refinement is to help the team understand what the stories are and how large the stories are in relation to each other. [Agile Practice Guide, 1st edition, Page 52] [Adaptive Planning]

34. C - Once the problem (variation) has been identified, the next step is to uncover the underlying root cause (sources). Fishbone diagrams break down the causes of the problem statement into discrete branches, helping to identify the main or root cause of the problem. [Derby, E. and Larsen, D., 2006. Agile Retrospectives: Making Good Teams Great. 1st ed. Texas: Pragmatic Bookshelf, Page 87] [Continuous Improvement]

35. B - Teams use stand-ups to micro-commit to each other, uncover problems, and ensure the work flows smoothly through the team. This is the most common and effective Agile communication tool. [Agile Practice Guide, 1st edition, Page 53] [Adaptive Planning]

36. A - Agile CPI = Completed features value/actual costs to date = $450,000 / $600,000 = 0.75. [Agile Practice Guide, 1st edition, Page 69] [Team Performance]

37. A - It is the responsibility of the Agile team to maintain confidentiality of protected or proprietary information. The project team should provide such confidential information only to the sponsor and to the vendor evaluation committee or whoever is involved in the evaluation. The team must not provide this information to any other employees within the organization or within the project. [PMI Code of Ethics and Professional Responsibility] [Stakeholder Engagement]

38. C - The purpose of the "Short Subjects" activity is to help discover differing perspectives on how the team is doing and provide variety in very short retrospectives. [Derby, E. and Larsen, D., 2006. Agile Retrospectives: Making Good Teams Great. 1st ed. Texas: Pragmatic Bookshelf, Page 111] [Continuous Improvement]

39. D - This role is equivalent to the product owner's role on Agile teams. [Agile Practice Guide, 1st edition, Page 154] [Value-driven Delivery]

40. C - As a general rule of thumb, people experience productivity losses somewhere between 20% and 40% when task switching. [Agile Practice Guide, 1st edition, Page 45] [Team Performance]

PMI-ACP Knowledge Area Quiz: Adaptive Planning Practice Questions

Test Name: Knowledge Area Test: Risk Management
Total Questions: 15
Correct Answers Needed to Pass: 11 (73.33%)
Time Allowed: 25 Minutes

Test Description

This practice quiz specifically targets your knowledge of the Risk Management exam topic area.

Test Questions

1. Story points are a unit of measure for expressing the overall size of a user story. When we estimate with story points we assign a point value to each item. Which of the following is the correct scale for estimating story points?

   A. Nominal scale

   B. Ordinal scale

   C. Agile scale

   D. Cardinal scale

2. When grooming and prioritizing the user stories in the product backlog, which of the following ranking approaches can be used?

   A. Ranking with story size multiplied with the number of team members.

   B. Ranking with story size divided by the number of sprints.

   C. Ranking with sprint size divided by the number of sprints.

   D. Ranking with value including the cost of delay divided by duration.

3. A product is required to be shipped in six months. If the release plan contains thirteen two-week iterations with on average twenty story points per iteration, what is the project size?

   A. 12 story points

   B. 260 story points

   C. 120 story points

   D. 40 story points

4. Which of the following is the main benefit of estimating ideal time rather than estimating elapsed time for user stories?

   A. Ideal time, measured in hours, is more accurate than elapsed time which is usually measured in days.

   B. It is almost always far easier and accurate to predict the duration of an event in ideal time than in elapsed time.

   C. Ideal time estimation allows Agile teams to individually size user stories.

   D. It is usually impossible to estimate a user story size in elapsed time.

5. Which of the following is the Agile view on detailed cost estimates for projects with high

degrees of uncertainty or those where the scope is not yet fully defined?

A. Agile projects do not involve detailed cost estimates due to frequent changes.

B. Agile projects do not involve detailed cost estimates due to the absence of a scope baseline.

C. Detailed cost estimates for the project are determined early but adjusted as new information becomes available.

D. Detailed cost estimates are reserved for short-term planning horizons.

6. Agile approaches do not require developing a formal scope management plan or a WBS. In Agile projects, which of the following makes up the high-level project scope?

A. Product backlog

B. Release plan

C. Burndown chart

D. Scope statement

7. The Kano model gives us an approach to separate features into three categories: must-have features, linear features, and delighters. The 'must have' features are also known as:

A. Threshold features

B. Exciting features

C. Boundary features

D. Baseline features

8. An Agile team working on a data center migration project has accrued substantial technical debt. What should be done now?

A. Re-prioritize the backlog.

B. Develop a minimum viable product.

C. Drop stories from the backlog.

D. Increase the team size.

9. Which of the following Agile tools is not targeted toward identifying problems and bottlenecks?

A. Product backlog

B. Daily standups

C. Retrospectives

D. Kanban board

10. Which of the following refers to the progressive elaboration of project requirements and the ongoing activity in which the team collaboratively reviews, updates, and writes requirements to satisfy the needs of the customer request?

A. Conditions of satisfaction determination

B. Backlog refinement

C. Process mapping

D. Root cause analysis

11. Which of the following Agile events is not primarily designed to generate feedback on either project approach or project deliverable?

A. Usability testing

B. Planning poker

C. Retrospective

D. Demonstration

12. According to the Kano model, which of the following statements regarding the "must-have" features is correct?

A. The "must-have" features only increase customer satisfaction if all delighters have been provided.

B. The increase in the number of "must-have" features is directly proportional to the increase of customer satisfaction.

C. The increase in the number of "must-have" features is inversely proportional to the increase of customer satisfaction.

D. Once some amount of a must-have feature has been implemented, customer satisfaction cannot be increased by adding more of that feature.

13. Which of the following planning activities is NOT part of release planning?

A. Prioritizing user stories.

B. Developing a milestone schedule.

C. Selecting an iteration length.

D. Assigning resources to tasks.

14. You and your Agile team are currently making team commitments regarding what features will be progressed or completed prior to the next planning meeting. Which meeting is this?

A. Backlog grooming

B. Daily meeting

C. Iteration planning

D. Sprint retrospective

15. You are leading an Agile team developing an enterprise automation system. You have scheduled the next project iteration planning meeting with the team members next week. Which of the following action items must be completed prior to the iteration planning meeting?

A. Nothing, the self-organizing Agile team will do everything themselves.

B. Conduct root cause analysis

C. Refine the backlog

D. Estimate the user stories

PMI-ACP Knowledge Area Quiz: Adaptive Planning Answer Key and Explanations

1. D - The raw value of story points we assign is unimportant. What matters is the relative values. A story that is assigned a 20 should be twice as much as a story that is assigned a 10. Nominal and ordinal scales cannot be used. Agile teams use cardinal scale to estimate story points. (NOTE: Nominal scales are used to "name," or label a series. Ordinal scales provide good information about the order of choices. Cardinal scales give us the order of values + the ability to quantify the difference between each one. There is no such thing as an Agile scale.) [Cohn, M., 2006. Agile Estimating and Planning. 1st ed. Massachusetts: Pearson Education. Page 36] [Adaptive Planning]

2. D - Many ranking methods exist but they all pivot around organizational value. Only one of the given choices pivots around value: ranking with value including cost of delay divided by duration. [Agile Practice Guide, 1st edition, Page 59] [Adaptive Planning]

3. B - There will be 13 two-week iterations in a six-month period. With an average of 20 story points per iteration, the project size will be 260 story points. [Cohn, M., 2006. Agile Estimating and Planning. 1st ed. Massachusetts: Pearson Education. Page 132] [Adaptive Planning]

4. B - Ideal time is the amount of time that something takes when stripped of all peripheral activities. Elapsed time is the amount of time from the start to finish of an activity. It is almost always far easier and accurate to predict the duration of an event in ideal time than in elapsed time. [Cohn, M., 2006. Agile Estimating and Planning. 1st ed. Massachusetts: Pearson Education. Page 43] [Adaptive Planning]

5. D - Agile projects with high degrees of uncertainty or those where the scope is not yet fully defined may not benefit from detailed cost calculations for the entire project due to frequent changes. However, detailed costs are estimated for short-term planning horizons in a just-in-time fashion. [Agile Practice Guide, 1st edition, Page 92] [Adaptive Planning]

6. A - The backlog is the ordered list of all the work, presented in story form, for a team. At any given point in time, the current produce backlog defines the current project scope. [Agile Practice Guide, 1st edition, Page 52] [Adaptive Planning]

7. A - Threshold features are those that must be present in the product for it to be successful. They are often referred to as "must-have features". [Cohn, M., 2006. Agile Estimating and Planning. 1st ed. Massachusetts: Pearson Education. Page 110] [Adaptive Planning]

8. A - Technical debt refers to the deferred cost of work not done at an earlier point in the product life cycle. This is sunk cost and cannot be recovered. However, the team must ensure that the current product backlog is updated with current organizational priorities. [Agile Practice Guide, 1st edition, Page 154] [Adaptive Planning]

9. A - During daily standups each team member gets an opportunity to discuss any impediments to his/her work. Kanban

boards visually show the team's WIP and highlight bottlenecks. The team discusses what went right and what went wrong during retrospectives. Product backlog in itself is least helpful in identifying any bottlenecks or issues. [Agile Practice Guide, 1st edition, Pages 50, 52, 53, 103] [Adaptive Planning]

10. B - Backlog refinement refers to the progressive elaboration of project requirements and the ongoing activity in which the team collaboratively reviews, updates, and writes requirements to satisfy the needs of the customer request. [Agile Practice Guide, 1st edition, Page 150] [Adaptive Planning]

11. B - Planning poker is an Agile estimating technique and not a feedback solicitation technique. Planning poker combines expert opinion, analogy, and disaggregation into an enjoyable approach to estimating that results in quick but reliable estimate. [Cohn, M., 2006. Agile Estimating and Planning. 1st ed. Massachusetts: Pearson Education. Page 56] [Adaptive Planning]

12. D - According to the Kano model, once some amount of a must-have feature has been implemented, customer satisfaction cannot be increased by adding more of that feature. Also, no matter how much of a must-have feature is added, customer satisfaction never rises above the mid-point. [Cohn, M., 2006. Agile Estimating and Planning. 1st ed. Massachusetts: Pearson Education. Page 110] [Adaptive Planning]

13. D - During release planning we do not want to create a plan that indicates which resources will be assigned to which tasks or the sequence in which work will be performed within an iteration. Creating a plan with that level of detail is dangerous and misleading during release planning. [Cohn, M., 2006. Agile Estimating and Planning. 1st ed. Massachusetts: Pearson Education. Page 132] [Adaptive Planning]

14. B - During daily planning teams make, assess, and revise their daily plans. During daily meetings, teams constrain the planning horizon to be no further away than the next day, when they will meet again. Daily meetings are also used to make team commitments. [Cohn, M., 2006. Agile Estimating and Planning. 1st ed. Massachusetts: Pearson Education. Page 28] [Adaptive Planning]

15. C - In iteration-based Agile, the product owner often works with the team to prepare some stories for the upcoming iteration. The purpose of these meetings is to groom enough stories so the team understands what the stories are and how large the stories are in relation to each other. [Agile Practice Guide, 1st edition, Page 52] [Adaptive Planning]

PMI-ACP Lite Mock Exam 13 Practice Questions

Test Name: PMI-ACP Lite Mock Exam 13
Total Questions: 40
Correct Answers Needed to Pass: 30 (75.00%)
Time Allowed: 60 Minutes

Test Description

This is a cumulative PMI-ACP Mock Exam which can be used as a benchmark for your PMI-ACP aptitude. This practice test includes questions from all exam topic areas, including sections from Agile Tools and Techniques, and all three Agile Knowledge and Skills areas.

Test Questions

1. During a sprint retrospective, the team found out that one particular item's cycle time was 10 days and the lead time was 30 days. Which of the following statements correctly explains the difference between the two numbers?

A. The item's waiting time in the "Done" state was 20 days.

B. The item's waiting time in the "WIP" state was 20 days.

C. The item's waiting time in the "Ready" state was 20 days.

D. The item's waiting time in the "Testing" state was 20 days.

2. During a retrospective, an Agile team defines a desired state they want to achieve. Small groups work to identify the factors that could either restrain or drive the change they want. The factors are listed on a poster, then the group assesses the strength of each supporting factor relative to the other supporting factors and repeats the process for inhibiting factors. Which Agile technique is the team using?

A. Fishbone analysis

B. Brainstorming

C. Force Field Analysis

D. Working agreements

3. You are managing an Agile project and just completed the third iteration of the project. During the iteration planning the team thinks that the original release plan has become outdated. What should you do next?

A. Update the release plan and notify the product owner.

B. Conduct a detailed feasibility study of the project and then update the release plan.

C. Update the release plan and notify the PMO.

D. Update the release plan and notify the end users.

4. You are responsible for analyzing and mapping an organization's core processes. The project is complex as it requires a lot of knowledge work. Due to the complexity of the project, the project team needs to be agile and respond quickly to change. Which of the following has a potential to impede the team's agility?

A. Change control boards

B. Kanban boards

C. Project sponsor

D. Scrum processes

5. You, your Agile team, and the product owner are currently prioritizing features, ranking them in order of their business value, and defining the scope of the project. Which planning meeting is this?

A. Daily scrum

B. Retrospective

C. Iteration planning

D. Release planning

6. You have been hired as a consultant to review the project management practices of an organization. You conduct a thorough review of project management methodology, tools and techniques used by the organization and found out all of these have been developed from scratch in the organization and none of these are well-established techniques in the Agile community. However all of these adhere to the mindset, values and principles of the Agile Manifesto. What is your view on the organization's approach to project management?

A. The organization's approach is not Agile since none of the practices are well-established Agile approaches.

B. The organization's approach is Agile as the project management approach is rooted in the Agile Manifesto.

C. The organization's approach is not Agile since all of the practices have been developed from scratch.

D. The organization's approach is not Agile since it is following a traditional approach.

7. Which of the following is an archetype user representing a set of similar end users described with their goals, motivations, and representative personal characterizes?

A. Plant

B. Guinea pig

C. Persona

D. Subject

8. You are conducting an ESVP activity during an iteration retrospective. People have cast their votes and handed over their slips to you. What should you do next?

A. Record individual responses on the responses log.

B. Distribute the slips to all team members.

C. Shuffle the slips, use the slips to mark a histogram and then tear up the slips.

D. Call out the people who haven't signed their names on the slips.

9. According to the Agile principles, all of the following are important factors to be considered when forming an Agile team EXCEPT:

A. Office environment

B. Motivation level

C. Trust level

D. Team RACI

10. Which of the following techniques doesn't help in identifying underlying root cause of a given problem?

A. Brainstorming

B. Burndown charts

C. Fishbone Diagrams

D. Five Whys

11. You are managing a productivity monitoring and reporting system. The stakeholders have historically required all projects to produce exhaustive documentation. You do not want to produce exhaustive documentation on your project as that impedes the team's agility. How should you approach this problem?

A. Work with stakeholders to review required documentation.

B. Ignore documentation requirements on all Agile projects.

C. Organize a briefing on the Agile Manifesto.

D. Park all documentation requirements and only consider them once the project is finished.

12. Which of the following is not a valid Agile estimating technique?

A. Expert opinion

B. Analogy

C. Disaggregation

D. Parametric estimation

13. If all features on a project have been classified by their risk and business value, which of the following group of themes would you recommend starting first?

A. The features that have low value, especially those that are also high risk.

B. The features that deliver high value but are less risky.

C. The features that deliver high value and eliminate the maximum risk from the project.

D. The features that have less impact on the total value and have low risk.

14. You are leading an Agile team developing a resource management application. Recently due to some unexplained events, some of the scheduled tasks got delayed and increased the project costs. You now want to investigate the root cause of this issue. Which of the following tool should you use?

A. Fishbone diagram

B. PDCA cycle

C. Sensitivity analysis

D. Histogram

15. During a project retrospective, the team expressed its concerns over the quality management processes. One percent of the produced deliverables had minor defects which required rework. What must the team do to bring the future project performance in line with the expected quality standards?

A. Investigate the root cause using critical chain diagram.

B. Investigate the root cause using a tornado diagram.

C. Investigate the root cause using a fishbone diagram.

D. Ignore the minor defects.

16. Which of the following is NOT a valid Scrum artifact?

A. Sprint backlog

B. Team charter

C. Increments

D. Product backlog

17. You are leading an Agile team developing an organizational system. The time-box for the current iteration has expired but only 50% of the iteration stories have been completed. What should you do next?

A. Calculate individual velocities and remove the weak performers from the team.

B. Conduct a demonstration and return the incomplete work to the backlog.

C. Request additional time to complete the incomplete work.

D. Cancel the demonstration and start the next iteration.

18. Which Agile role is primarily responsible for determining the business value of stories in an Agile project?

A. Agile team

B. Servant-leader

C. Product owner

D. Functional manager

19. Agile teams often conduct time-boxed research experiments to learn some critical technical or functional element of the project. What are these researches called?

A. Spikes

B. Reflections

C. Root cause analysis

D. Retrospectives

20. Which of the following is NOT an established Scrum event?

A. Spring retrospective

B. Sprint review

C. Daily sprint

D. Daily scrum

21. Organizations are structured on a spectrum ranging from highly projectized to matrixed to highly functionalized. Projects within which of the following organizational structures are more likely to find general resistance to collaboration?

A. Matrix structures.

B. Highly projectized structures.

C. Highly functionalized structures.

D. Weak matrix structures.

22. A feeding buffer, like the schedule buffer, protects the on-time delivery of a set of new capabilities. However, which of the following is the main disadvantage of using feeding buffers?

A. It generally increases the cost of the project.

B. It generally decreases the control of the project.

C. It generally increases the scope of the stories.

D. It generally extends the expected duration of the project.

23. If a product owner adds new stories to an iteration plan halfway through an iteration, which of the following may happen?

A. Story size increases.

B. Iteration gets terminated.

C. Risk increases.

D. Velocity decreases.

24. Which of the following statements regarding Agile teams is generally NOT considered a good practice?

A. Establishing a team having no more than seven to ten members.

B. Assigning full-time resources to Agile projects.

C. Breaking larger teams into smaller Agile teams.

D. Establishing a single 100-person team.

25. A project team is currently struggling with clarity around the project's context and boundaries. Which of the following, most probably, did NOT happen for this project?

A. Agile chartering

B. Storyboarding

C. Time boxing

D. Backlog grooming

26. You have recently been hired in an organization as the database expert on a critical project. The organization is currently managing all of its projects using Agile methodologies. You overheard one of the project managers saying that he values staff utilization over rapid feature delivery to the customer. What is wrong with this?

A. The database administrator role needs to be filled prior to hiring a database expert.

B. There shouldn't be any role of a project manager in an Agile environment.

C. Emphasis should be on rapid feature delivery to the customer instead of staff utilization.

D. The database expert should be consulted before allocating work.

27. You are managing an Agile project. As the team learns more about the product they are building, new features are added to the release plan. If the team's story size estimates are consistent and nothing else changes, which of the following is LEAST likely to happen:

A. The team's velocity might get reduced.

B. Total story points might get increased.

C. A burnup can appear on the release burndown chart.

D. The number of iterations might get increased.

28. Which of the following contract types shares the financial risk between the buyer and the supplier?

A. Graduated time and materials

B. Cost plus incentive fee

C. Firm fixed-price

D. Cost plus fixed fee

29. You are the servant-leader for an Agile team developing a procurement system. The team wants to explore a new technology that would allow direct access to suppliers' databases. The product owner is concerned that this might cause delays on the project. What should you do?

A. Convince the team to drop the idea and follow the product owner's recommendations.

B. Have the team collaborate with the product owner to find a suitable way.

C. Engage an Agile coach to resolve this conflict.

D. Convince the product owner that Agile teams thrive on new technologies.

30. How much should be invested in a long-term bond, offering an annual interest rate of 5%, so that there is $1,000,000 by the end of 10 years?

A. 613913

B. 1458277

C. 1628895

D. 1500012

31. Backlog refinement in Agile projects helps in realizing which of the following Agile Manifesto values?

A. "Individuals and interactions over processes and tools" and "Responding to change over following a plan".

B. "Working software over comprehensive documentation" and "Responding to change over following a plan".

C. "Working software over comprehensive documentation" and

"Individuals and interactions over processes and tools".

D. "Individuals and interactions over processes and tools" and "Customer collaboration over contract negotiation".

32. For a complex project with a loosely defined scope, which of the following contracting approaches can help an Agile team define a contractual relationship in a way that the team gets control over the expenditure while at the same time limiting the supplier's financial risk of over-commitment?

A. Aggregating the scope into a fixed-price contract.

B. Decomposing the scope into cost-reimbursable macro-deliverables.

C. Decomposing the scope into fixed-price micro-deliverables.

D. Aggregating the scope into a time & materials contract.

33. If an Agile team planned to complete 30 story points in an iteration but worked at only 83% of the rate planned. What is the project's SPI?

A. 0.83

B. SPI cannot be determined from the given information.

C. 36 story points

D. 25 story points

34. An Agile team is progressing a little slower than what was planned at the start of the iteration. Which of the following Agile metrics will this effect?

A. Actual duration

B. Ideal time

C. Velocity

D. Story points

35. An Agile team is currently engaged in an enterprise-wide system development project. The team is struggling to complete user stories by the end of the iteration. What can be a potential root cause and potential solution to this problem?

A. The stories are too large and need to be split.

B. The conditions of satisfaction were not identified and the team needs to reschedule the work.

C. Low value stories were selected which now need to be replaced with higher value stories.

D. The stories were underestimated and need to be merged.

36. Traditional project management approaches included multiple KPIs that predicted the success of a project. How do we demonstrate success of an Agile project?

A. By demonstrating that a working product has been delivered to the customer.

B. By maintain a productive team velocity.

C. By release on time.

D. By reusing the traditional KPIs and measures.

37. Which of the following Agile techniques requires splitting a user story or feature into smaller, easier-to-estimate pieces?

A. Disaggregation

B. Grooming

C. Analogy

D. Expert opinion

38. During a retrospective, a team member has reported degrading production quality. What should you do to get to the bottom of this?

A. Adopt stricter quality control processes.

B. Create a fishbone diagram with the team members.

C. Ask the team member to submit a detailed report.

D. Develop a value stream map of the production process.

39. According to the Kano model, which of the following statements regarding the "delighters" is incorrect?

A. These are also known as the threshold features.

B. These features allow premium pricing.

C. The lack of a delighter will not decrease customer satisfaction below neutral.

D. These features provide the greatest satisfaction.

40. Traditional teams initially face difficulties in understanding how Agile teams can determine expected project completion time given that they do not spend sufficient time in upfront project planning. What is your opinion regarding predicting project completion on Agile projects?

A. The Agile team predicts completion time using displacement and mean distance.

B. The Agile team predicts completion time using velocity and average cycle time.

C. The Agile team predicts completion time using project baselines.

D. The Agile team predicts completion time using speed and average acceleration.

PMI-ACP Lite Mock Exam 13 Answer Key and Explanations

1. C - Lead time is the total time it takes to deliver an item, measured from the time it is added to the board to the moment it is completed. Cycle time is the time required to process an item. The difference between the two is the item's waiting time in the "Ready" state. [Agile Practice Guide, 1st edition, Page 64] [Continuous Improvement]

2. C - This is an example of Force Field Analysis. During this activity, the team discusses which factors they can influence either by increasing the strength of a supporting factor or by reducing the strength of an inhibiting factor. [Derby, E. and Larsen, D., 2006. Agile Retrospectives: Making Good Teams Great. 1st ed. Texas: Pragmatic Bookshelf, Page 81] [Continuous Improvement]

3. A - If the release plan is based on outdated information or on assumptions that are now false, update it and notify the product owner. The product owner can then decide the future course for the project. [Cohn, M., 2006. Agile Estimating and Planning. 1st ed. Massachusetts: Pearson Education. Page 248] [Problem Detection and Resolution]

4. A - The question does not provide enough context to determine if a project sponsor has the potential to impede the team's agility. Scrum processes and Kanban boards are Agile techniques which should, in fact, enable agility. However a change control board and the associated formal change control processes have the potential to impede any team's responsiveness to change. [Agile Practice Guide, 1st edition, Page 35] [Agile Principles and Mindset]

5. D - Release planning considers the user stories, features or themes that will be developed for a new release of a product or system. The goal of this planning is to determine an appropriate answer to the questions of scope, schedule, and resources for a project. [Cohn, M., 2006. Agile Estimating and Planning. 1st ed. Massachusetts: Pearson Education. Page 28] [Adaptive Planning]

6. B - The organization's approach is Agile as the project management approach is rooted in the Agile Manifesto. It is not necessary to use any of the established Agile approaches; an Agile approach can be developed from scratch as long as it adheres to the mindset, values, and principles of the Agile Manifesto. [Agile Practice Guide, 1st edition, Page 99] [Agile Principles and Mindset]

7. C - A persona defines an archetypical user of a system, an example of the kind of person who would interact with it. The idea is that if you want to design effective software, then it needs to be designed for a specific person. [Agile Practice Guide, 1st edition, Page 153] [Adaptive Planning]

8. C - With the ESVP activity, you need to be careful about conducting anonymous polling. If voters fear that their names will be called out, they might not cast an honest vote, especially the prisoners and the vacationers. Once you receive the slips, you must shuffle the slips, use the slips to create a histogram and then tear up the slips. [Derby, E. and Larsen, D., 2006. Agile Retrospectives: Making Good Teams Great. 1st ed. Texas: Pragmatic Bookshelf, Page 46] [Continuous Improvement]

9. D - Build projects around motivated individuals. Give them the environment and support they need and trust them to get the job done. Agile teams are supposed to be self-organizing and to work as a unit, developing a team RACI doesn't support this view. [Agile Practice Guide, 1st edition, Page 9] [Agile Principles and Mindset]

10. B - Brainstorming can be used to identify root causes by generating a number of divergent ideas. This is usually an underpinning technique for more accurate root cause analysis techniques such as Five Whys and Fishbone diagrams. [Derby, E. and Larsen, D., 2006. Agile Retrospectives: Making Good Teams Great. 1st ed. Texas: Pragmatic Bookshelf, Pages 85, 87] [Continuous Improvement]

11. A - If the stakeholders require extensive documentation, the role of a servant-leader is to work with them to review the required documentation, assist with creating a shared understanding of how Agile deliverables meet those requirements, and evaluate the amount of documentation required so team can spend more time delivering a valuable product instead of producing exhaustive documentation. [Agile Practice Guide, 1st edition, Page 35] [Problem Detection and Resolution]

12. D - Parametric estimating is a more accurate technique for estimating cost and duration; it uses the statistical relationships between variables to calculate the cost or duration. Although this method is frequently used in predictive approaches, it is not considered an Agile estimating approach. The rest of the choices are valid Agile estimation approaches. [Cohn, M., 2006. Agile Estimating and Planning. 1st ed. Massachusetts: Pearson Education. Page 54] [Adaptive Planning]

13. C - "Do first" is recommended for the features that have been classified as "High Risk" and "High Value". Such features deliver the maximum business value while lowering the maximum risk on the project. [Cohn, M., 2006. Agile Estimating and Planning. 1st ed. Massachusetts: Pearson Education. Page 85] [Adaptive Planning]

14. A - Root cause analysis using a fishbone diagram is the recommended approach. The rest of the tools are not designed around root cause analysis. [Derby, E. and Larsen, D., 2006. Agile Retrospectives: Making Good Teams Great. 1st ed. Texas: Pragmatic Bookshelf, Page 87] [Continuous Improvement]

15. C - Once the problem (variation) has been identified, the next step is to uncover the underlying root cause (sources). Fishbone diagrams break down the causes of the problem statement into discrete branches, helping to identify the main or root cause of the problem. [Derby, E. and Larsen, D., 2006. Agile Retrospectives: Making Good Teams Great. 1st ed. Texas: Pragmatic Bookshelf, Page 87] [Continuous Improvement]

16. B - Although team chartering is an established Agile technique, it is not a Scrum artifact. [Agile Practice Guide, 1st edition, Page 101] [Value-driven Delivery]

17. B - If the team wasn't able to complete the planned work, the incomplete work will be returned to the backlog and the current iteration will not be stretched to complete the work. Further a demonstration needs to

be arranged at the end of each iteration. [Cohn, M., 2006. Agile Estimating and Planning. 1st ed. Massachusetts: Pearson Education. Page 66] [Problem Detection and Resolution]

18. C - The product owner is primarily responsible for determining the business value of stories in an Agile project. [Cohn, M., 2006. Agile Estimating and Planning. 1st ed. Massachusetts: Pearson Education. Page 23] [Value-driven Delivery]

19. A - Such events are called spikes. Spikes are useful for learning and may be used in circumstances such as estimation, acceptance criteria definition, and understanding the flow of a user's action through the product. [Agile Practice Guide, 1st edition, Page 56] [Continuous Improvement]

20. C - Scrum events include sprint, sprint planning, daily scrum, sprint review and sprint retrospectives. [Agile Practice Guide, 1st edition, Page 101] [Value-driven Delivery]

21. C - Projects with highly functionalized structures may find general resistance to collaboration across its organization. [Agile Practice Guide, 1st edition, Page 83] [Value-driven Delivery]

22. D - Feeding buffers are created by introducing lag to successor activities. In most cases, adding feeding buffers will extend the expected duration of a project. [Cohn, M., 2006. Agile Estimating and Planning. 1st ed. Massachusetts: Pearson Education. Page 204] [Adaptive Planning]

23. C - This increases the project risk. If new stories are added beyond the team capacities, all assigned stories might not get completed during the current sprint. [Cohn, M., 2006. Agile Estimating and Planning. 1st ed. Massachusetts: Pearson Education. Page 5] [Problem Detection and Resolution]

24. D - Agile teams are often describe as having no more than seven to ten members. Instead of providing a single large team to projects requiring larger teams, required resources are divided into multiple smaller Agile teams. [Cohn, M., 2006. Agile Estimating and Planning. 1st ed. Massachusetts: Pearson Education. Page 199] [Agile Principles and Mindset]

25. A - An Agile project and team charter should provide enough clarity at the start of the project around project's vision and mission. Further, these should provide clarity around team working agreements, project boundaries and context. [Agile Practice Guide, 1st edition, Page 58] [Value-driven Delivery]

26. C - For this question, two of the choices are irrelevant and should easily be eliminated; "consultation with the database expert for the work allocation" and "filling the database administrator role". Although, the role of the project manager has not been clearly articulated in many Agile frameworks, pragmatic Agile practitioners realize that project managers can add significant value in many situations. In the given scenario, the problem is with the emphasis on staff utilization rather than rapid feature delivery to the customer, which doesn't foster an Agile environment. [Agile Practice Guide, 1st edition, Page 38] [Value-driven Delivery]

27. A - If the size estimation is consistent, the team velocity should remain consistent. Although the total story points on the project might get increased which will show up as a burnup on the burndown chart and might require additional iterations to complete the project. [Cohn, M., 2006. Agile Estimating and Planning. 1st ed. Massachusetts: Pearson Education. Page 244] [Problem Detection and Resolution]

28. A - Firm fixed-price contracts hedge the buyer's financial risk, while cost plus contracts hedge the supplier's financial risk. Graduated time and material contracts share the financial risk between the two parties. [Agile Practice Guide, 1st edition, Page 78] [Value-driven Delivery]

29. B - It is your responsibility to find a solution to this conflict. Encouraging collaboration to determine the best way is the best approach to take. This will result in a win-win situation for both parties. [Agile Practice Guide, 1st edition, Page 34] [Problem Detection and Resolution]

30. A - We need to determine the Present Value (PV) of $1,000,000 at 5% for 10 years. The formula for Present Value is: PV = FV / (1+r)^n. So to calculate, PV = $1,000,000 / (1+0.05)^10 = $613,913. [Cohn, M., 2006. Agile Estimating and Planning. 1st ed. Massachusetts: Pearson Education. Page 100] [Value-driven Delivery]

31. B - "Working software over comprehensive documentation" and "Responding to change over following a plan" is the correct response. [Agile Practice Guide, 1st edition, Page 97] [Adaptive Planning]

32. C - A fixed price contract will hedge the buyer's risk but will not limit the supplier's financial risk. On the other hand, a time & materials or a cost-reimbursable arrangement will not give the buyer any control over the cost. The recommended approach is to decompose the project scope into fixed-price micro-deliverables, such as user stories. For the buyer, this gives more control over how the money is spent. For the supplier, it limits the financial risk of over-commitment to a single feature or deliverable. [Agile Practice Guide, 1st edition, Page 77] [Value-driven Delivery]

33. A - If the team worked at only 83% story points the SPI is 0.83. Productivity of 83% means that the team was only able to complete 25 story points during the iteration. [Agile Practice Guide, 1st edition, Page 69] [Team Performance]

34. C - Story points and ideal time are sizing/estimating metrics; these do not change with actual performance. Velocity, however, would get reduced if the team is delivering fewer story points than planned. Actual duration is an absolute number you get at the end of an activity, it can be different than the planned duration, but the final value doesn't change. [Agile Practice Guide, 1st edition, Page 61] [Team Performance]

35. A - The scenario doesn't give enough information to determine if the stories being worked on are low value stories or whether the conditions of satisfaction were not identified earlier. If the team has unfinished stories at the end of the iteration, most probably the team is working with features or stories that are too large. Splitting these larger stories into smaller stories will lead to a steady flow through the development process. [Cohn, M., 2006. Agile Estimating and Planning. 1st ed. Massachusetts: Pearson Education. Page 212] [Problem Detection and Resolution]

36. A - For Agile teams, working product is the primary measure of progress. [Agile Practice Guide, 1st edition, Page 9] [Agile Principles and Mindset]

37. A - Disaggregation refers to splitting a story or feature into smaller, easier-to-estimate pieces. [Cohn, M., 2006. Agile Estimating and Planning. 1st ed. Massachusetts: Pearson Education. Page 55] [Adaptive Planning]

38. B - Here you want to investigate the root cause of the reported problem. You can do that by analyzing the problem with the team using a fishbone diagram. [Derby, E. and Larsen, D., 2006. Agile Retrospectives: Making Good Teams Great. 1st ed. Texas: Pragmatic Bookshelf, Page 87] [Continuous Improvement]

39. A - Delighters are those features that provide great satisfaction, often adding a price premium to a product. However, the lack of an exciter or delighter will not decrease customer satisfaction below neutral as in the case of "must-have" features, also known as the threshold features. [Cohn, M., 2006. Agile Estimating and Planning. 1st ed. Massachusetts: Pearson Education. Page 110] [Adaptive Planning]

40. B - Project baselines are not established on Agile projects. Once Agile teams establish a reliable velocity (average stories or story points per iteration) or the average cycle time, the teams can predict how much long the project will take. [Agile Practice Guide, 1st edition, Page 61] [Team Performance]

PMI-ACP Lite Mock Exam 14 Practice Questions

Test Name: PMI-ACP Lite Mock Exam 14
Total Questions: 40
Correct Answers Needed to Pass:
30 (75.00%)
Time Allowed: 60 Minutes

Test Description

This is a cumulative PMI-ACP Mock Exam which can be used as a benchmark for your PMI-ACP aptitude. This practice test includes questions from all exam topic areas, including sections from Agile Tools and Techniques, and all three Agile Knowledge and Skills areas.

Test Questions

1. A project team is struggling with a number of technical obstacles and impediments on the project. The servant-leader was able to remove some of the initial obstacles, but now some of these need to be escalated. What is recommended next?

   A. Consult the coach.

   B. Consult the project manager.

   C. Consult the HR department.

   D. Consult the product owner.

2. You have been hired by as a Project Manager in an organization that has recently transitioned to Agile practices. During your first week at work, you have noticed that your team hasn't fully embraced Agile. What should you do?

   A. Set WIP limits.

   B. Put on the Agile coach hat.

   C. Escalate the matter to product owner.

   D. Negotiate for better qualified resources.

3. While companies are moving toward open, collaborative work environments, organizations also need to create quiet spaces for workers who need uninterrupted time to think and work. Companies are now designing their offices to balance common and social areas sometimes called:

   A. Caves and gardens.

   B. Caves and common.

   C. Pounds and common.

   D. Pounds and gardens.

4. Your project team has recently completed the 3rd iteration on the project. So far 45 story points have been successfully delivered to the customer. For this project, the iteration size is fixed at three weeks. The team (six team members) is dedicated to working five days per week. Looking at the backlog, you have 150 story points remaining to be delivered. How many more iterations are required to complete the project?

   A. 30

   B. 15

   C. 10

   D. 1

5. Individuals add padding to estimates because:

A. It is a good project management practice.

B. They expect to be beaten up if they are wrong.

C. It is a recognized scheduling risk mitigation method.

D. Scheduling buffers cannot be created until the activities are padded.

6. Halfway through the iteration, a senior team member has expressed his concern regarding a major risk. Although the probability of the risk occurrence is very low, the impact will be significant if the risk does occur. The team member has some mitigation ideas that need to be tested before being implemented. What should you do?

A. Ignore the risk as the probability is very low.

B. Organize an exploratory spike.

C. Add the risk to your watch-list.

D. Immediately implement the mitigation actions.

7. On Agile projects, how frequently is a release plan updated?

A. Updated every week or, at worst, after each iteration.

B. Updated on a daily basis as an output of daily standups.

C. The release plan is never updated during the course of the project.

D. Either after each iteration or, at worst, after every few iterations.

8. Chief architect, Chief programmer, Class owner, and Domain expert are some of the primary roles in which of the following Agile methods?

A. FDD

B. Kanban

C. Scrum

D. XP

9. Which of the following is a valid Agile project delivery framework?

A. Plan Do Check Act (PDCA)

B. Dynamic Systems Development Method (DSDM)

C. Define Measure Analyze Design Verify (DMADV)

D. Precedence Diagraming Method (PDM)

10. Which of the following activities mark the closure of an Agile project?

A. Project closure

B. Project retrospective

C. Release planning

D. Closure spike

11. The leader of a project that your company is running in another country is at the corporate headquarters for a company-wide project management meeting. During a break, you overhear the project lead discussing payments made to local municipal governments for construction permits for the project. Your company has a strict policy about paying or taking bribes. What should you do?

A. Report him to his manager.

B. Report him to PMI.

C. Notify his project stakeholders.

D. Do nothing.

12. During a planning poker meeting, estimators drew different cards for a particular story. What is the recommended next step if estimators come up with estimates that differ significantly?

A. The high and low estimators are asked to explain their estimates.

B. The high and low estimates are removed as outliers and average of the rest of the estimates is used.

C. The draw is declared invalid and a call for re-draw is made.

D. The median of all estimates is used as the story size.

13. You are leading an Agile project. The project includes producing a number of web apps for your customer. You collected performance data to help identify the causes of defects in the development process. Which technique should you use to analyze this data to determine the main source of the defects?

A. Statistical sampling

B. Defect repair review

C. Kaizen

D. Fishbone diagram

14. You are leading an Agile team developing a mission-critical healthcare system. You need to adapt an approach that requires developing detailed tests prior to commencing project work so that the work in progress is validated continuously. Which Agile approach should you consider?

A. Scrum

B. Scrum of Scrums

C. Test-Driven Development

D. Swarming

15. An Agile team is currently working with the product owner to define the release plan. Which of the following approaches would produce the highest return on investment (ROI)?

A. Allowing the Agile team to prioritize the backlog items.

B. Define a minimum viable product and prioritizing associated features.

C. Estimate the backlog items in ideal days instead of story points.

D. Estimate the expected velocity and the number of change requests per iteration.

16. Which of the following is NOT a typical advantage associated with estimating with story points in comparison to estimating with ideal days?

A. Estimating in story points is typically faster.

B. Estimating in story points results in consistent estimates across different teams and projects.

C. Story points are a pure measure of size.

D. Story point estimates do not decay with the change of team's skillset.

17. What are SMART goals?

A. Specific, Measurable, Attainable, Relevant, and Timely.

B. Sizeable, Methodological, Agile, Risk-free, and Tested.

C. Specific, Measurable, Agile, Relevant, and Timely.

D. Specific, Methodological, Agile, Robust and Time-boxed.

18. Jill is managing an organizational re-design project. Although the higher level operating model was approved by the project's steering committee, most of the project stakeholders lack a clear understanding of their requirements and are struggling to envision future processes and workflows. This has brought a great deal of uncertainty around project requirements and how to fulfil those requirements. Which of the following is a major project risk at this stage?

A. Initial project budget cannot be determined.

B. Initial project duration cannot be determined.

C. These uncertainties can contribute to high rates of change and project complexity.

D. These uncertainties would result in a big number of layoffs.

19. Which of the following is not an Agile recommended strategy regarding smoothing the flow of work?

A. Plan to the team's capacity.

B. Rank the user stories by business value.

C. Ask the team to work in pairs.

D. Stop multi-tasking and be dedicated to one team.

20. Your project team has recently been formed and is ready to initiate a website development project. The team now needs a product backlog to commission the project work. How many user stories need to be created at this stage of the project?

A. Only enough to understand the first release.

B. No more than 50 user stories should be created.

C. No more than 10 user stories should be created.

D. To cover the entire project scope.

21. For a particular outsourcing arrangement, the project team decided to keep mostly fixed items, e.g. warranties and arbitration, in the master agreement. However, more dynamic items such as scope, schedule, and budget can be formalized in a:

A. Team charter

B. Product backlog

C. Project charter

D. Lightweight statement of work

22. When project managers act as servant-leaders, the emphasis shifts from:

A. Managing coordination to facilitating collaboration.

B. Penalizing the worst to rewarding the best.

C. Planning project work to executing project work.

D. Executing project work to planning project work.

23. For a particular outsourcing arrangement, the project team decided to keep mostly fixed items, e.g. warranties and arbitration, in the master agreement. However, to allow flexibility in the customer-supplier relationship, other items subject to change, e.g. services rates and product descriptions, were listed separately in the schedule of services. When the entire contracting relationship is split across multiple documents, how can these documents be linked?

A. The master agreement can reference all other documents including the schedule of services.

B. When the entire contracting relationship is split across multiple documents these documents cannot be linked.

C. The schedule of services can reference all other documents including the master agreement.

D. When the entire contracting relationship is split across multiple documents these documents can be linked through a team charter.

24. Agile teams focus on rapid product development so that they get:

A. Detailed scope.

B. Continuously funded.

C. User stories.

D. Continuous feedback.

25. You are leading an Agile team developing a marketing website for a new entrant in the telecommunication industry. For this project, who is accountable for the development of the underlying database management system?

A. The Agile team

B. The database administrator

C. The product owner

D. The programmer

26. What is the present value of $100,000, paid exactly five years from now, if the investment's rate of return is 9%?

A. 45000

B. 145000

C. 64993

D. 153862

27. Team standup is considered one of the key Agile tools. What are these called in the Scrum framework?

A. Sprint

B. Sprint planning

C. Daily scrum

D. Increments

28. Which of the following are three common Agile roles?

A. Planners, developers and testers.

B. Cross-functional team members, product owner, and team facilitator.

C. Scrum masters, Scrum servants, and collaborators.

D. Generalists, specialists, and the project manager.

29. Agile teams use which of the following platforms to report work in process issues?

A. Daily standups

B. Sprint backlog

C. Risk register

D. Issue log

30. You have recently been hired by a construction company to help transform a traditional PMO into an Agile PMO. You want to schedule daily stand-ups but the team has no prior exposure to Agile methods. You call a quick training session on daily stand-ups. Which of the following should be included on the agenda?

A. Stand-ups vs. backlog grooming.

B. Stand-ups vs. retrospectives.

C. Stand-ups vs. sprints.

D. Stand-ups vs. status meetings.

31. Who do we call an "Agilist"?

A. Product owner

B. Agile practitioner

C. Agile coach

D. Agile Manifesto holder

32. You have asked a publisher to print some Agile principles on posters. When the posters were delivered, you found out that some of them had incorrect Agile principles printed on them. Which of the following posters has an incorrect Agile principle printed on it?

A. "Plan conservatively and deliver aggressively".

B. "Continuous delivery of valuable software".

C. "Focus on technical excellence".

D. "Working software is the primary measure of progress".

33. An Agile team is working on a SCM project. At the end of the 3rd iteration, the team had successfully delivered 81 story points. The team was able to successfully address some improvement opportunities and during the 4th iteration the team was able to deliver 39 story points. What was the team's velocity at the end of the 3rd iteration?

A. 30 story points per iteration.

B. 39 story points per iteration.

C. 120 story points per iteration.

D. 27 story points per iteration.

34. On a project involving multiple teams, which of the following Agile techniques helps in coordinating work and accommodating inter-team dependencies?

A. Rolling look-ahead planning.

B. Estimating expected velocity and comparing with observed velocity.

C. Merging related themes together into epics.

D. Merging related stories together into themes.

35. Who is responsible for task estimating during an iteration planning event?

A. The Agile team.

B. The servant-leader.

C. The team member responsible for the task.

D. The product owner.

36. Forecasting velocity based on the observed velocity on a project generally produces reliable estimates. If the project team has completed its first iteration and the observed velocity was 20 story points per iteration, what would be a reasonable estimate of velocity for the next iteration?

A. 12 to 32 story points per iteration.

B. 18 to 22 story points per iteration.

C. 16 to 25 story points per iteration.

D. 17 to 23 story points per iteration.

37. A project manager in a seller organization discovered that certain deliverables had been delivered to the buyer without undergoing proper testing. Recalling the deliverables will result in a cost overrun on the project. What should the project leader do in such a case?

A. Terminate the project.

B. Approach management to obtain additional funding to handle the potential cost overrun.

C. Recall the deliverables even though there will be a cost overrun.

D. Wait for the procuring organization to get back with their list of defects in the deliverables.

38. All of the following are valid Agile techniques to gather data about feelings in an iteration, release or project retrospective except:

A. Mad Sad Glad

B. Triple Nickels

C. Color Code Dots

D. Locate Strengths

39. The traditional project management approaches place the project manager at the center of coordination for the project and makes them responsible for the project tracking and reporting. However this approach is not suitable for:

A. Projects where detailed schedules are required to be developed and approved by the clients.

B. Low-change projects where detailed scope has been provided by the client organization.

C. High-change projects where there is more complexity than one person can manage.

D. Projects that require front-loaded planning work.

40. "Responding to change over following a plan" is one of the key Agile Manifesto values. Which of the following Agile approaches helps in achieving this value?

A. Servant-leader

B. Kanban boards

C. Backlog refinement

D. Self-organizing teams

PMI-ACP Lite Mock Exam 14 Answer Key and Explanations

1. A - The project manager is the servant-leader. The product owner can clarify requirements but usually cannot remove technical impediments. Consulting the HR department will be insane. It is recommended to consult a coach at this stage. [Agile Practice Guide, 1st edition, Page 58] [Problem Detection and Resolution]

2. B - When working on an Agile project, project managers shift from being the center to serving the team and the management. In an Agile environment, project managers are servant leaders, changing their emphasis to coaching people who want help, fostering greater collaboration on the team, and aligning stakeholder needs. [Agile Practice Guide, 1st edition, Page 38] [Agile Principles and Mindset]

3. B - While companies are moving toward open, collaborative work environments, organizations also need to create quiet spaces for workers who need uninterrupted time to think and work. Companies are now designing their offices to balance common and social areas sometimes called "caves and common". [Agile Practice Guide, 1st edition, Page 46] [Team Performance]

4. C - Since the team has successfully delivered 45 stories in three iterations, the velocity is 15 stories per iteration. There are 150 more story points to be delivered, which will require another 10 iterations (150/15). [Agile Practice Guide, 1st edition, Page 61] [Team Performance]

5. B - Individuals add padding to an estimate if they expect to be beaten up if they are wrong. A schedule buffer is different: A schedule buffer is a necessary margin of safety added to the sum of estimates from which local safety has been removed. [Cohn, M., 2006. Agile Estimating and Planning. 1st ed. Massachusetts: Pearson Education. Page 197] [Adaptive Planning]

6. B - If the impact is significant, the risk cannot be ignored. However, since the mitigation actions needs to be tested, an exploratory spike needs to be arranged. [Agile Practice Guide, 1st edition, Page 56] [Continuous Improvement]

7. D - The release plan is updated either after each iteration or, at worst, after every few iterations. [Cohn, M., 2006. Agile Estimating and Planning. 1st ed. Massachusetts: Pearson Education. Page 243] [Adaptive Planning]

8. A - Chief architect, Chief programmer, Class owner, and Domain expert are some of the primary roles in a Feature-Driven Development (FDD) project. [Agile Practice Guide, 1st edition, Page 108] [Value-driven Delivery]

9. B - Dynamic Systems Development Method (DSDM) is an Agile project delivery framework. Other choices are not Agile approaches. [Agile Practice Guide, 1st edition, Page 151] [Value-driven Delivery]

10. B - In Agile projects, typically a project retrospective is the last Agile event conducted. [Agile Practice Guide, 1st edition, Page 51] [Continuous Improvement]

11. D - Do nothing. Paying fees to government organizations to cover the administrative costs associated with issuing various types of permits is a common practice in many parts of the world. These payments are not considered bribes. PMI's code prohibits project managers from engaging in bribery, and it requires Agile team members to report others who do to the appropriate management. In this case, however, there is nothing to report. [PMI Code of Ethics and Professional Conduct] [Stakeholder Engagement]

12. A - If the estimates differ significantly, the high and low estimators explain their estimates. This helps the team in adjusting their estimates. [Cohn, M., 2006. Agile Estimating and Planning. 1st ed. Massachusetts: Pearson Education. Page 56] [Problem Detection and Resolution]

13. D - Fishbone diagrams break down the causes of the problem statement into discrete branches, helping to identify the main or root cause of the problem. [Derby, E. and Larsen, D., 2006. Agile Retrospectives: Making Good Teams Great. 1st ed. Texas: Pragmatic Bookshelf, Page 87] [Continuous Improvement]

14. C - Test-Driven Development is a technique where tests are defined before work is begun, so that work in progress is validated continuously, enabling work with a zero defect mindset. [Agile Practice Guide, 1st edition, Page 154] [Problem Detection and Resolution]

15. B - Through defining a minimum viable product and prioritizing associated features, the Agile team can quickly deliver a basic product that meets the basic needs of the stakeholders. Building a basic product and then enhancing it produces the highest return on investment (ROI). [Agile Practice Guide, 1st edition, Page 23] [Value-driven Delivery]

16. B - Story points are a pure measure of size and is typically faster than estimating in ideal days. Further, unlike ideal days estimates, story point estimates do not decay with the change of team's skillset. However, estimating in story points does not result in consistent estimates across different teams and projects, since there is no unit standard or baseline for estimating in story points. [Cohn, M., 2006. Agile Estimating and Planning. 1st ed. Massachusetts: Pearson Education. Pages 70-72] [Adaptive Planning]

17. A - SMART goals are Specific, Measurable, Attainable, Relevant, and Timely. [Derby, E. and Larsen, D., 2006. Agile Retrospectives: Making Good Teams Great. 1st ed. Texas: Pragmatic Bookshelf, Page 107] [Agile Principles and Mindset]

18. C - Initial project budget and duration might be difficult to determine, but it should still be possible. Rough order of magnitude estimates can be used if detailed requirements are not known early during the project. The project might or might not result in layoffs and no relevant information has been provided to determine this. However, since the project has significant uncertainties, this can contribute to high rate of change and project complexity. [Agile Practice Guide, 1st edition, Page 13] [Problem Detection and Resolution]

19. B - Ranking the user stories by business value is a product backlog grooming technique. However, this doesn't help in smoothing the work flow. On the other hand, the rest of the choices are valid work flow smoothing techniques. [Agile Practice Guide, 1st edition, Page 59] [Adaptive Planning]

20. A - There is no magic number regarding the number of user stories to be created at the start of any project. However, the entire project scope is not documented at this stage. Only enough user stories are created to understand the first project release. [Agile Practice Guide, 1st edition, Page 52] [Adaptive Planning]

21. D - It is recommended to separate more dynamic items such as scope, schedule and budget in a lightweight statement of work. None of the other choice capture this contracting information. [Agile Practice Guide, 1st edition, Page 77] [Value-driven Delivery]

22. A - Agile practices focus on collaboration. Planning and executing are critical activities and are part of any project regardless of the chosen delivery methodology. Penalizing or rewarding a few doesn't create an environment that helps everyone succeed. [Agile Practice Guide, 1st edition, Page 35] [Agile Principles and Mindset]

23. A - When the entire contracting relationship is split across multiple documents, the master agreement can reference all other documents including the schedule of services and link all document with each other. [Agile Practice Guide, 1st edition, Page 77] [Value-driven Delivery]

24. D - Agile teams focus on rapid product development so they can obtain feedback. [Agile Practice Guide, 1st edition, Page 39] [Agile Principles and Mindset]

25. C - On Agile projects, while some specialist might be engaged to develop some specific parts of the project, the overall team is responsible for the entire system development and all its components. However the accountability lies with the product owner. [Agile Practice Guide, 1st edition, Page 153] [Value-driven Delivery]

26. C - The formula is Present Value (PV) = Future Value (FV) / (1 + interest rate) ^ periods. So to calculate, PV = $100,000 / (1+9%)^5 = $64,993. [Cohn, M., 2006. Agile Estimating and Planning. 1st ed. Massachusetts: Pearson Education. Page 100] [Value-driven Delivery]

27. C - In the Scrum framework, daily standups are knows as daily scrums. [Agile Practice Guide, 1st edition, Page 101] [Value-driven Delivery]

28. B - Three common Agile roles are cross-functional team members, product owner, and team facilitator. [Agile Practice Guide, 1st edition, Page 40] [Value-driven Delivery]

29. A - Since the most effective and efficient way of conveying information to and within a team is face-to-face conversation, Agile teams report all work in process issues during the daily standups. [Agile Practice Guide, 1st edition, Page 98] [Problem Detection and Resolution]

30. D - The training session is on daily stand-ups so there is no point comparing these with retrospectives, backlog grooming, and sprints. Further, these comparisons don't even make any sense. However, stand-ups can be compared with traditional status meetings as teams who have traditionally worked in predictive environments may tend to fall into the trap of status reporting. [Agile Practice Guide, 1st edition, Page 54] [Adaptive Planning]

31. B - An Agilist is a person embracing the Agile mindset who collaborates with the like-minded colleagues in cross-functional teams. Also known as an Agile practitioner. [Agile Practice Guide, 1st edition, Page 150] [Value-driven Delivery]

32. A - "Plan conservatively and deliver aggressively" is not a valid Agile principle. The rest of the choices are all valid Agile principles. [Agile Practice Guide, 1st edition, Page 9] [Agile Principles and Mindset]

33. D - Velocity = average story points per iteration. At the end of the 3rd iteration, the team had delivered 81 story points. The velocity was 81/3 = 27 story points per iteration. [Agile Practice Guide, 1st edition, Page 61] [Team Performance]

34. A - On a project involving multiple teams, coordinate their work through rolling look-ahead planning. By looking ahead and allocating specific features to specific upcoming iterations, inter-team dependencies can be planned and accommodated. [Cohn, M., 2006. Agile Estimating and Planning. 1st ed. Massachusetts: Pearson Education. Page 250] [Adaptive Planning]

35. A - Although the best estimates come from those who will do the work, task estimating on an Agile project should be a group endeavor. Tasks are not allocated to individuals during iteration planning. [Cohn, M., 2006. Agile Estimating and Planning. 1st ed. Massachusetts: Pearson Education. Page 155] [Adaptive Planning]

36. A - The cone of uncertainty can be used to calculate the ranges of the estimates. If the team has completed the first iteration, the multipliers are 0.6 and 1.6. If the team has completed two iterations, the multipliers are 0.8 and 1.25. If the team has completed three iterations, the multipliers are 0.85 and 1.15. [Cohn, M., 2006. Agile Estimating and Planning. 1st ed. Massachusetts: Pearson Education. Page 178] [Team Performance]

37. C - It is the project team's primary responsibility to ensure that deliverables are tested and have gone through the process outlined in the test plan. The project leader should recall the deliverables, even if it involves a cost overrun. Approaching management may be the next step. Terminating the project is not called for, and it will be unethical to wait for the procuring organization to do their testing and find out the defects in deliverables. [PMI Code of Ethics and Professional Conduct] [Stakeholder Engagement]

38. B - All of the given choices except Triple Nickels are valid Agile techniques to gather data about feelings in an iteration, release or project retrospective. [Derby, E. and Larsen, D., 2006. Agile Retrospectives: Making Good Teams Great. 1st ed. Texas: Pragmatic Bookshelf, Pages 59, 61, 63] [Continuous Improvement]

39. C - Agile approaches are recommended for high-change projects. Such projects require cross-functional teams to coordinate their own work because usually such projects have more complexity than one person can manage. [Agile Practice Guide, 1st edition, Page 38] [Agile Principles and Mindset]

40. C - Backlog refinement allows the product owner to change project priorities in line with evolving business needs. This changes the focus from following a predefined plan to responding to change. [Agile Practice Guide, 1st edition, Page 97] [Agile Principles and Mindset]

PMI-ACP Knowledge Area Quiz: Agile Principles and Mindset Practice Questions

Test Name: Knowledge Area Test: Process Improvement
Total Questions: 15
Correct Answers Needed to Pass: 11 (73.33%)
Time Allowed: 25 Minutes

Test Description

This practice test specifically targets your knowledge of the Process Improvement knowledge area.

Test Questions

1. According to the Agile principles, the best architectures, requirements and designs emerge from the:

   A. Product owner.

   B. Project customers.

   C. Self-organizing team.

   D. Scrum master.

2. You have just been assigned as the project manager for a new project. The goal of the project is to improve the business operations so that the corporate ROI is increased by 5% in the next three years. What is the problem with this objective?

   A. It is not attainable.

   B. It is not specific.

   C. It is not measurable.

   D. It is not time bound.

3. You have been assigned a new project. The project involves disruptive technologies. The project scope is not clear which has introduced a lot of risk into the project. You have requested to use Agile to manage this project. Why?

   A. Agile techniques and approaches effectively manage disruptive technologies, scope changes and project risk.

   B. Agile techniques and approaches effectively manage disruptive technologies.

   C. Agile techniques and approaches effectively manage project risk.

   D. Agile techniques and approaches effectively manage scope changes.

4. What is the recommended risk attitude for Agile teams?

   A. Delay the development of risky items as much as possible.

   B. Avoid risk until more information becomes available.

   C. Take on the risk as early as possible.

   D. For any given iteration, select a mix of risky and risk-free features to be developed.

5. The Agile practices, tools and techniques are geared towards projects operating in environments that:

A. Control changes through a change request process.

B. Require upfront collection and definition of the bulk of the requirements.

C. Have high rates of change, complexity and risk.

D. Involve project work that heavily is driven by industry standards.

6. Which of the following roles doesn't fit the definition of an Agile servant-leader?

A. Team facilitator

B. Business owner

C. Project manager

D. Scrum master

7. Which of the following item is of highest priority for an Agile project?

A. An item that is required the most urgently.

B. An item that has the highest NPV.

C. An item that has the maximum number of assigned story points.

D. An item has the highest return on investment.

8. You are an Agile consultant hired by a construction firm. The firm wants to adopt Agile management approaches for all of its internal process improvement projects. You are currently developing a number of checklists that the organization can use while initiating projects. Which of the following doesn't influence the effectiveness of an Agile team?

A. Team members' locations

B. Team size

C. Project complexity

D. Team members' availability

9. One of the 12 Agile principles requires that, "At regular intervals, the team reflects on how to become more effective, then tunes and adjusts its behavior accordingly". Which of the following Agile techniques help achieve this?

A. Chartering the project and the team

B. Backlog refinement

C. Retrospectives

D. Daily standups

10. One of the 12 Agile principles states that, "Business people and developers must work together daily throughout the project". Which of the following Agile techniques helps achieve this?

A. Kanban boards

B. Retrospectives

C. Backlog preparation and refinement

D. Daily standups

11. According to the Agile principles, when should the business people interact with the project team?

A. During the start and the end of the project.

B. Daily throughout the project.

C. During the release and iteration planning.

D. During the release planning.

12. All Agile teams need servant-leadership on the team. Which of the following is usually not considered a servant-leadership skill?

A. Facilitation

B. Impediment removal

C. Backlog grooming

D. Coaching

13. Which of the following attributes of an Agile team help the team develop and deliver often?

A. Dedicated people.

B. Collocation.

C. Cross-functional team members.

D. Stable work environment.

14. "Simplicity – the art of maximizing the amount of work not done is essential" is one of the 12 fundamental principles of Agile. Which of the following Agile techniques helps realize this principle?

A. Retrospectives

B. Backlog preparation and refinement

C. Kanban boards

D. Daily standups

15. Agile approaches could be alternatively defined as a:

A. Continuous cost management approach

B. Continuous risk management approach

C. Continuous stakeholder management approach

D. Continuous time management approach

PMI-ACP Knowledge Area Quiz: Agile Principles and Mindset Answer Key and Explanations

1. C - According to the Agile principles, the best architectures, requirements, and designs emerge from self-organizing teams. [Agile Practice Guide, 1st edition, Page 9] [Agile Principles and Mindset]

2. B - The objective is measurable (ROI to be increased by 5%) and time-bound (to be achieved in three years). The scenario doesn't give further information to determine if this is attainable or not, generally speaking this doesn't look like a daunting task. The problem with the goal is that it is not specific as it doesn't address which operations to target. Are we aiming to increase revenue or decrease cost? [Derby, E. and Larsen, D., 2006. Agile Retrospectives: Making Good Teams Great. 1st ed. Texas: Pragmatic Bookshelf, Page 107] [Agile Principles and Mindset]

3. A - Agile techniques and approaches effectively manage disruptive technologies, scope changes and project risk. [Agile Practice Guide, 1st edition, Page 2] [Agile Principles and Mindset]

4. C - One of the greatest risk to most projects is the risk of building the wrong product. This risk can be dramatically reduced by developing those features early. [Cohn, M., 2006. Agile Estimating and Planning. 1st ed. Massachusetts: Pearson Education. Page 83] [Agile Principles and Mindset]

5. C - The Agile practices are geared towards high-uncertainty projects that have high rates of change, complexity and risk. Traditional approaches require upfront scope definition and performing an integrated change control process. [Agile Practice Guide, 1st edition, Page 7] [Agile Principles and Mindset]

6. B - A servant-leader on Agile projects may be called a project manager, scrum master, project team lead, team coach, or team facilitator. Business owners are external to Agile teams. [Agile Practice Guide, 1st edition, Page 41] [Agile Principles and Mindset]

7. A - This is a tricky question. Although higher ROI and NPV are always desirable scenarios, all business priorities do not have to be financially lucrative, e.g., a new government legislation requiring a business change. An item that is required the most urgently, due to any reason, will always be the highest priority item. [Agile Practice Guide, 1st edition, Page 56] [Agile Principles and Mindset]

8. C - Project complexity might influence the project durations, costs, risks and other attributes. However, the project complexity should not influence the effectiveness of an Agile team. However, the team size, members' locations and availability can influence the team's effectiveness. [Agile Practice Guide, 1st edition, Page 39] [Agile Principles and Mindset]

9. C - Retrospectives are used by Agile teams to reflect upon their way of working and to continuously improve it. Daily standups on the other hand, are used to communicate and make team commitments. Backlog refinement and chartering activities do not have a focus on continuous improvement. [Agile Practice Guide, 1st edition, Page 98] [Agile Principles and Mindset]

10. C - Backlog preparation and refinement are the activities where the business (product owner) and the developers (Agile team) work together to define and prioritize project objectives. The rest of the choices are tools used by Agile teams not necessarily with the direct involvement of the business. [Agile Practice Guide, 1st edition, Page 98] [Agile Principles and Mindset]

11. B - According to the Agile principles, business people and developers must work together daily throughout the project. [Agile Practice Guide, 1st edition, Page 9] [Agile Principles and Mindset]

12. C - Servant-leadership skills include facilitation, coaching, and impediment removal. Backlog grooming is a usually associated with product owners. [Agile Practice Guide, 1st edition, Page 41] [Agile Principles and Mindset]

13. C - An Agile Team consists of cross-functional members who have the capability and power to deliver business value in short Iterations. The team includes the individuals necessary to successfully deliver business value. [Agile Practice Guide, 1st edition, Page 40] [Agile Principles and Mindset]

14. B - Kanban boards are used to manage an Agile team's work in progress. Retrospectives are team reflection points conducted at regular intervals. Daily standups are used by Agile teams to communicate and make team commitments. Backlog preparation and refinement are the activities conducted jointly by Agile teams and the product owner to prioritize project deliverables by the order of business value. This allows Agile teams to focus only on high-value deliverables. [Agile Practice Guide, 1st edition, Page 98] [Agile Principles and Mindset]

15. B - Agile approaches could be alternatively defined as a continuous risk management approach. Risk management is a distinct component of traditional project management and teams new to Agile are sometimes concerned that Agile approaches do not address risk management. This is not correct since risk management is built into Agile approaches and are not separate processes and procedures. The short iterations, single-minded focus on working product, hefty emphasis on testing and validation, and frequent customer deliveries help teams manage project risks. [Cohn, M., 2006. Agile Estimating and Planning. 1st ed. Massachusetts: Pearson Education. Page 5] [Agile Principles and Mindset]

PMI-ACP Lite Mock Exam 15 Practice Questions

Test Name: PMI-ACP Lite Mock Exam 15
Total Questions: 40
Correct Answers Needed to Pass:
30 (75.00%)
Time Allowed: 60 Minutes

Test Description

This is a cumulative PMI-ACP Mock Exam which can be used as a benchmark for your PMI-ACP aptitude. This practice test includes questions from all exam topic areas, including sections from Agile Tools and Techniques, and all three Agile Knowledge and Skills areas.

Test Questions

1. During which stage of a retrospective event, should you conduct the ROTI activity?

A. Setting the stage

B. Generate insights

C. Gathering data

D. Closing

2. If an Agile team has got a solid release plan and each iteration is started with a robust iteration plan, what is the need for the team do conduct daily planning?

A. Daily planning is still required to make team commitments.

B. Daily planning is still required to fine-tune the release plan.

C. Daily planning is still required to fine-tune the product backlog.

D. Daily planning is not required if robust release and iteration plans have been developed.

3. A relative asks you to submit his resume for a job opening at the company where you work as an Agile coach. You know this position will also be used as a resource on your project. What do you do?

A. Submit the resume but do not disclose that you are a relative.

B. Submit the resume and notify the appropriate management and stakeholders that you are a relative of the person.

C. Ask another coworker to submit the resume.

D. Advise your relative it is a conflict of interest for you to submit the resume.

4. Which of the following represents the expected money (revenue) the project will generate once completed?

A. Discounted cash flows

B. Net cash flows

C. Net present value

D. Return on investment

5. A government agency has awarded your company a massive software project. This project has an early completion incentive, and your company has a policy of paying a bonus to the project team if such an incentive is awarded. However, this particular government agency has a reputation for being extremely difficult to work with; there is a great deal of bureaucracy within this agency and stonewalling and hostility toward contractors are common. The project leader will need to have excellent political skills to lead this project successfully. You have been asked to lead the project because of your expertise with this type of project. However, you have never worked within such a highly charged and political environment. What should you do?

A. Decline the project citing lack of experience.

B. Accept the project.

C. Accept the project and request that a corporate liaison be assigned to your project.

D. Accept the project but disclose your lack of experience in this type of environment.

6. An Agile team has been working on a system design and development project for the last 8 months. The project sponsor is not happy as he though the project would be completed within 6 months. Although the team's throughput has been steady, a number of features have been added during the course of the project which pushed the project completion. Which of the following tools can be used by the project team to show this scenario to the project sponsor?

A. Feature burnup/burndown chart

B. Daily standup minutes

C. Team charter

D. Product backlog

7. Most projects have either too little or too many features. It is often impossible to do everything that everyone wants in the time allowed. If you face such a challenge on your project, how would you resolve this?

A. Ask the customers to prioritize the features based on their desirability.

B. Ask the Agile team to prioritize the features based on their convenience.

C. Ask the servant-leader to prioritize the features based on story points.

D. Ask the product owner to prioritize the features based on business value.

8. You have recently joined an organization that has recently adopted Agile methods for project management. Since these tools and methods are new to the organization, most of the project teams are currently going through a steep learning curve. For most of the internal projects, the project team lacks a clear purpose or mission for the project. How can this issue be resolved?

A. Develop project and team charters for all on-going projects.

B. Conduct daily standups.

C. Encourage communications.

D. Arrange professional training in Agile.

9. You are leading an Agile team currently analyzing and documenting enterprise-level processes for an organization. In order to review drafted processes as early as possible and get a just-in-time feedback, which XP technique can be tailored and applied?

A. Sensitivity analysis

B. Backlog grooming

C. Demonstrations

D. Pair programming

10. For any given user story, which of the following equations always holds?

A. Lead time = response time + cycle time

B. Cycle time = lead time + response time

C. No equation can be established

D. Response time = lead time + cycle time

11. Some projects may require tailoring to Agile approaches. However, prior to attempting tailoring, care must be taken to ensure:

A. Tailoring is undertaken by the project team.

B. Tailoring is undertaken by the servant-leader and approved by the product owner.

C. Tailoring is undertaken by experienced practitioners who have been successfully using Agile approaches.

D. Tailoring is either undertaken or approved by the product owner.

12. You have recently been hired by a pharmaceutical company to design and build an ERP system for the company. The system is supposed to cover the end-to-end operations of the business. Due to the complexity and size of the project, the project team needs a product roadmap that shows the anticipated sequence of deliverables over time. Who is responsible for producing this roadmap?

A. Scrum master

B. Product owner

C. Agile team

D. Servant-leader

13. You have just finished your meeting with the project sponsor who has identified new project priorities. You have worked with the sponsor to assign relative priorities of the newly identified features. What should you do next?

A. Work with the sponsor and estimate ideal days.

B. Ask the project sponsor to provide a formal change request.

C. Re-estimate the items in the backlog.

D. Perform integrated change control.

14. You have recently taken over a project that is halfway through the execution. You are not happy with the team's throughput. You have also noticed that each team member is multi-tasking and has, on average, five concurrently assigned tasks. What should you do?

A. Reschedule the project so that each team member has only one task to perform at any given point in time.

B. Add new team members so that overall project productivity gets increased.

C. Call a team meeting and discuss ways to limit multi-tasking to two tasks.

D. Increase the number of task assignments per team member so that overall project productivity gets increased.

15. Few project members are disgruntled about the technology selected for use on your project and are venting their frustration in the daily standup meeting. What do you do?

A. Ask them to escalate the issue to the product owner.

B. Ask them to explain how the technology they are advocating will be a bigger benefit to the project than the selected technology.

C. Do nothing. The decision is already made.

D. Remind them that the technology was selected as a team effort.

16. What is the "cycle time" of an item?

A. The time that an item waits until the work starts.

B. The time required to process an item.

C. Average story points per iteration.

D. The total time it takes to deliver including the waiting time.

17. Which of the following approaches CANNOT be used to show the variability in the estimates?

A. Providing a mean and the standard deviation of the estimate.

B. Providing a range of estimates.

C. Providing the mean and the median of the estimate.

D. Drawing hurricane-style charts.

18. Some projects may require tailoring to Agile approaches. Which of the following is NOT a tailoring good practice?

A. Evaluating a change on an iteration or two first before adopting it permanently.

B. Discussing the change with the people it will impact and agree on a course of action.

C. Reviewing the effectiveness of tailoring during retrospectives.

D. Undertaking tailoring in collaboration with the product owner instead of the project team.

19. Which of the following is a set of related user stories treated as a single entity for either estimating or release planning?

A. Theme

B. Account

C. Epic

D. Tale

20. Some projects are undertaken to generate revenue, cut expenses or both. On such projects, financial analysis plays an important role in prioritizing themes and features. Who is primarily responsible for forecasting the financial value of a theme or a feature?

A. Scrum master

B. Agile coach

C. Agile team

D. Product owner

21. During a backlog grooming event, the Agile team has tagged a couple of user stories as high-risk features due to the involved untested technology and ambiguous customer requirements. How should you deal with these high-risk items?

A. Conduct a detailed quantitative risk analysis.

B. Schedule these features to be developed during the early project iterations.

C. Conduct a detailed sensitivity analysis.

D. Schedule these features to be developed during the later project iteration.

22. Which of the following is a predictability measure for an Agile team?

A. Story points

B. Cycle time

C. Burnups

D. Burndowns

23. All of the following approaches can be adopted to improve velocity EXCEPT:

A. Extend iteration duration.

B. Increase stakeholder engagement.

C. 100% allocated resources to the project.

D. Limit work in process.

24. You are leading a complex knowledge work project in an organization with 20,000+ employees. Due to the magnitude of the project, ever-changing stakeholder requirements, and evolving organizational priorities, you decided to schedule bi-weekly team events aimed at improving project processes. What are these events called?

A. Kaizen

B. Poka-Yoke

C. 5S

D. Muda

25. You are leading a complex Agile project. During the project kick-off meeting, the team is considering the frequency of delivery. Based on the project conditions, you and the team believe that the delivery frequency can be planned from a couple of weeks to a couple of months. What frequency should you select?

A. One month; this will be the expected average.

B. This cannot be determined based on the information provided.

C. Couple of weeks; this is shortest possible timescale.

D. Couple of months; this will allow the least distraction.

26. Which of the following is NOT recommended when splitting large user stories in order to fit an iteration?

A. Splitting a large story by separating the functional and non-functional aspects into separate stories.

B. Splitting a large story along the boundaries of the data supported by the story.

C. Splitting a large story into smaller stories if the priorities of the smaller stories are different.

D. Splitting a large story into its constituent tasks.

27. You are leading an enterprise-wide project than involves a lot of knowledge work. You and the team are currently determining the ideal project management approach for the project. Which of the following Agile measures for estimating user stories is generally recommended if the external stakeholders interested in project estimates are not well-versed with Agile methods?

A. Cycle time

B. Velocity

C. Story points

D. Ideal days

28. Which of the following is a unit-less Agile metric?

A. Story Point

B. Lead Time

C. Cycle Time

D. Ideal Days

29. The HR Policies and Procedures project team has just submitted a progress report. The Agile team has completed 120 features so far and the project's SPI is 1.2. What is the number of planned features the team was supposed to complete?

A. 144 features.

B. 120 features.

C. 100 features.

D. This figure cannot be computed with the given data.

30. An Agile team is currently developing an inventory control system. Two programmers on the team are arguing and recommending different development approaches. One is of the view that the system should be built from scratch, while the other believes that the existing system should be enhanced and patched. How should you resolve this conflict?

A. Select the patch work approach as that will save time for the organization.

B. Ask the entire team to analyze both approaches and select the one that will deliver higher business value.

C. Ask the product owner to choose the right approach.

D. Develop the product from scratch as that will bring the system closer to requirements.

31. Agile approaches recommend keeping estimates of size and duration separate by:

A. Using different teams to estimate size and duration.

B. Using different units.

C. Estimating size at the start of an iteration and estimating duration by the end of the iteration.

D. Using historical data to estimate size and using the Agile teams to estimate the duration.

32. While forming an Agile team for a complex project, which of the following is desirable?

A. Self-organized, cross-functional team.

B. Focus on individual throughput.

C. Specialists for each function.

D. Majority of I-shaped team members.

33. You were halfway through your project when the product owner left the company. The new product owner has been assigned to the project but they come from a different part of the business. What should you do first?

A. Send a copy of all project documents created so far on the project to the new product owner.

B. Don't engage the product owner until the current iteration finishes and you are ready to demonstrate the results.

C. Give a detailed progress presentation to the product owner and invite them to the daily standups.

D. Meet with the new product owner and groom the entire product backlog.

34. A new CEO has taken office and has assigned you an interesting project. The goal of the project is to identify ways to increase the revenue and/or decrease the costs in a way that the stock price of the company increases by 100% on an annual basis for the next five years (which is the term of the new CEO). What might be a problem with this objective?

A. It is not attainable.

B. It is not time bound.

C. It is not specific.

D. It is not measurable.

35. A team is currently engaged with a complex software product development. This team has completed similar projects in the past on a waterfall approach, however this time the team has decided to try an Agile approach. The team decided to use Agile to deliver this project because:

A. Earlier projects were not successful.

B. The project involves knowledge work and involves learning while delivering value.

C. Earlier projects were not completed under budget.

D. Earlier projects were not completed by the deadlines.

36. Which of the following is the correct core property of the Kanban method?

A. Limit work in progress.

B. Accelerate work in progress.

C. Slowdown work in progress.

D. Halt work in progress.

37. Which of the following Agile methods provides a product development framework that is an adaption of Toyota Product System (TPS) principles and practices to the software development domain and is based on a set of principles and practices for achieving quality, speed, and customer alignment?

A. Toyota Software Development (TSD)

B. TPS Enabled Software Lifecycle (TSL)

C. Large Scale Scrum (LeSS)

D. Lean Software Development (LSD)

38. An organization has historically rewarded managers for departmental efficiencies rather than end-to-end flow of organizational processes. This has resulted in departments working in silos. If you have to undertake an Agile project in this organization, which of the following challenges are you most likely to face?

A. Creating cross-functional teams and acquiring the top-performing resources.

B. Developing the project and the team charter.

C. Collecting user stories and developing a feature chart.

D. Training the team members on effective use of Agile methods.

39. Impact mapping helps organizations determine which products to develop. It is a technique for building shared understanding between leaders and project teams. In Agile projects, who leads this work?

A. Servant-leader

B. Product owner

C. Scrum master

D. Agile team

40. Your organization can either invest $50,000 in upgrading a production control system or invest this money in a bond that yields a 6% annual interest, compounded monthly. What is the future value of $50,000 invested in the bond at the end of three years?

A. 59000

B. 50000

C. 9834

D. 59834

PMI-ACP Lite Mock Exam 15 Answer Key and Explanations

1. D - ROTI stands for Return on Time Invested. This technique is used in the closing retrospective phase for iteration or release retrospectives. It helps generate feedback on the retrospective process and gauge the effectiveness of the session from the team members' perspectives. At the end of retrospective, the retrospective leader asks the team members to give feedback on whether they spent their time well. [Derby, E. and Larsen, D., 2006. Agile Retrospectives: Making Good Teams Great. 1st ed. Texas: Pragmatic Bookshelf, Page 124] [Team Performance]

2. A - Daily planning is still required. Teams make, assess, and revise their plans during these meetings. During daily meetings, teams constrain the planning horizon to be no further away than the next day, when they will meet again. Daily meetings are also used to make team commitments. [Cohn, M., 2006. Agile Estimating and Planning. 1st ed. Massachusetts: Pearson Education. Page 28] [Adaptive Planning]

3. B - Submit the resume and notify all appropriate management and project stakeholders that the candidate is a relative. Once they have been advised of the circumstances, they can best determine how to proceed. PMI's Code of Ethics and Professional Conduct mandates that Agile practitioners refrain from participating in any decision-making process where there is a possible conflict of interest. [PMI Code of Ethics and Professional Conduct] [Stakeholder Engagement]

4. D - Return on Investment (ROI) is the expected money the project will generate once completed. On the other hand, NPV and discounted cash flows are future cash flows represented in present values and are usually less than the sum of actual cash flows. [Cohn, M., 2006. Agile Estimating and Planning. 1st ed. Massachusetts: Pearson Education. Page 100] [Value-driven Delivery]

5. D - Accept the position but disclose your lack of experience with this type of environment. PMI's Code of Ethics and Professional Conduct requires that Agile practitioners accept only those projects for which they have the appropriate qualifications and background. However, if the project stakeholders receive full disclosure and still give their consent, it is permissible to accept a stretch assignment. [PMI Code of Ethics and Professional Conduct] [Stakeholder Engagement]

6. A - Team charter and daily standup minutes cannot help much in addressing the issue at hand. The product backlog can only show the current state and how it has changed over time. A feature burnup/burndown chart can show how requirements grew during the project. The total features line shows how the project's total features changed over time. [Agile Practice Guide, 1st edition, Page 67] [Team Performance]

7. D - Although asking the end users to prioritize the features based on their desirability looks tempting, many times the project team does not have direct access to the end users. In Agile projects, the product owner, representing the business/customers, is asked to prioritize the features based on their business value. [Cohn, M., 2006. Agile Estimating and Planning. 1st ed.

Massachusetts: Pearson Education. Page 134] [Adaptive Planning]

8. A - The problem at hand is lack of clarity on project's purpose and mission. This clarity can be provided by developing project and team charters. Other choices are good things to do, but these don't solve the problem at hand. [Agile Practice Guide, 1st edition, Page 58] [Problem Detection and Resolution]

9. D - Pair programming is an XP technique that requires one programmer to review the code as the second programmer writes the code. This allows just-in-time feedback. This technique can be tailored to process work as one process analyst is drafting a process, a second analyst reviews the work. [Agile Practice Guide, 1st edition, Page 153] [Problem Detection and Resolution]

10. A - Response time is the time that an item waits until work starts. Cycle time is the time required to process the item. Lead time is the total time it takes to deliver an item, measured from the time it is added to the board to the moment it is completed (response time + cycle time). [Agile Practice Guide, 1st edition, Page 64] [Value-driven Delivery]

11. C - The key success factor with regards to tailoring is that it must be undertaken by experienced practitioners who have been successfully using Agile approaches. What role does it is a secondary consideration. [Agile Practice Guide, 1st edition, Page 119] [Value-driven Delivery]

12. B - The product owner is responsible for grooming the product backlog and producing the roadmap. [Agile Practice Guide, 1st edition, Page 52] [Value-driven Delivery]

13. C - You have got new priorities and their relative rankings. What you don't have is the priorities of these new items relative to the items already in the backlog. You need to work with your team now and re-estimate these new items together with the items in the backlog. [Cohn, M., 2006. Agile Estimating and Planning. 1st ed. Massachusetts: Pearson Education. Page 61] [Stakeholder Engagement]

14. C - Adding new team members may be required but first you need to eliminate the waste from the current work practice. Multi-tasking exacts a horrible toll on productivity. Clark and Wheelwright (1993) studied the effect of multi-tasking and found that the time an individual spends on value-adding work drops rapidly when the individual is working on more than two tasks. With two value-adding tasks, if a team member becomes blocked on one task, he/she can switch to the other task. Productivity increases as the number of concurrent assigned tasks decreases until the optimal point is reached (80% productivity) when an individual only performs two independent value-adding tasks. (Note that observed productivity while performing a single task is only 70%.) [Cohn, M., 2006. Agile Estimating and Planning. 1st ed. Massachusetts: Pearson Education. Page 15] [Team Performance]

15. B - Ask them to explain how the technology will provide a bigger benefit to the project. PMI's Code of Ethics requires Agile practitioners to listen to the points of view of others and seek to understand them. [PMI Code of Ethics and Professional Conduct] [Stakeholder Engagement]

16. B - Cycle time is the time required to process an item. [Agile Practice Guide, 1st edition, Pages 61, 64] [Value-driven Delivery]

17. C - Variation can be statistically be shown using standard deviation. Agile approaches provide a range of estimates to show the variation. Hurricane-style charts are also used to graphically show the magnitude of the variation. However, both the mean and the median are measures of central tendency and do not show variance. [Agile Practice Guide, 1st edition, Page 61; Cohn, M., 2006. Agile Estimating and Planning. 1st ed. Massachusetts: Pearson Education. Pages 175, 193] [Adaptive Planning]

18. D - Tailoring should be undertaken in collaboration with the team members or whoever the change is likely to impact. Ignoring the project team is not a good practice. [Agile Practice Guide, 1st edition, Page 120] [Value-driven Delivery]

19. A - A set of related user stories combined together (usually by a paper clip if working with note cards) and treated as a single entity for either estimating or release planning is referred to as a theme. [Cohn, M., 2006. Agile Estimating and Planning. 1st ed. Massachusetts: Pearson Education. Page 53] [Adaptive Planning]

20. D - Forecasting the financial value of a theme is the responsibility of the product owner. Agile teams do share the responsibility but the primary responsibility sits with the product owner. [Cohn, M., 2006. Agile Estimating and Planning. 1st ed. Massachusetts: Pearson Education. Page 89] [Value-driven Delivery]

21. B - One of the greatest risk to most projects is the risk of building the wrong product. This risk can be dramatically reduced by developing those features early. [Cohn, M., 2006. Agile Estimating and Planning. 1st ed. Massachusetts: Pearson Education. Page 83] [Adaptive Planning]

22. B - Burnups and burndowns are capacity measures, while lead time and cycle time are predictability measures. Measuring story points is not the same as measuring completed stories or features which is against Agile Principles. [Agile Practice Guide, 1st edition, Page 66] [Value-driven Delivery]

23. A - Agile requires time-boxed iterations; extending iteration duration is not allowed. The rest of the choices will help improve the team's velocity. [Agile Practice Guide, 1st edition, Pages 25, 61] [Team Performance]

24. A - Kaizen are small events attended by the owners and operators of a process to make improvements to that process which are within the scope of the process participants. [Agile Practice Guide, 1st edition, Page 152] [Continuous Improvement]

25. C - According to the Agile principles, the shortest possible delivery timescale should be selected. [Agile Practice Guide, 1st edition, Page 9] [Adaptive Planning]

26. D - You can choose any method that can help you split a large user story into smaller user stories that fit project iterations. However, it is not recommended to split a user story into its constituent tasks and fitting tasks to iterations. [Cohn, M., 2006. Agile Estimating and Planning. 1st ed.

Massachusetts: Pearson Education. Page 125] [Adaptive Planning]

27. D - Cycle time and velocity are not user stories sizing measures. In this case, ideal days is recommended because it makes intuitive sense and is easier to explain outside the team. [Cohn, M., 2006. Agile Estimating and Planning. 1st ed. Massachusetts: Pearson Education. Page 72] [Adaptive Planning]

28. A - A Story Point is a unit-less measure used in relative user story estimation techniques. The rest of choices are all time-based units. [Agile Practice Guide, 1st edition, Page 154] [Adaptive Planning]

29. C - Since SPI = completed features/planned features this means Planned Features = Completed Features/SPI = 120/1.2 = 100 features. This means the team delivered more stories than planned. [Agile Practice Guide, 1st edition, Page 69] [Team Performance]

30. B - This has to be a team decision. Ask the entire team to analyze both approaches and select the one that will deliver higher business value. [Agile Practice Guide, 1st edition, Page 4] [Value-driven Delivery]

31. B - The best way to maintain a clear distinction between an estimate of size and one of duration is to use separate units that cannot be confused. Estimating size in story points and translating size into duration using velocity is an excellent way of doing this. [Cohn, M., 2006. Agile Estimating and Planning. 1st ed. Massachusetts: Pearson Education. Page 248] [Adaptive Planning]

32. A - In Agile teams, we prefer a team of self-organizing, T-shaped, cross-functional team generalists. The focus is on team's throughput rather than on individual throughputs. [Agile Practice Guide, 1st edition, Page 42] [Value-driven Delivery]

33. D - The product owner is the owner of the product backlog and is ultimately accountable for the outcome of the project. At this stage, it is critical for you to review the entire backlog with the new product owner and ensure that they agree with the current ranking of stories. [Agile Practice Guide, 1st edition, Page 41] [Problem Detection and Resolution]

34. A - The objective is time-bound (five years), measurable (100% increase on a year to year basis), and specific (increase in the stock price). However, such a sustained rate of increase seems highly unlikely. [Derby, E. and Larsen, D., 2006. Agile Retrospectives: Making Good Teams Great. 1st ed. Texas: Pragmatic Bookshelf, Page 107] [Agile Principles and Mindset]

35. B - The scenario doesn't given enough information regarding the previous projects' outcomes. We cannot determine if the previous projects were completed on time or not. Similarly, we cannot determine if the previous projects were completed under the budget or not. The answer to this question should be a general benefit of using Agile approaches on software development projects. Software product development, like other knowledge work, is about learning while delivering value. This is most probably the reason why the team has selected Agile on this project. [Agile Practice Guide, 1st edition, Page 61] [Value-driven Delivery]

36. A - Kanban boards also help in increasing productivity and quality by limiting work in progress. [Agile Practice Guide, 1st edition, Page 103] [Value-driven Delivery]

37. D - Lean Software Development (LSD) is an adaption of Toyota Product System (TPS) principles and practices to the software development domain and is based on a set of principles and practices for achieving quality, speed, and customer alignment. [Agile Practice Guide, 1st edition, Page 152] [Continuous Improvement]

38. A - Developing charters, collecting user stories, and training the project team do not depend on the organizational culture. We need to look for a choice that has a direct relation with the problem at hand; departmental silos. In this organization, the biggest challenge will be to form a cross-functional team and acquire top-performing resources as functional managers are more focused on departmental KPIs rather than organizational excellence. [Agile Practice Guide, 1st edition, Page 74] [Agile Principles and Mindset]

39. B - Typically the product owner leads the impact mapping work. A servant-leader may facilitate any necessary meeting as a way of serving the project. [Agile Practice Guide, 1st edition, Page 52] [Value-driven Delivery]

40. D - The formula is: Future Value (FV) = Present Value (PV) * (1 + interest rate)^periods. So to calculate, FV = $50,000 * (1 + 6%/12) ^ 36 = $59,834. [Cohn, M., 2006. Agile Estimating and Planning. 1st ed. Massachusetts: Pearson Education. Page 100] [Value-driven Delivery]

PMI-ACP Lite Mock Exam 16 Practice Questions

Test Name: PMI-ACP Lite Mock Exam 16
Total Questions: 40
Correct Answers Needed to Pass:
30 (75.00%)
Time Allowed: 60 Minutes

Test Description

This is a cumulative PMI-ACP Mock Exam which can be used as a benchmark for your PMI-ACP aptitude. This practice test includes questions from all exam topic areas, including sections from Agile Tools and Techniques, and all three Agile Knowledge and Skills areas.

Test Questions

1. You are your Agile team are currently decomposing the stories into smaller stories and tasks to be completed in the next three weeks. Which Agile planning meeting is this?

   A. Retrospective

   B. Daily scrum

   C. Iteration planning

   D. Release planning

2. Mike is the chief programmer on a software development project. He has been asked to prepare some compliance documentation for the upcoming ISO audit. Mike somehow managed to expand the scope of the programming work so that it filled almost all of his time and left him with the bare minimum of time to prepare for the audit. This behavior is commonly known as:

   A. Pareto's Law

   B. Parkinson's Law

   C. Programmer's Law

   D. Boyles' Law

3. Which of the following tasks is generally recommended to be performed prior to starting an iteration?

   A. Developing a precise story development schedule.

   B. Specifying the requirements in detail.

   C. Establishing a formal change control process.

   D. Identification of the conditions of satisfaction for the user stories.

4. An Agile team is currently working on a complex ERP customization and deployment project. The team is currently facing an issue with deploying a couple of features as the recipient department is not yet ready for the changeover. Which Scrum role is responsible for removing this impediment?

   A. Development team

   B. Business analyst

   C. Scrum master

   D. Product owner

5. Agile teams complete the features usually in the form of user stories. The teams periodically demonstrate the working product to the product owner who accepts or declines the stories. In flow-based Agile, when are these demonstrations conducted?

   A. At the end of the iteration.

   B. When enough features have accumulated into a set that is coherent.

   C. At the end of the project.

   D. During retrospectives.

6. You are managing a complex project with loosely defined requirements. By the end of each iteration, the number of story points delivered is offset by the addition of new requirements. Using a burndown chart in this situation is not indicating the team's actual progress. What alternative method can be used in this case?

   A. Show the burndown chart as a histogram and show additional scope below the horizontal axis.

   B. Show the burndown chart as a histogram and show additional scope above the bars.

   C. Show the burndown chart without the additional scope.

   D. Show the burndown chart as a histogram and show additional scope next to the bars.

7. Which of the following statements correctly describes the attitude of Agile teams towards changing requirements?

   A. Agile teams do not welcome change but not changing requirements.

   B. Agile teams welcome changing requirements during the start of the project.

   C. Agile teams welcome changing requirements during project planning.

   D. Agile teams welcome changing requirements, even late in development.

8. A common misconception is that Agile teams do not estimate work as traditional teams do. This is incorrect. Which of the following statements is correct regarding estimating in Agile projects?

   A. The team limits its estimation to the next four to six weeks at most.

   B. The team limits its estimation to the next few sprints at most.

   C. The team limits its estimation to the next few weeks at most.

   D. The team limits its estimation to the next three to four weeks at most.

9. A dedicated Agile team is currently working on an ERP system customization and deployment project five days a week. Each iteration is time-boxed at three weeks. A total of 500 story points were estimated at the start of the project. The team has recently completed its 4th iteration on the project and have successfully delivered 30 story points during this iteration. So far, the team has delivered a total of 120 story points on the project. If no new stories have been added to the project since initiation, what

was the cycle time (in days) for the 30 stories delivered during the last iteration?

A. 9

B. 12

C. 2

D. 0.5

10. During a sprint retrospective, you are conducting a Five Whys activity to unearth underlying causes to some of the issues. Surprisingly, after the forth "Why?" you all seem to be agreeing on the identified root cause. What needs to be done?

A. Continue and ask the fifth "Why".

B. There is nothing wrong with this–root causes can be identified earlier than the fifth "Why".

C. There is something wrong about your assumptions–engage the product owner.

D. There is something wrong with your approach–restart the activity.

11. Which of the following is a prime responsibility of a servant-leader in an Agile organization?

A. Hiring and firing of employees.

B. Designing the rewards and penalties program.

C. Developing organizational policies and procedures.

D. Facilitate team's discovery and definition of Agile.

12. Agile's approach to project management is more suitable for projects that involve:

A. Definable work.

B. Exploratory work.

C. Procedures that have proven successful on past projects.

D. Low level of execution uncertainty and risk.

13. Which of the following is not a valid philosophy of the Agile Manifesto?

A. Individuals and interactions are valued over change control.

B. Customer collaboration is valued over contract negotiation.

C. Responding to change is valued over following a plan.

D. Working software is valued over comprehensive documentation.

14. You need to send out meeting invitations for your project's first retrospective meeting. Who should be on your mandatory participants list?

A. The team, the servant-leader, and the product owner.

B. The team and the servant-leader.

C. The team

D. The team, the servant-leader, the product owner, and the customer.

15. The only project artifacts you have is a project charter, a team charter and a product roadmap. You need the product backlog to move ahead. How do you get your product backlog?

A. By directing the team to develop the backlog from the team charter.

B. By requesting the product owner to provide the backlog.

C. By progressively decomposing the roadmap into smaller requirements.

D. By directing the team to develop the backlog from the project charter.

16. What is the time-box of an iteration?

A. The average time a story takes to get developed.

B. The time period assigned for an iteration to complete.

C. The time it takes for an average size story to get developed.

D. The maximum time allowed for an iteration to be stretched.

17. An Agile team has been divided into small groups. In the groups, each person has five minutes to brainstorm and write down ideas individually. At the end of five minutes, each person passes the paper to the person on his or her right. That person has five minutes to write down ideas that build on the ideas already written on the paper. This process is repeated until the paper returns to the original writer. The team is conducting which of the following Agile activities?

A. Affinity diagrams

B. Triple Nickels

C. Precedence diagrams

D. Working agreements

18. Which of the following is NOT a typical output of the release planning process?

A. Identified risks

B. Backlog

C. Product vision

D. Release plan

19. What enables an Agile team to deliver successful projects?

A. Detailed planning

B. Self-organization

C. Collocation

D. Contract negotiation

20. The payback period measures the amount of time required to earn back the initial investment and doesn't consider any further cash inflows. Despite this disadvantage, this method is used on projects that have:

A. High upfront costs

B. Long execution duration

C. Significant risk

D. Limited resources

21. Your team has just completed the first sprint on the project and is preparing for a demonstration of the completed features. Who do you need to invite for the demonstration to accept or reject the features?

A. Scrum master

B. Project manager

C. Sponsor

D. Product owner

22. An organization has been successfully using Agile approaches on all of its projects for the last three years. It has been proposed to develop standardized templates for user stories, test cases, cumulative flow diagrams, etc. to add further value to the organization. What is the best approach to develop these standardized tools and templates?

A. Use the tools and templates used on the most recent project.

B. Use the tools and templates from the most successful project.

C. Hire a consultant to design Agile tools and templates.

D. Setup an Agile PMO with a mandate to develop standardized tools and templates.

23. You are helping a software development team transition from traditional to Agile approaches. You tell the team that the single most important attribute of any product or feature is:

A. The velocity at which the team takes on the development of that product or feature.

B. The time required to deliver the product or feature.

C. The value customers associate with that product or feature.

D. The ideal days estimated to develop the minimum viable product or feature.

24. Ideally all Agile team members should be 100% dedicated to the project. While this condition is ideal, it sometimes cannot be met. What is the key problem when team members are not 100% dedicated?

A. Multi-tasking and task switching impacts the team's ability to delivery consistently.

B. It creates a conflict of interest.

C. Team cannot focus on high-value requirements.

D. Individual throughput per hour is reduced.

25. Some projects may require tailoring to Agile approaches. However, a team that is new to Agile approaches needs to start using established Agile approaches before tailoring these approaches or to invent a new custom approach. This concept is in line to which of the following improvement model?

A. Kaizen model

B. Shu-Ha-Ri model

C. Salience model

D. PDCA model

26. You are managing a critical project for your organization. The board of directors has asked for a quick presentation on the project and has asked you to show the anticipated sequence of project deliverables over time. What should you present to the board?

A. Product roadmap

B. Product backlog

C. Iteration burndown chart

D. User stories

27. Most projects with multiple teams will benefit from estimating in a common unit and establishing a baseline meaning for that unit. Which of the following activities is NOT considered a good practice in this regards?

A. Estimates should be equivalent regardless of which team estimates the work.

B. Sub-teams are responsible for establishing a common baseline for their estimates.

C. Each user story is estimated by all sub-teams.

D. All sub-teams meet at the start of the project and choose between story points and ideal days.

28. The law of diminishing marginal returns is applicable to which type of the following features?

A. Delighters

B. Must-have

C. Exciters

D. Performance

29. Your organization is currently going through tough times. Due to the recent increase in prices of raw materials the overall production cost has gone up and the company cannot increase the price of finished goods due to intense market competition. The CEO has asked you to deploy a state-of-the-art ERP system. The goal of the project is to automate the management and control processes so that employees' morale is raised and the company can couple up with current economic challenges. The CEO has allowed you a reasonable duration of eight months to implement the new system. What is the problem with the project's objective?

A. It is not relevant.

B. It is not attainable.

C. It is not specific.

D. It is not time bound.

30. Which of the following statements regarding Agile approaches is correct?

A. An Agile approach can be developed from scratch as long as it adheres to the mindset, values and principles of the Agile Manifesto.

B. Agile approaches mandate the use of a Kanban board to manage the team's work in progress.

C. Agile approaches mandate preparing and refining a product backlog and then developing it in small batches.

D. Agile approaches mandate the use of daily standups and end of sprint retrospectives.

31. Which of the following is a product quality technique whereby the design of a product is improved by enhancing its maintainability and other desired attributes without altering its expected behavior?

A. Design of Experiments

B. Refactoring

C. Monte Carlo Analysis

D. House of Quality

32. You are managing a complex enterprise-wide project. If the project completion date has been fixed, how would you reflect the project uncertainty in the release plan?

A. Reverting back to traditional project management approaches.

B. Pushing the team to crash the project and shifting the focus from quality control.

C. Classifying the requested features as "must have" and "good to have".

D. Developing the release plan in a way that 90% or more of the team effort is spent on development.

33. The time-box for the current iteration has expired. All of the following activities must now be organized except:

A. Grooming the backlog

B. Conducting a spike event

C. Conducting a retrospective

D. Conducting a demonstration

34. Which of the following Agile tools is used to visualize the progress of work items through a project?

A. Poke Yoke

B. Spike

C. Andon

D. Kanban

35. Which retrospective activity will you perform if you want to help the team gauge how well they are doing on a variety of measures, such as engineering practices, team values, or other processes?

A. Working agreements

B. Team charter

C. Mad Sad Glad

D. Team radar

36. If an Agile project's SPI is greater than the project's CPI, and the CPI is less than 1.0, what can you infer about the project's schedule performance?

A. The project is behind schedule.

B. This cannot be determined with the given data.

C. The project is ahead of schedule.

D. Agile projects do not have Earned Value measurements.

37. Once the problem (variation) has been identified, the next step is to uncover the underlying root cause (source). Fishbone diagrams break down the causes of the problem statement into discrete branches, helping to identify the main or root cause of the problem. All of the following are acceptable ways to label the "bones" of the fish EXCEPT:

A. Stories, Epics, Themes, Backlogs

B. Surroundings, Suppliers, Systems, Skills

C. Place, Procedures, People, Policies

D. Methods, Machines, Materials, Staffing

38. Which of the following is LEAST helpful in estimating the financial return on a theme?

A. Estimating story points.

B. Estimating the timing of sales increases.

C. Estimating the average value of a sale.

D. Estimating number of sales.

39. "Customer collaboration over contract negotiation" is one of the key Agile Manifesto values. Which of the following Agile approaches helps in achieving this value?

A. Agile measurements

B. Daily standups

C. Backlog refinement

D. Backlog preparation

40. An Agile team has recently been assigned to design and deploy an ERP system for an external organization. During the project kick-off meeting, the team stressed the flow of value through rapid feature delivery to the customer. All of the following are the benefits of this mindset except:

A. Teams finish valuable work faster.

B. Teams waste much less time because they multi-task.

C. People are more likely to collaborate.

D. Teams deliver earlier return on investment through rapid feature delivery.

PMI-ACP Lite Mock Exam 16 Answer Key and Explanations

1. C - Iteration planning is conducted at the start of each iteration. During iteration planning we talk about the tasks that will be needed to transform a feature request into working and tested software during the iteration, which is typically 2 to 6 weeks in duration. [Cohn, M., 2006. Agile Estimating and Planning. 1st ed. Massachusetts: Pearson Education. Page 28] [Adaptive Planning]

2. B - This is commonly known as Parkinson's Law (1957), which states that, "Work expands so as to fill the time available for its completion." [Cohn, M., 2006. Agile Estimating and Planning. 1st ed. Massachusetts: Pearson Education. Page 12] [Team Performance]

3. D - Usually, an Agile team begins an iteration with vaguely defined requirements and turns those vague requirements into functioning, tested software by the end of the iteration. Developing a detailed schedule and a formal change control process is generally not recommended. However it is recommended to define the conditions of satisfaction for the user stories that are planned to be developed during the iteration. [Cohn, M., 2006. Agile Estimating and Planning. 1st ed. Massachusetts: Pearson Education. Page 201] [Adaptive Planning]

4. C - The scrum master is responsible for ensuring the Scrum process is upheld and works to ensure the Scrum team adheres to the practices and rules as well as coaches the team on removing impediments. [Agile Practice Guide, 1st edition, Page 101] [Value-driven Delivery]

5. B - In flow-based Agile, the team demonstrates completed work when it is time to do so, usually when enough features have accumulated into a set that is coherent. [Agile Practice Guide, 1st edition, Page 55] [Value-driven Delivery]

6. A - Showing the burndown chart without the additional scope is not recommended. A reasonable approach would be to show the burndown chart as a histogram and show additional scope below the horizontal axis. That way the team's progress can be shown according to the original scope and, at the same time, the increase in scope can also be shown. [Cohn, M., 2006. Agile Estimating and Planning. 1st ed. Massachusetts: Pearson Education. Page 214] [Team Performance]

7. D - Agile teams welcome changing requirements, even late in development. Agile processes harness change for the customer's competitive advantage. [Agile Practice Guide, 1st edition, Page 9] [Agile Principles and Mindset]

8. C - There is no fixed duration for the estimation span. However, the team limits its estimation to the next few weeks at most. [Agile Practice Guide, 1st edition, Page 61] [Adaptive Planning]

9. D - Cycle time = number of days per delivered story. 30 stories were delivered in three weeks; that is 10 stories per week. Since the dedicated team works five days a week, the cycle time per story was 5 days / 10 stories = 0.5 days per delivered story. [Agile Practice Guide, 1st edition, Pages 61, 64] [Team Performance]

10. B - There is nothing wrong with this–root causes can be identified earlier than the fifth "Why". [Derby, E. and Larsen, D., 2006. Agile Retrospectives: Making Good Teams Great. 1st ed. Texas: Pragmatic Bookshelf, Page 85] [Continuous Improvement]

11. D - The question is explicitly asking for a responsibility of servant-leadership in an Agile setting, which is facilitating the team's discovery and definition of Agile. The rest of the choices are typical responsibilities of any leadership and cannot be attributed to the Agile servant-leadership mindset. [Agile Practice Guide, 1st edition, Page 33] [Agile Principles and Mindset]

12. B - The Agile practices are geared towards high-uncertainty projects that have high rates of change, complexity and risk. [Agile Practice Guide, 1st edition, Page 7] [Agile Principles and Mindset]

13. A - According to the Agile Manifesto, individuals and interactions are valued over processes and tools and not over change control. [Agile Practice Guide, 1st edition, Page 8] [Agile Principles and Mindset]

14. B - The team and servant-leader are required to attend the retrospective meeting. The participation of the product owner is optional. The customers do not attend the retrospectives. [Agile Practice Guide, 1st edition, Page 51] [Continuous Improvement]

15. C - The product backlog is developed by bringing the team and the product owner together and progressively decomposing the product roadmap. [Agile Practice Guide, 1st edition, Page 58] [Value-driven Delivery]

16. B - The iteration time-box is the period assigned for each project iteration to complete. Each iteration is terminated at the expiry of the time-box. [Agile Practice Guide, 1st edition, Page 25] [Value-driven Delivery]

17. B - This is an example of "Triple Nickels". The purpose of the "Triple Nickels" activity is to generate ideas for actions or recommendations and uncover important topics about the project history. [Derby, E. and Larsen, D., 2006. Agile Retrospectives: Making Good Teams Great. 1st ed. Texas: Pragmatic Bookshelf, Page 56] [Continuous Improvement]

18. C - The project vision is developed prior to the commencement of release planning. It is an input to the release planning process and is not an output of this process. [Cohn, M., 2006. Agile Estimating and Planning. 1st ed. Massachusetts: Pearson Education. Page 131] [Adaptive Planning]

19. B - One attribute that makes Agile teams stand out from traditional teams is self-organization. In Agile, the team manages its work process and its work product. That self-management and self-organization applies to everyone serving and supporting the organization and project. [Agile Practice Guide, 1st edition, Page 36] [Agile Principles and Mindset]

20. C - There are two primary advantages to using a payback period: first, the calculations and interpretations are straightforward; second, it measure the amount and duration of financial risk taken on by the organization. The larger the payback period, the riskier the project because anything could change during that period. [Cohn, M., 2006. Agile Estimating and Planning. 1st ed.

Massachusetts: Pearson Education. Page 104] [Value-driven Delivery]

21. D - The product owner sees the demonstration and accepts or declines developed features. [Agile Practice Guide, 1st edition, Page 55] [Value-driven Delivery]

22. D - Setup an Agile PMO with a mandate to develop standardized tools and templates. Once the PMO has been setup, it can decide the source of the tools and templates and can help standardization. [Agile Practice Guide, 1st edition, Page 82] [Problem Detection and Resolution]

23. C - A successful project, product or feature is the one that delivers value to the customer. Customers usually do not care how teams develop products, however they do care if the product delivers value to them or not. [Agile Practice Guide, 1st edition, Page 4] [Value-driven Delivery]

24. A - Focusing on high-value requirements is an absolute must on Agile projects, regardless of the presence of a dedicated team. The project's overall throughput gets increased due to dedicated team members but that shouldn't affect individual throughput per hour. Further, this doesn't create any conflicts of interest. In the absence of a dedicated team, the project's throughput is decreased which impacts the team's ability to deliver consistently. [Agile Practice Guide, 1st edition, Page 43] [Value-driven Delivery]

25. B - The Shu-Ha-Ri model of skills acquisition describes progression from obeying the rules (Shu means to obey and protect), through consciously moving away from the rules (Ha means to change or digress), and finally through steady practice and improvement finding an individual path (Ri means to separate or leave). [Agile Practice Guide, 1st edition, Page 119] [Value-driven Delivery]

26. A - A product roadmap shows the anticipated sequence of deliverables over time. [Agile Practice Guide, 1st edition, Page 52] [Stakeholder Engagement]

27. C - It is recommended that each user story is estimated by one team, however care must be taken to ensure that estimates are consistent and equivalent. [Cohn, M., 2006. Agile Estimating and Planning. 1st ed. Massachusetts: Pearson Education. Page 200] [Adaptive Planning]

28. B - According to the Kano model, once some amount of a must-have feature has been implemented, customer satisfaction cannot be increased by adding more of that feature. Also, no matter how much of a must-have feature is added, customer satisfaction never rises above the mid-point. We can observe the law of diminishing marginal returns on such features. [Cohn, M., 2006. Agile Estimating and Planning. 1st ed. Massachusetts: Pearson Education. Page 110] [Value-driven Delivery]

29. A - The problem with the project objective is that it is not relevant. Even if the new ERP system somehow results in increased employee morale, this doesn't contribute to the current economic problem associated with the increased cost of raw materials. [Derby, E. and Larsen, D., 2006. Agile Retrospectives: Making Good Teams Great. 1st ed. Texas: Pragmatic Bookshelf, Page 107] [Agile Principles and Mindset]

30. A - It is not necessary to use any of the established Agile approaches; an Agile approach can be developed from scratch as long as it adheres to the mindset, values, and principles of the Agile Manifesto. [Agile Practice Guide, 1st edition, Page 99] [Agile Principles and Mindset]

31. B - Refactoring is a product quality technique whereby the design of a product is improved by enhancing its maintainability and other desired attributes without altering its expected behavior. [Agile Practice Guide, 1st edition, Page 153] [Continuous Improvement]

32. C - If the date is fixed, the project uncertainty is expressed about the exact functionality to be delivered. Classifying the requested features as "must have" and "good to have" allows the team some degree of flexibility. [Cohn, M., 2006. Agile Estimating and Planning. 1st ed. Massachusetts: Pearson Education. Page 248] [Adaptive Planning]

33. B - Spikes events are organized when required. These do not need to be organized at the end of each iteration. The rest of the choices are the activities that need to be organized after each iteration. [Agile Practice Guide, 1st edition, Page 56] [Problem Detection and Resolution]

34. D - A Kanban board provides a means to visualize the flow of work, make impediments easily visible, and allow flow to be managed by adjusting the work in process limits. [Agile Practice Guide, 1st edition, Page 31] [Value-driven Delivery]

35. D - Team radars help the team gauge how well they are doing by tracking individual and group ratings for specific factors about process or development practices they want to examine. [Derby, E. and Larsen, D., 2006. Agile Retrospectives: Making Good Teams Great. 1st ed. Texas: Pragmatic Bookshelf, Page 71] [Continuous Improvement]

36. B - This cannot be determined with the given data. For example CPI can be 0.5 and the SPI can be 0.6 implying the project is behind schedule. Similarly the CPI can be 0.9 and SPI can be 1.1 implying the project is ahead of schedule. [Agile Practice Guide, 1st edition, Page 69] [Team Performance]

37. A - Typical categories are: methods, machines, materials, staffing; places, procedures, people, policies; and surroundings, suppliers, systems, skills. [Derby, E. and Larsen, D., 2006. Agile Retrospectives: Making Good Teams Great. 1st ed. Texas: Pragmatic Bookshelf, Page 87] [Continuous Improvement]

38. A - Estimating story points helps in sizing user stories and themes. However, this doesn't help much in estimating the financial return on a theme. [Cohn, M., 2006. Agile Estimating and Planning. 1st ed. Massachusetts: Pearson Education. Page 80] [Adaptive Planning]

39. A - Agile measurements measure value delivered to the customer rather than how the project is performing against project baselines. This shifts the focus from the contract to the customer. [Agile Practice Guide, 1st edition, Page 97] [Agile Principles and Mindset]

40. B - The optimized flow of value results due to reduction in waste by tackling one thing at a time instead of multi-tasking. [Agile

Practice Guide, 1st edition, Page 39] [Agile Principles and Mindset]

PMI-ACP Lite Mock Exam 17 Practice Questions

Test Name: PMI-ACP Lite Mock Exam 17
Total Questions: 40
Correct Answers Needed to Pass: 30 (75.00%)
Time Allowed: 60 Minutes

Test Description

This is a cumulative PMI-ACP Mock Exam which can be used as a benchmark for your PMI-ACP aptitude. This practice test includes questions from all exam topic areas, including sections from Agile Tools and Techniques, and all three Agile Knowledge and Skills areas.

Test Questions

1. Which of the following is an acceptable use of Gantt charts for Agile projects?

A. Each project task on the Gantt chart has a dedicated task calendar.

B. Gantt charts stop at the feature level and does not decompose each user story into its constituent tasks.

C. All project tasks are estimated before being mapped on a Gantt chart.

D. All project tasks mapped on the Gantt chart are resource loaded.

2. Project "ERP" has a duration of 10 years and an NPV of $600,000, Project "Database" has a duration of two years and an NPV of $580,000, Project "Restructure" has a duration of eight years and an NPV of $550,000 and project "Cost Saving" has a duration of seven years and an NPV of $500,000. Which project is the most lucrative?

A. Project "Restructure"

B. Project "Database"

C. Project "ERP"

D. Project "Cost Savings"

3. You have been hired by an organization to introduce Agile to its project management office. During one of your initial presentations to the team you have been asked a tough question: Is Agile an approach, a method, a practice, a technique, or a framework? What should be your response?

A. Agile is neither an approach nor a framework, however it contains some methods and techniques.

B. Agile is an approach and not a framework, it contains methods and techniques.

C. Any or all of these terms could apply depending on the situation.

D. Agile is a framework that contains methods and techniques.

4. Which of the following is not an Agile mitigation strategy for the risk of degraded code quality?

A. Agile modeling.

B. Refactoring.

C. Choice of programming language.

D. Definition of done.

5. You are currently managing a complex project that requires a lot of knowledge work. You want some sort of visual management system that can help you visualize the flow of work, make impediments easily visible, and allow flow to be managed by adjusting the work-in-process limits. Which of the following tools can help you in this regard?

A. 5S

B. Sprint retrospective

C. Kanban board

D. Product backlog

6. Which of the following is the ordered list of all the work, presented in story form, for a team?

A. Backlog

B. Team charter

C. Epics

D. User stories

7. When Agile teams provide their own units of measure for story points, teams are better able to assess and estimate and deliver their work. However, the downside of relative estimation is that:

A. There is no way to compare teams or add velocity across teams.

B. Project risk is increased due to indigenously crafted units.

C. This is a violation of the Agile Manifesto.

D. Various tools such as burndown charts and Kanban boards cannot be used.

8. An Agile team is currently not meeting the product owner's throughput requirements. The team proposes creating smaller features so that the net throughput can be increased. What is your view on this demand?

A. Cycles times do not change with feature size.

B. The team's demand is not legitimate.

C. Smaller features have smaller cycle times.

D. Bigger features should have smaller cycle times.

9. What is the difference between IRR and NPV?

A. IRR is expressed as a percentage value, while the NPV is not.

B. IRR is risk-free measure, while the NPV is not.

C. IRR is used for capital budgeting, while the NPV is not.

D. IRR is a financial measure, while the NPV is not.

10. You have recently acquire a new team member. Today the team member came to you and suggested trying a new planning approach. How should you respond?

A. Advise the team member to focus on responding to change rather than following a plan.

B. Discard the current approach and adopt the new approach.

C. Try the new planning approach at the next opportunity.

D. Coach the team member on Agile estimating techniques used by the team.

11. Which of the following events is typically the ending point of an Agile project?

A. Planning poker.

B. Project retrospective.

C. End of project spike.

D. Backlog cleaning.

12. If an Agile team discovers a new management approach that could potentially reduce the cycle time of all stories. Which of the following Agile metrics will subsequently be impacted?

A. The lead time will be negatively impacted.

B. The response time will be positively impacted.

C. The lead time will be positively impacted.

D. The response time will be negatively impacted.

13. Which of the following is NOT a correct interpretation of the Agile Manifesto:

A. Business people and developers must work together daily throughout the project.

B. Customer satisfaction is the highest priority.

C. Shorter delivery cycles are preferred.

D. Changing requirements are welcomed more at the start of the project than late in development.

14. Which of the following conditions may stop a team from pulling work from the "Ready" state to the "WIP" state?

A. WIP limits are met.

B. Team's velocity starts to drop.

C. Product demonstration generated negative feedback.

D. New scope has been added.

15. The interest rate used to discount future values into present values is also known as:

A. Direct cost

B. Cost of quality

C. Opportunity cost

D. Total cost of ownership

16. Which of the following is a hybrid framework that allows teams to use Scrum as a framework and Kanban for process improvement?

A. Agile UP

B. Crystal

C. Scrumban

D. DSDM

17. Rather than formalizing an entire contracting relationship in a single document, Agile teams recommend documenting the mostly fixed items in a master agreement and separating all other items subject to change. Isolating the more changing elements of a contractual relationship:

A. Simplifies modifications and thus flexibility.

B. Encourages modifications and thus makes the contract redundant.

C. Over-simplifies contracting and thus increases risk.

D. Complicates contracting and thus decreases risk.

18. You have just completed a solid waste management project in an underdeveloped country. The contractor you are working for has a strict policy of abiding by local laws and rules although the local resources working on the project have a much laxer approach to following laws and policies. Now at the end of the project, you are handing over the operational equipment to the local operators and disposing of the leftover inventory and other materials that were used during the project. More than 50 percent of the toxic materials used during the project remains in your inventory. There is no law that would prohibit you from disposing of either the type or quantity of remaining materials in the local sewage system. What should you do?

A. Do not dispose of the materials improperly.

B. Abandon the materials in the project facility you are handing over to the local operators.

C. Give the material to local resources to dispose of by selling it to a recycling facility.

D. Dispose of the material in the local sewage system; there is no law applicable here.

19. You are responsible for designing and a new handheld gadget followed by a mass rollout to the market. The project has been requested as a result of your organization's blue ocean strategy, and if successful, will creating a market for its own. However there is a high degree of uncertainty around the requirements which can only be uncovered through prototyping. Which of the following approaches is most likely to succeed?

A. Using an Agile approach for both design and rollout.

B. Using a predictive approach for both design and rollout.

C. Using a hybrid model; predictive approach for the design phase followed by an Agile approach for the rollout.

D. Using a hybrid model; Agile approaches for the design phase followed by a predictive approach for the rollout.

20. Forming a cross-functional and dedicated Agile team is recommended for complex and high-change projects. This helps in:

A. Shortening development cycles.

B. Providing feedback from inside the team.

C. Limiting work in progress.

D. Creating bigger teams.

21. Traditional approaches such as Gantt charts, PERT charts, or WBS focus on the tasks needed to create a product. On the other hand, Agile approaches focus on:

A. Agility

B. Speed

C. Change

D. Features

22. You have just taken over a project from another project lead about six months into a 12-month project. As you get to know the staff on the project, you become aware that five staff members are relatives of the previous project lead. What do you do?

A. Report the HR manager to PMI.

B. Interview these five employees.

C. Notify your project stakeholders there is a possibility that nepotism was behind some of the staffing decisions made on your project.

D. Check recruitment records of all employees.

23. George is the project manager managing an ERP implementation project for a client organization. Given the complexity of the project, George must rely on tailored project management processes and tools. However, at the same time, George needs to be agile and quickly adapt to requested changes. According to the Agile Manifesto, which of the following should take preference over the project management processes and tools?

A. Comprehensive documentation.

B. Contract negotiation.

C. Individuals and interactions.

D. Project management plan.

24. When conducting a Five Whys analysis, you as the retrospective leader, must ensure that:

A. The team has collected the necessary data to support the analysis.

B. The team is disintegrated prior to using this technique.

C. The team is aware of the technique.

D. The team is penalized upon discovery of lapses.

25. Which of the following is a simplistic version of the Rational Unified Process (RUP) and is an understandable approach to developing business application software using Agile techniques and concepts?

A. Agile Unified Process

B. Agility Driven Rational Unified Process

C. Rational Rose Process

D. Agile Rational Process

26. The best task estimates come from:

A. The Agile coach.

B. The entire team.

C. Those who will do the work.

D. The product owner.

27. You are leading a green-field ERP system design and development project. It is critical that each team member's work products are frequently integrated and validate with one another. Which Agile technique should you encourage the team to use?

A. Continuous WIP

B. Continuous Integration

C. Continuous Improvement

D. Continuous Delivery

28. What is the "lead time" of an item?

A. Average story points per iteration.

B. The total time it takes to deliver an item including the wait time.

C. The time that an item waits until the work starts.

D. The time required to process an item.

29. During the first iteration, your team developed four features (sized at three story points each) but was only able to test and deliver three features. The testing and delivery activities for each user story was estimated at two story points. What was your team's velocity for the first iteration?

A. 15 story points

B. 6 story points

C. 12 story points

D. 18 story points

30. At a sprint retrospective the Agile team has identified a number of risks that can have serious implications on the project. Unfortunately there is no way these risks can be mitigated. How should you manage these risks?

A. Add the risks to your watch list and continuously monitor these risks.

B. Add the risks to the iteration backlog.

C. Add the risks to the product backlog.

D. Do nothing as these risks cannot be mitigated.

31. Halfway during a project, the product owner hands over a high-priority list of features that need to be urgently developed. These features are large in size and none of these can be fully developed in any single iteration. What should you do?

A. Decompose the big features into smaller stories and prioritize these at the top of the backlog.

B. Decompose the big features into smaller stories and schedule all of them for the next iteration.

C. Group the related features into themes and increase the iteration duration.

D. Reject the features unless the product owner comes up with manageable story sizes.

32. Which of the following is a project acceleration and collaboration technique whereby any team member is authorized to modify any project work product or deliverable?

A. Extreme Programming.

B. Chaotic Development.

C. Collective Code Ownership.

D. Kanban Development.

33. Which of the following is a critical problem with traditional approaches to planning?

A. Traditional approaches are plan-driven.

B. Traditional approaches focus on the completion of activities rather than on the delivery of features.

C. Traditional approaches measure the progress against plans.

D. Traditional approaches use Gantt charts instead of a product backlog.

34. Agile teams frequently refer to a "Servant-Leadership" model. What does this mean?

A. Providing enterprise-wide training sessions.

B. Hiring servants for the organizational leadership.

C. Practice of leading through service to the team.

D. Providing leadership to organizational servants.

35. During the first iteration, the Agile team realizes that the project is not as easy as they earlier estimated. There is an immediate need for review of the project management approach. What should you do?

A. Re-estimate the backlog.

B. Reprioritize the backlog.

C. Call a retrospective.

D. Try a spike event.

36. Which of the following is not one of the eight guiding principles of the DSDM framework?

A. Develop a detailed project schedule

B. Focus on the business need

C. Deliver on time

D. Never compromise quality

37. A product backlog, a sprint backlog, and increments are Agile project artifacts in which of the following Agile approaches?

A. XP

B. Kanban

C. Scrum

D. Lean

D. DA

38. Your project team has recently completed the 3rd iteration on the project. So far 45 story points have been successfully delivered to the customer. For this project, the iteration size is fixed at three weeks. The team (six team members) is dedicated to working five days per week. Looking at the backlog, you have 150 story points remaining to be delivered. What is the project's current velocity?

A. 30

B. 10

C. 1

D. 15

39. Which of the following techniques can be used to identify underlying root causes and can be used in conjunction with an activity that generates themes or a list of potential problems, for example Patterns and Shifts?

A. Five Whys

B. 7Ws

C. Kanban

D. Kaizan

40. Which of the following is NOT considered a scaled Agile or Lean framework?

A. Scrum

B. LeSS

C. SAFe

PMI-ACP Lite Mock Exam 17 Answer Key and Explanations

1. B - The difference between traditional and Agile approaches to Gantt charts is that, in Agile approach, the chart stops at the feature level and does not decompose each use story into its constituent tasks. [Cohn, M., 2006. Agile Estimating and Planning. 1st ed. Massachusetts: Pearson Education. Page 231] [Stakeholder Engagement]

2. C - When the NPV of a project is computed, the duration of the project is factored in to the calculations. Therefore, the project with the highest NPV, Project "ERP", is the most lucrative. [Cohn, M., 2006. Agile Estimating and Planning. 1st ed. Massachusetts: Pearson Education. Page 100] [Value-driven Delivery]

3. C - Agile can be viewed as an approach, a method, a practice, a technique, or a framework depending on the context of use. [Agile Practice Guide, 1st edition, Page 11] [Agile Principles and Mindset]

4. C - The choice of programming language doesn't influence the quality of the code. The rest of the choices are valid mitigation strategies. [Agile Practice Guide, 1st edition, Page 58] [Value-driven Delivery]

5. C - A Kanban board provides a means to visualize the flow of work, make impediments easily visible, and allow flow to be managed by adjusting the work-in-process limits. [Agile Practice Guide, 1st edition, Page 31] [Problem Detection and Resolution]

6. A - Backlog is the ordered list of all the work, presented in story form, for a team. [Agile Practice Guide, 1st edition, Page 52] [Adaptive Planning]

7. A - When Agile teams provide their own units of measure for story points, teams are better able to assess and estimate and deliver their work. However, the downside of relative estimation is that there is no way to compare teams or add velocity across teams. [Agile Practice Guide, 1st edition, Page 67] [Team Performance]

8. C - Each feature is unique, so its cycle time is unique. However, smaller features have smaller cycle times. Further, the scenario doesn't provide enough context to determine the legitimacy of the team's demand. [Agile Practice Guide, 1st edition, Page 66] [Value-driven Delivery]

9. A - Subtracting the present value of all future cash inflow from the initial investment provides the net present value (NPV) of the investment, it's a numeric value and not expressed as a percentage. [Cohn, M., 2006. Agile Estimating and Planning. 1st ed. Massachusetts: Pearson Education. Pages 100, 101] [Value-driven Delivery]

10. C - Agility is all about responding to changes in environment. If the team member has come up with a new idea, that must be tested at the next opportunity. Discarding the current approach without testing the new one would be irrational. [Agile Practice Guide, 1st edition, Page 8] [Adaptive Planning]

11. B - The final event should be a project retrospective where the team discusses its processes and improvement opportunities for the future projects. Planning poker is a planning activity that happens during the

project. The other two choice are just made up terms. [Agile Practice Guide, 1st edition, Page 51] [Continuous Improvement]

12. C - The lead time is the total time it takes to deliver an item, measured from the time it is added to the board to the moment it is delivered. Cycle time is the time required to process an item. Lead time = response time + cycle time. If the cycle time is reduced, the lead time should also reduce. [Agile Practice Guide, 1st edition, Page 64] [Problem Detection and Resolution]

13. D - Changing requirements are welcomed, even late in development. [Agile Practice Guide, 1st edition, Page 9] [Agile Principles and Mindset]

14. A - When the work in progress (WIP) limits are reached, the team cannot pull further work. [Agile Practice Guide, 1st edition, Page 66] [Value-driven Delivery]

15. C - The interest rate used to discount future values into present values is also known as opportunity cost. [Cohn, M., 2006. Agile Estimating and Planning. 1st ed. Massachusetts: Pearson Education. Page 100] [Value-driven Delivery]

16. C - Scrumban is an Agile approach originally designed as a way to transition from Scrum to Kanban. As additional Agile frameworks and methodologies emerged, it became an evolving hybrid framework in and of itself where teams use Scrum as a framework and Kanban for process improvement. [Agile Practice Guide, 1st edition, Page 108] [Value-driven Delivery]

17. A - Isolating the more changing elements of a contract into a single document simplifies modifications and thus flexibility. [Agile Practice Guide, 1st edition, Page 77] [Stakeholder Engagement]

18. A - Although there is no law restricting disposal, the material is still toxic and must not be disposed of improperly. Abandoning it or giving it to local recyclers may also result in improper disposal. PMI's Code of Ethics and Professional Conduct requires Agile practitioners to make decisions based on the interests of public safety and the environment. Failing to ensure proper disposal of toxic materials is a violation of this code. [PMI Code of Ethics and Professional Conduct] [Stakeholder Engagement]

19. D - Since the product requirements are not known upfront and can only be discovered through a series of prototyping iterations, an Agile approach is suitable for the design phase. Once the product is developed, the mass rollout can be manage using a predictive life cycle. [Agile Practice Guide, 1st edition, Page 26] [Agile Principles and Mindset]

20. B - Shorter development cycles and limited work in progress are desirable Agile approaches. However, these are not directly influenced by the presence of a cross-functional team (a specialist team can also implement these approaches). A cross-functional team provides feedback from inside the team due to a wider range of collective team expertise. [Agile Practice Guide, 1st edition, Page 40] [Value-driven Delivery]

21. D - The question is comparing traditional to Agile approaches. Although Agile approaches do focus on speed, agility and change, here we are comparing traditional "tasks" to the Agile equivalent. An Agile team focuses on the "features" that will be needed in the product, instead of "tasks" that are required for the development. [Cohn, M., 2006. Agile Estimating and Planning. 1st ed. Massachusetts: Pearson Education. Page 245] [Value-driven Delivery]

22. C - Notify your project stakeholders of the situation. Once they are aware of the circumstances, a plan of action can be developed. It is possible the stakeholders may already be aware of the situation and had actually approved the hiring of these resources. Therefore, you should involve your stakeholders to resolve this issue. [PMI Code of Ethics and Professional Conduct] [Stakeholder Engagement]

23. C - According to the Agile Manifesto, individuals and interactions are valued more than processes and tools. The rest of the choices, like processes and tools, are valued less in an Agile setting. [Agile Practice Guide, 1st edition, Page 8] [Agile Principles and Mindset]

24. C - The team should be aware of how the technique works. Otherwise asking "Why?" five times might seem intimidating and the team might feel as though they are being reprimanded. [Derby, E. and Larsen, D., 2006. Agile Retrospectives: Making Good Teams Great. 1st ed. Texas: Pragmatic Bookshelf, Page 85] [Continuous Improvement]

25. A - Agile Unified Process is a simplistic version of the Rational Unified Process (RUP) and is an understandable approach to developing business application software using Agile techniques and concepts. [Agile Practice Guide, 1st edition, Page 150] [Value-driven Delivery]

26. C - The question is asking about the source of best estimates and not about who estimates tasks on an Agile project. The best estimates come from those who will do the work. (Lederer and Prasad 1992). (However, it must also be noted that task estimating on an Agile project should be a group endeavor as tasks are not allocated to individuals during iteration planning.) [Cohn, M., 2006. Agile Estimating and Planning. 1st ed. Massachusetts: Pearson Education. Page 155] [Adaptive Planning]

27. B - Continuous Integration is a practice in which each team member's work products are frequently integrated and validated with one another. [Agile Practice Guide, 1st edition, Page 151] [Value-driven Delivery]

28. B - Lead time is the total time it takes to deliver an item, measured from the time it is added to the board to the moment it is completed (response time + cycle time). [Agile Practice Guide, 1st edition, Pages 61, 64] [Value-driven Delivery]

29. A - Points counted toward velocity are only for those stories or features that are complete at the end of the iteration. In this case three features were complete so the velocity was 3 x (3 + 2) = 15 story points. [Cohn, M., 2006. Agile Estimating and Planning. 1st ed. Massachusetts: Pearson Education. Page 211] [Team Performance]

30. A - The scenario doesn't give enough information to determine if these risks are feature-related. Adding backlog items might not be the right choice. The best strategy is to add these risks to a watch list and continuously monitor these risks. If the risks cannot be mitigated, appropriate workarounds can be identified upon the risk occurrence. [Cohn, M., 2006. Agile Estimating and Planning. 1st ed. Massachusetts: Pearson Education. Page 5] [Problem Detection and Resolution]

31. A - Large stories are known as epics. Epics are decomposed into smaller stories before being developed. Since the list contains urgently needed features, these need to be prioritize at the top of the backlog. [Cohn, M., 2006. Agile Estimating and Planning. 1st ed. Massachusetts: Pearson Education. Page 249] [Problem Detection and Resolution]

32. C - Collective Code Ownership is a project acceleration and collaboration technique whereby any team member is authorized to modify any project work product or deliverable, thus emphasizing team-wide ownership and accountability. [Agile Practice Guide, 1st edition, Page 151] [Value-driven Delivery]

33. B - A critical problem with traditional approaches to planning is that they focus on the completion of activities rather than on the delivery of features. Features are the unit of customer value while activities are not. Feature-based Gantt charts can still be used on Agile projects. Agile teams also measure progress against plans. [Cohn, M., 2006. Agile Estimating and Planning. 1st ed. Massachusetts: Pearson Education. Page 12] [Agile Principles and Mindset]

34. C - Servant leadership is the practice of leading through service to the team, by focusing on understanding and addressing the needs and development of team members in order to enable the highest possible team performance. [Agile Practice Guide, 1st edition, Page 33] [Agile Principles and Mindset]

35. C - Reprioritizing or re-estimating the backlog will not produce any desirable results if review of the project management approach is required. In this case, you need to call a retrospective. [Agile Practice Guide, 1st edition, Page 50] [Problem Detection and Resolution]

36. A - Developing a detailed schedule is not an Agile technique. The eight guiding principles of DSDM framework are: focus on the business need, deliver on time, collaborate, never compromise quality, build incrementally from firm foundations, develop iteratively, communicate continuously and clearly, and demonstrate control. [Agile Practice Guide, 1st edition, Page 110] [Value-driven Delivery]

37. C - A product backlog, a sprint backlog, and increments are Agile project artifacts used in the Scrum approach. [Agile Practice Guide, 1st edition, Page 101] [Value-driven Delivery]

38. D - Velocity = average story points per iteration. Since the team had delivered 45 story points in three iterations, the velocity is 45/3 = 15 story points per iteration. [Agile Practice Guide, 1st edition, Page 61] [Team Performance]

39. A - The keyword for this question is "underlying root causes". The Five Whys technique helps in discovering underlying conditions that contribute to an issue. Team members ask "Why?" five times to get beyond habitual thinking. The rest of the choices are not root cause analysis techniques. [Derby, E. and Larsen, D., 2006. Agile Retrospectives: Making Good Teams

Great. 1st ed. Texas: Pragmatic Bookshelf, Page 85] [Continuous Improvement]

40. A - Disciplined Agile (DA), Scaled Agile Framework (SAFe), and Large Scale Scrum (LeSS) are scaled Agile approaches. Scrum is a single-team framework. [Agile Practice Guide, 1st edition, Pages 112, 113, 114, 121] [Value-driven Delivery]

]

PMI-ACP Lite Mock Exam 18 Practice Questions

Test Name: PMI-ACP Lite Mock Exam 18
Total Questions: 40
Correct Answers Needed to Pass:
30 (75.00%)
Time Allowed: 60 Minutes

Test Description

This is a cumulative PMI-ACP Mock Exam which can be used as a benchmark for your PMI-ACP aptitude. This practice test includes questions from all exam topic areas, including sections from Agile Tools and Techniques, and all three Agile Knowledge and Skills areas.

Test Questions

1. You are leading an Agile project heading into its third sprint. The third sprint contains 15 stories with an average story size of 3 points. The observed velocities for the first and second sprints were 30 and 35 story points respectively. What is the theoretically possible maximum story size in this sprint?

A. 45 points.

B. 31 points.

C. 3 points.

D. 4 points.

2. You are reviewing the Agile project management practices of an organization and find out that Agile teams are rolling forward incomplete stories in one iteration to the next. How would you document this in your report to the senior leadership?

A. Team should learn from its mistakes and not over estimate. Further, any rolled over work needs to be completed first in the next iteration.

B. The teams should not leave incomplete work and should stretch the iterations in order to complete all scheduled stories.

C. Automatic rollover of incomplete works is not a good Agile practice as each iteration should be planned afresh.

D. A second Agile team needs to be setup to take care of the incomplete work while the primary team should move on with the release plan.

3. Which of the following is a collection of lightweight Agile software development methods focused on adaptability to a particular circumstance?

A. Crystal

B. Critical Chain

C. Kanban

D. Fishbone

4. You are analyzing and automating end-to-end business processes for a manufacturing facility. It is critical that you form a team that includes practitioners with all the skills necessary to deliver valuable product increments. What kind of team you should look for?

A. Members who have served as an Agile coach in the past.

B. Team with multiple product owners.

C. Team form from existing organizational resources.

D. Cross-functional team.

5. Which of the following is NOT a recognized Scrum role?

A. Scrum master

B. Winger

C. Development team

D. Product owner

6. Flow-based Agile has a different approach to stand-ups than iteration-based Agile. Which of the following is one of the typical areas addressed during these stand-ups?

A. What do we need to finish as a team?

B. What am I planning to complete between now and the next stand-up?

C. What are my impediments?

D. What did I complete since the last stand-up?

7. Which of the following is considered a waste in Agile environments?

A. Multi-tasking

B. Change management

C. Planning

D. Scope management

8. Using historical values for estimating a team's velocity on a new project is risky because:

A. Historical values might not look desirable to the product owner.

B. Each project is unique.

C. Historical values were only valid for the historical projects.

D. Historical values cannot produce a reliable estimate.

9. George is considered a super-star programmer in an organization. Over time, he has also acquired some business analysis skills that complement his programming skills. George is:

A. H-shaped

B. I-shaped

C. T-shaped

D. U-shaped

10. Which of the following is the practice of using a lightweight set of tests to ensure that the most important functions of the system under development work as intended?

A. Acceptance testing

B. Smoke testing

C. Box testing

D. Regression testing

11. XP's evolution was the result of designing and adopting techniques through the filter of core values and informed by key principles. Which of the following are the core values of XP?

A. Collaboration, complexity, communication, faith and discipline.

B. Communication, simplicity, feedback, courage, and respect.

C. Planning, executing, monitoring and controlling.

D. Unity, faith, agility and discipline.

12. AgileUP is an offshoot of the:

A. Scrumban

B. Rational Rose

C. Object-oriented design

D. Unified Process

13. You are leading a software development project that has recently been initiated. You have just finished with your release plan covering approximately the next six months. What is your next activity?

A. Plan a sprint retrospective.

B. Expand the release plan to the next six months.

C. Plan the first iteration.

D. Conduct a feasibility study.

14. You have analyzed all the themes of your project and have assigned each one of them to one of the four quadrants of a risk-value matrix that has a risk rating (high and low) on the y-axis, and a business value rating (high and low) on the x-axis. What is the recommend approach to be taken for the themes that fell under the "High Risk" and "Low Value" quadrant?

A. Do second

B. Do first

C. Do last

D. Avoid

15. A large university has a contract with you to run a large transformation project, which you expect to last 15 months. While developing the project charter, you discover that it did not address several compliance requirements in the business case. Failure to meet these requirements could result in legal action against the company. However, implementing the technology to comply with these regulations could exceed the project's expected budget, which could lead to the project's cancellation. What should you do?

A. Disclose the discovery to the project sponsor and stakeholders immediately.

B. Write up a change request for the work.

C. Add this risk to the product backlog.

D. Wait until a few sprints are completed, when you have a better idea of what resources and funding could be allocated to addressing these requirements.

16. Which of the following Agile approaches involves techniques such as 10-minute build, continuous integration, and test-first?

A. XP

B. Scrum

C. Kanban

D. Lean

17. Which of the following helps in establishing a set of behaviors that will support the team in having productive discussions and establishing that team members are responsible for monitoring their interactions?

A. Product backlog

B. Spikes

C. Kanban board

D. Working agreements

18. Which of the following is an iterative and lightweight Agile method?

A. PDM

B. FDD

C. WBS

D. EVM

19. You are introducing Agile approaches to a team new to Agile. You recently carried out the first team retrospective event and while soliciting team responses regarding future improvement opportunities, you felt that the team took that negatively. Which of the following activities should be conducted, in such circumstances, to close off the retrospective?

A. Appreciations

B. Planning Poker

C. Pair work

D. Root cause analysis

20. You have recently been asked to design and build a "complex" project that is supposed to somehow reduce the production costs by 20% or more. Together with the product owner, you developed a product roadmap using user story mapping, and impact mapping techniques. Now you want to assign business values to each user story. How should you proceed?

A. Bring the product owner and the team together again and determine the business value.

B. Ask the product owner to email you the business values for each user story.

C. Randomly assign business values to the user stories so that you get a fine mix of user stories.

D. Ask the team to estimate the business value for each user story.

21. An Agile team is currently estimating user stories in ideal days. For a particular user story, the team estimated two ideal days from a programmer, one ideal day from a database engineer, one ideal day from a user interaction designer, and two ideal days from a tester. What should be done next?

A. Assign three ideal days for development effort and three ideal days for design and testing effort.

B. Assign six ideal days as an aggregated estimate to the user story.

C. Capture all four estimates on the story card and track them individually.

D. Assign one ideal day for design, three ideal days for development, and one ideal day for testing.

22. Two programmers are working on a story originally estimated at 40 ideal hours. If a third programmer with a similar skillset is added, which of the following might happen?

A. The iteration duration will get reduced.

B. The cycle time might get reduced.

C. The lead time might get reduced.

D. The individual velocity might get increased.

23. Your company has recently been awarded a complex project and you have started to acquire project resources. You want to create a project charter so that the project team develops an understanding of how to work together. At a minimum, for an Agile project, what needs to be included on the charter?

A. Product and sprint backlog.

B. Project assumption, constraints and scope.

C. Project risks and timelines.

D. Project vision or purpose and a clear set of working agreements.

24. An Agile team is currently experimenting with some new technology that can be utilized on the current project. If the results are favorable, the team might be able to significantly cut the delivery timeline. Which Agile event is the team currently conducting?

A. Retrospective

B. Spike

C. Iteration planning

D. Release planning

25. You have recently setup an Agile PMO in your organization. The organization has been successfully using Agile on all organizational projects for a while but it was thought that a central PMO will add further value. You are considering to setup an invitation-oriented PMO. What is the main benefit of this approach?

A. Inviting only those interested to engage with PMO services results in higher engagement with PMO practices.

B. Invitation-oriented PMOs usually invite higher value projects to engage with them and maximizes value per project ratio.

C. An invitation-oriented PMO focuses on business goal alignment instead of employee engagement and delivers higher business value.

D. An invitation-oriented PMO mandates certain solutions or approaches to get some quick wins.

26. You are managing a complex project with loosely defined requirements. By the end of each iteration, the number of story points delivered are offset by the addition of new requirements. How would that effect your burndown chart?

A. The slope of the burndown line will become positive.

B. The slope of the burndown line will become negative.

C. The slope of the burndown line will not change.

D. The slope of the burndown line will become zero.

27. Which of the following statements regarding an Agile PMO is incorrect?

A. An Agile PMO is value-driven.

B. An Agile PMO is multidisciplinary.

C. An Agile PMO is a control center.

D. An Agile PMO is invitation-oriented.

28. According to the Agile Manifesto customer collaboration is valued more than:

A. Following a plan

B. Processes and tools

C. Contract negotiation

D. Comprehensive documentation

29. You are leading a complex knowledge work project. You need to select a tool to document and share the knowledge work created by the project. A number of options were discussed and the team ended with two options that look equally good. What should you do next to help you make the right choice?

A. Request the product owner to make the final call.

B. Organize a spike event to study both of the options.

C. Use a fishbone diagram to determine the best tool.

D. Organize a planning poker event to identify the best option.

30. Which of the following techniques is used by Agile teams to convert epics into stories?

A. Decomposition

B. Root cause analysis

C. Backlog grooming

D. Design of experiments

31. An organization is currently struggling during its transition from traditional to Agile project management approaches. Teams are still working in silos instead of coming together and forming a cross-functional team. If you are the servant-leader, what should you do first?

A. Hire a coach to help the organization transition through the change.

B. Use servant-leadership skills to help the managers understand why Agile needs cross-functional teams.

C. Use the product owner's authority to influence team members to abolish their silos.

D. Include non-conformance penalties in the team charter.

32. The product owner has asked you to report on project's ROTI. What does ROTI mean?

A. Subcontinental bread

B. Rapid Organizational Transformation Impact

C. Return on Time Invested

D. Rough Order Turnover Index

33. You have recently been asked to lead the development of a complex supply chain management system for your organization. You are currently acquiring your project team. Which type of resources should you prefer for this project?

A. H-shaped team members

B. Z-shaped team members

C. T-shaped team members

D. I-shaped team members

34. Which of the following fosters better team communication, improved team dynamics, knowledge sharing, and reduced cost of learning?

A. Kanban board.

B. Cross-functional teams.

C. Mixed team of generalists and specialists.

D. Collocated team.

35. You are leading an XP software development project. Recently you found out that the underlying technology being used is unstable and has impacted several features already released. What should you do first?

A. Replace the unstable technology with a more stable one.

B. Explain the impact to the product owner.

C. Apply pair programming technique.

D. Call a retrospective and discuss how such problems can be avoided in the future.

36. An Agile team is currently struggling with a number of issues including false starts and wasted efforts. On a number of occasions, a number of user stories selected for development were not actually required by the business. Which of the following, most likely, is the root cause of this problem?

A. External experts haven't been hired.

B. Servant-leader's soft skills are limited.

C. Project team's technical competence is limited.

D. Product owner's engagement is either minimal or doesn't exist at all.

37. An Agile team is discussing each user story in the iteration backlog and documenting the conditions of satisfactions for each story. These conditions are then written on the back of the story cards. What is the team doing?

A. Determining the definition of done for stories.

B. Playing planning poker.

C. Testing the user stories.

D. Estimating the stories.

38. A particular user story has very low business value. However, if not implemented properly this story can have serious consequences on the project. How should you deal with this story?

A. Prioritize this story at the top of the backlog.

B. Order the backlog based on business value.

C. Calculate the ideal days involved with this particular story.

D. Sort the backlog based on story points.

39. An organization has historically rewarded managers for departmental efficiencies rather than end-to-end flow of organizational processes. This has resulted in departments working in silos. Which type of resources will be difficult to find in this organization?

A. H-Shaped

B. T-shaped

C. I-Shaped

D. U-Shaped

40. An Agile project is currently suffering from major delays. During the project retrospective you asked for the underlying reason for this. There is a general team consensus that poor story estimation caused major delays on the project. What should you do next?

A. Document this as a lesson learned so that future projects might benefit from the experience.

B. Do not accept this excuse and reprimand the team members.

C. Investigate which team members provided inaccurate estimates.

D. Conduct a Five Whys exercise to uncover the underlying root cause.

PMI-ACP Lite Mock Exam 18 Answer Key and Explanations

1. A - A sprint can have stories having a size of zero story points. The theoretical maximum can be 45 story points for one story and 0 story points for the remaining 14 stories and still the average story size will be 3 story points. [Cohn, M., 2006. Agile Estimating and Planning. 1st ed. Massachusetts: Pearson Education. Page 271] [Team Performance]

2. C - One of the reasons why Agile planning succeeds is that all work in process is eliminated at the end of each iteration. Because work is not automatically rolled forward from one iteration to the next, each iteration is planned afresh. This means that work on a feature not fully implemented in one iteration will not necessarily be continued in the next. [Cohn, M., 2006. Agile Estimating and Planning. 1st ed. Massachusetts: Pearson Education. Page 247] [Stakeholder Engagement]

3. A - The Crystal family of methodologies is a collection of lightweight Agile software development methods focused on adaptability to a particular circumstance. [Agile Practice Guide, 1st edition, Page 151] [Value-driven Delivery]

4. D - Selection of the right team members depends on a number of factors. However, a critical requirement of an Agile team is to have cross-functional team members. A cross-functional team includes practitioners with all the skills necessary to deliver valuable product increments. [Agile Practice Guide, 1st edition, Page 151] [Value-driven Delivery]

5. B - The Scrum team consists of a product owner, development team, and scrum master. [Agile Practice Guide, 1st edition, Page 101] [Value-driven Delivery]

6. A - "What did I complete since the last stand-up", "what am I planning to complete between now and the next stand-up", and "what are my impediments" are typical questions for iteration-based Agile and not flow-based Agile. [Agile Practice Guide, 1st edition, Pages 53, 54] [Adaptive Planning]

7. A - Planning, scope and change management are part of all projects regardless of the environment. However, the project environment and the selected management methodology influence how teams approach these. Multi-tasking is considered a waste in Agile environments. [Agile Practice Guide, 1st edition, Page 39] [Agile Principles and Mindset]

8. B - Historical values are great–if you have them. The problem with historical values is that they're of the greatest value when very little has changed between the old project and team and the new project and team. The fact that each project is unique introduces risk in this estimating approach. [Cohn, M., 2006. Agile Estimating and Planning. 1st ed. Massachusetts: Pearson Education. Page 176] [Adaptive Planning]

9. C - In Agile communities, people with expertise in one domain, less-developed skills in associated areas and good collaboration skills are known as T-shaped people. [Agile Practice Guide, 1st edition, Page 42] [Value-driven Delivery]

10. B - Smoke testing is the practice of using a lightweight set of tests to ensure that the

most important functions of the system under development work as intended. [Agile Practice Guide, 1st edition, Page 154] [Problem Detection and Resolution]

11. B - XP's foundational core values are communication, simplicity, feedback, courage and respect. [Agile Practice Guide, 1st edition, Page 102] [Value-driven Delivery]

12. D - The Agile Unified Process (AgileUP) is an offshoot of the Unified Process (UP) for software projects. [Agile Practice Guide, 1st edition, Page 111] [Value-driven Delivery]

13. C - Since the project has already been initiated, it is safe to assume that a feasibility study would already have been completed. According to the scenario, a six-month release plan has already been established, so there is no need to expand it to include the next six-months. The next step is to start planning your first project iteration. [Cohn, M., 2006. Agile Estimating and Planning. 1st ed. Massachusetts: Pearson Education. Page 30] [Adaptive Planning]

14. D - "Avoiding" is recommended for themes that have been classified as "High Risk" and "Low Value". [Cohn, M., 2006. Agile Estimating and Planning. 1st ed. Massachusetts: Pearson Education. Page 85] [Problem Detection and Resolution]

15. A - Notifying the stakeholders immediately that there has been a significant oversight in the business case is the appropriate response. Agile practitioners are required by PMI's Code of Ethics to comply with all laws and regulations. Failure to immediately and actively disclose that a compliance requirement has not been addressed could put the company and the team in the position of breaking the law. [PMI Code of Ethics and Professional Responsibility] [Stakeholder Engagement]

16. A - 10-minute build, continuous integration, and test-first techniques are used in XP projects. [Agile Practice Guide, 1st edition, Page 102] [Value-driven Delivery]

17. D - Working agreements establish a set of behaviors that will support the team in having productive discussions and establishing that team members are responsible for monitoring their interactions. [Derby, E. and Larsen, D., 2006. Agile Retrospectives: Making Good Teams Great. 1st ed. Texas: Pragmatic Bookshelf, Page 48] [Continuous Improvement]

18. B - Feature-Driven Development (FDD) is an iterative and incremental software development process. FDD was developed to meet the specific needs of large software development projects. [Agile Practice Guide, 1st edition, Page 108] [Value-driven Delivery]

19. A - Appreciations allow team members to notice and appreciate each other and end the retrospective on a positive note. [Derby, E. and Larsen, D., 2006. Agile Retrospectives: Making Good Teams Great. 1st ed. Texas: Pragmatic Bookshelf, Page 117] [Team Performance]

20. A - The product owner should assign the business value. However, it is better that this is done in collaboration with (and presence of) the team. [Agile Practice Guide, 1st edition, Page 58] [Value-driven Delivery]

21. B - If you choose to estimate in ideal days, assign one aggregate estimate to each user story. Some teams are tempted to estimate a

number of ideal days for each individual or group who will work on a story. In such cases, it is recommended to aggregate individual estimates and do not track them individually. Tacking at the role-level shifts the team's focus away from "We're all in this together." [Cohn, M., 2006. Agile Estimating and Planning. 1st ed. Massachusetts: Pearson Education. Page 46] [Problem Detection and Resolution]

22. B - An estimate in ideal days/hours can change based on the team's experience with technology, the domain, and themselves, among other factors. Additional team members can positively (completing stories faster) or negatively (too many communication channels) affect the story. In this case, adding a third resource means adding 50% capacity while the team size is still manageable. [Cohn, M., 2006. Agile Estimating and Planning. 1st ed. Massachusetts: Pearson Education. Page 70] [Problem Detection and Resolution]

23. D - The charting process helps the team learn how to work together and coalesce around the project. At a minimum, for an Agile project, the team needs the project vision or purpose and a clear set of working agreements. [Agile Practice Guide, 1st edition, Page 49] [Value-driven Delivery]

24. B - This is an example of a spike. A spike is a task included in an iteration plan that is being undertaken specifically to gain knowledge or answer a question. [Cohn, M., 2006. Agile Estimating and Planning. 1st ed. Massachusetts: Pearson Education. Page 154] [Continuous Improvement]

25. A - Invitation-oriented PMOs invite only those interested to engage with PMO services. This usually results in higher engagement with PMO practices and makes it easier for those practices to be "sticky". [Agile Practice Guide, 1st edition, Page 81] [Value-driven Delivery]

26. D - If the number of story points added offsets the number of story points delivered, the remaining story points on the project will not change. The slope of the burndown line will become zero and the line will become perfectly flat in the horizontal direction. [Cohn, M., 2006. Agile Estimating and Planning. 1st ed. Massachusetts: Pearson Education. Page 214] [Team Performance]

27. C - Since Agile teams are self-organizing, Agile PMOs have to be collaborative and supportive rather than being control centers. Agile PMOs are value-driven, invitation-oriented and multidisciplinary. [Agile Practice Guide, 1st edition, Pages 81, 82] [Value-driven Delivery]

28. C - According to the Agile Manifesto, customer collaboration is valued over contract negotiation. [Agile Practice Guide, 1st edition, Page 8] [Agile Principles and Mindset]

29. B - You need to organize a spike event to study both of the options. Spikes are useful for learning and may be used in circumstances such as estimation, acceptance criteria definition, and understanding the flow of a user's action through the product. [Agile Practice Guide, 1st edition, Page 56] [Continuous Improvement]

30. A - Large stories are known as epics. Epics are decomposed into smaller stories before being developed. [Cohn, M., 2006. Agile Estimating and Planning. 1st ed.

Massachusetts: Pearson Education. Page 249] [Adaptive Planning]

31. B - As the first step you need to make the initial effort. Engaging the product owner or an external coach is not recommended as the first step. You should use your servant-leadership skills to help the functional managers understand why Agile needs a cross-functional team. The functional manager can then help you in forming cross-functional teams. [Agile Practice Guide, 1st edition, Page 59] [Problem Detection and Resolution]

32. C - ROTI stands for Return on Time Invested. This technique is used in the closing retrospective phase for iteration or release retrospectives. It helps generate feedback on the retrospective process and gauge the effectiveness of the session from the team members' perspectives. [Derby, E. and Larsen, D., 2006. Agile Retrospectives: Making Good Teams Great. 1st ed. Texas: Pragmatic Bookshelf, Page 124] [Team Performance]

33. C - Many successful Agile teams are made up of generalizing specialists, or "T-Shaped" people. In Agile communities, people with expertise in one domain, less-developed skills in associated areas and good collaboration skills are known as T-shaped people. [Agile Practice Guide, 1st edition, Page 42] [Value-driven Delivery]

34. D - Collocated teams enable better communication, improved team dynamics, knowledge sharing, and reduced cost of learning. [Agile Practice Guide, 1st edition, Page 40] [Stakeholder Engagement]

35. C - Right now you have a major issue at hand that has impacted a big number of features that have already been released. Since the product owner is ultimately responsible for the system development, the first thing you need to do is present the impact to the product owner. [Agile Practice Guide, 1st edition, Page 153] [Problem Detection and Resolution]

36. D - The problem at hand is inadequately groomed product backlog, which is a responsibility of the product owner. In this scenario it seem like the product owner's engagement is either minimal or doesn't exist at all. [Agile Practice Guide, 1st edition, Page 59] [Problem Detection and Resolution]

37. A - Since the team is analyzing and documenting the conditions of satisfaction, they are determining the definition of done for the stories in the iteration. [Agile Practice Guide, 1st edition, Page 151] [Adaptive Planning]

38. A - Although this particular story doesn't have much business value, this story is critical for the success of the project. Hence, this story needs to be prioritized and developed the earliest. [Cohn, M., 2006. Agile Estimating and Planning. 1st ed. Massachusetts: Pearson Education. Page 5] [Adaptive Planning]

39. B - When an organization is decomposed into departmental silos, employees become more and more specialized with their departmental work but are not able to diversify their skills. People with deep specializations in one domain but limited knowledge in other domains are known as "I-shaped people". On the other hand, people with expertise in one domain, some skills in associated areas and good collaboration skills are known as "T-shaped people". There is no such thing as H-shaped or U-shaped people. [Agile Practice Guide, 1st edition, Pages 42, 74] [Agile Principles and Mindset]

40. D - Poor estimation would have resulted in delay on the project, but this information is not enough to fix such problems in future. You need to understand the exact reasons behind the poor estimation effort. The Five Whys technique can be really helpful in this situation. [Derby, E. and Larsen, D., 2006. Agile Retrospectives: Making Good Teams Great. 1st ed. Texas: Pragmatic Bookshelf, Page 85] [Continuous Improvement]

PMI-ACP Lite Mock Exam 19 Practice Questions

Test Name: PMI-ACP Lite Mock Exam 19
Total Questions: 40
Correct Answers Needed to Pass:
30 (75.00%)
Time Allowed: 60 Minutes

Test Description

This is a cumulative PMI-ACP Mock Exam which can be used as a benchmark for your PMI-ACP aptitude. This practice test includes questions from all exam topic areas, including sections from Agile Tools and Techniques, and all three Agile Knowledge and Skills areas.

Test Questions

1. Which of the following are predefined roles in Scrumban?

   A. There are no predefined roles in Scrumban.

   B. Project manager, project team, and project sponsor.

   C. Dev team, test team, and deployment team.

   D. Product owner, Agile team, and Scrum master.

2. An Agile project has a total of 700 story points and each project iteration has a fixed duration of three weeks. At the end of the 4th iteration, the team had successfully delivered 76 story points. The team was able to successfully address some improvement opportunities and during the 5th iteration the team was able to deliver additional 24 story points. Assuming that the team can maintain its 5th iteration's throughput for the rest of the project, and no more story points are added to the project, how many more weeks are required to complete the project?

   A. 96 weeks

   B. 90 weeks

   C. 87 weeks

   D. 75 weeks

3. You are analyzing your project requirements and classifying them as "Must have", "Should have", "Could have", and "Won't have" requirements. Which Agile activity are you performing?

   A. Iteration planning

   B. Project scoping

   C. MoSCoW analysis

   D. Story estimating

4. You have recently been assigned a new project. This is a big project, $2M in budget and 12 months in duration. However, the uncertainty involved with the project is very low. Which project management approach would you select?

   A. Adaptive approach due to high budget.

   B. Incremental approach due to project duration.

C. Agile approach due to project complexity.

D. Predictive approach due to low risk.

5. In iteration-based Agile, each team member responds to which of the following three questions during the daily stand-ups?

A. Last sprint's achievements, this sprint's targets, and any risks.

B. Yesterday's individual achievement, today's individual target, and any impediments.

C. Last iteration's achievements, this iteration's targets, and any risks.

D. Yesterday's team achievement, today's team target, and any impediments.

6. What is the philosophy behind the design of Kanban boards?

A. Encourage change management.

B. Increase velocity.

C. Decrease waiting time.

D. Boost performance.

7. Which of the following statements regarding burndown and burnup charts is incorrect?

A. Burnup charts show the work completed.

B. Both charts are based on the same data but displayed in two different ways.

C. A burndown chart is an Agile tool while a burnup chart is not.

D. Burndown charts show story points remaining.

8. Which of the following is a collection of practices for creating a smooth flow of delivery by improving collaboration between development and operations staff?

A. Burndown chart

B. DevOps

C. Kanban

D. Retrospectives

9. What type of people are known as "Paint-Drip"?

A. People who are effective communicators but weak negotiators.

B. People who are effective in business as usual but not in project atmospheres.

C. People who have various depths of specialization in multiple skills.

D. People who specialize in one area.

10. Retrospectives are important team events which help in team-building, learning from past experiences and improving processes. Who chairs the retrospectives?

A. Retrospective leader

B. Servant-leader

C. Product owner

D. Project manager

11. Your Agile team is collocated except one of the team members who is based at the client location. How should you conduct your daily standups with this constraint?

A. Do not use daily standups and rely on formal written communications.

B. Conduct the face-to-face daily standups without the remotely located team member.

C. Since all of the team members are not collocated, this is not an Agile project. It is recommended reverting back to traditional project management approaches.

D. Use video conferencing technology to accommodate the remote team member.

12. What does "triangulation" mean?

A. Measuring the distance between user stories, themes and epics.

B. Decomposing epics and themes into smaller user stories.

C. Estimating user stories against an assortment of those that have already been estimated.

D. Progressively elaborating epics and themes.

13. You just carried out ESVP activity during an iteration retrospective and prepared a histogram of the responses. If the majority of the people in the room are found to be vacationers, what should you do?

A. Escalate the matter to the product owner.

B. Proceed with the rest of the agenda items.

C. Turn on a dime and make that the major topic of discussion.

D. Immediately close the meeting.

14. You are considering adopting an Agile project management approach in your construction business. You are not sure how to do this as a number of Agile techniques are more suitable to software development. For this initiative, what is the first thing the organization needs to adopt?

A. An Agile mindset.

B. 12 Agile Principles.

C. Agile Manifesto.

D. Agile Methods.

15. You are inspecting your project's Kanban board. You observe that, even though WIP limits are set, a big number of tasks are getting stuck in the "Road blocks" section. What should you do?

A. Reprioritize the backlog

B. Call a retrospective

C. Conduct a planning poker event

D. Schedule a spike

16. During a retrospective meeting, you asked the team members to write cards that represent events and interactions from the iteration that they feel proud about and events and interactions they feel sorry about.

You asked them to stick these cards either to a "Prouds" poster or a "Sorries" poster. Which Agile activity this example closely resembles?

A. Mad Sad Glad

B. Retrospective

C. Affinity diagram

D. Process analysis

17. You are your team are executing a knowledge work project. The project has started to suffer some delays and overruns due to insufficiently refined product backlog items. A number of actions can be recommended at this stage EXCEPT:

A. Schedule a backlog refinement workshop with the product owner and the team.

B. Split stories into smaller stories.

C. Create a definition of "ready" for the stories.

D. Conduct critical path analysis for the project.

18. Which of the following is the first stage of a FDD project?

A. Design by feature

B. Develop features list

C. Plan by feature

D. Develop high-level models

19. The process of moving future amounts back into their present value, taking the time value of money into account, is generally known as discounting. Which of the following measures is critical in determining the present value of future amounts?

A. Stock Beta

B. Return on investment

C. Interest rate

D. Discount window

20. When is a user story considered finished?

A. When the users start using the product.

B. When it can be demonstrated to meet all of the conditions of satisfaction.

C. When the stories are included in a particular release.

D. When the go-ahead from the testers is obtained.

21. An Agile team uses a Kanban board to manage its work in progress. Which of the following information can be used to determine the team's velocity during the last iteration?

A. Stories moved into "Testing" during the iteration.

B. Stories moved from 'In Progress" to "Complete" during the iteration.

C. Stories moved into "Ready" during the iteration.

D. Stories moved from "Ready" to "In Progress" during the iteration.

22. You are leading an ERP system development project for your organization. The Chief Financial Officer is the product owner of the project. Today, the CEO of the company has recommended some changes to the scope. What should you do?

A. Prioritize the changes as these are requested by the product owner's boss.

B. Reject the change request as only the product owner has the authority to request changes.

C. Ask the CEO to work with the CFO to prioritize the change.

D. Discuss the changes with the product owner.

23. An Agile team has estimated a story at 5 story points. If new team members are included, how would that impact the story size?

A. The story size will change, but the direction cannot be determined unless the old and new team sizes are provided.

B. The story size will not change.

C. The story size will increase in direct proportion to the increase in team members.

D. The story size will decrease in direct proportion to the increase in team members.

24. You are responsible of designing a new lessons learned management system for an organization. As a part of the project, you need to consult with a number of senior stakeholders and assess their needs and requirements. You then have to facilitate consensus on the system features, workflows, processes and procedures. Once the system is developed, it has to be rolled out across the organization and all employees have to be trained in effective use of the system. You have chosen to use a hybrid project life cycle. Which of the following life cycles should be adopted for the design and build phase of the project?

A. Iterative

B. Incremental

C. Agile

D. Predictive

25. Which of the following Agile techniques requires the entire team to get together and discuss the acceptance criteria for a work product (The team then creates the tests and writes enough code and automated tests to meet the criteria)?

A. Test at all levels.

B. Acceptance Test Driven Development (ATDD).

C. Continuous integration.

D. Behavior Driven Development (BDD).

26. Mobbing requires that multiple team members focus simultaneously and coordinate their contributions on a particular work item. This technique is also known as:

A. Swarming

B. Technical Debt

C. Pair Working

D. Rolling Wave

27. Which of the following is an example of an epic?

A. A very large user story that may span several iterations.

B. A very large user story not relevant to the project.

C. A user story that is common on all projects.

D. A user story that has more risk than the stakeholders' tolerance.

28. When teams attempt to measure story points without completing the actual feature or story, they are:

A. Measuring capacity and finished work.

B. Neither measuring capacity nor finished work.

C. Measuring capacity not finished work.

D. Measuring finished work not capacity.

29. You are leading an Agile project. Halfway during the first iteration of the project, the team has developed and tested all of the assigned stories. What should be done next?

A. Continue testing the features till the end of the iteration.

B. Terminate the iteration early.

C. Gold plate developed features.

D. Consult with the product owner and include more stories to fit the current iteration.

30. An Agile team is working on a SCM project with a total of 600 story point to deliver. At the end of the 3rd iteration, the team had successfully delivered 81 story points. The team was able to successfully address some improvement opportunities and during the 4th iteration the team was able to deliver 39 story points. Assuming that the team maintains its current velocity and no more story points are added to the project, which of the following statements is correct?

A. The velocity has decreased, which implies that the team would require another 16 iterations to complete the project.

B. The velocity has increased, which implies that the team would require another 16 iterations to complete the project.

C. The velocity has decreased, which implies that the team would require another 18 iterations to complete the project.

D. The velocity has increased, which implies that the team would require another 18 iterations to complete the project.

31. An Agile team is managing its work in progress on a Kanban board. Recently the WIP limits have been met and the team cannot pull further work from the "Ready"

column into the "WIP" column. How should the team deal with this situation now?

A. Team increases the WIP limits and work overtime.

B. Team removes the "Ready" items to the "Cannot be done" column.

C. Team tries to move work from "WIP" column to the "Done" column.

D. Team pushes the work from "Ready" column to the "WIP" column without changing the WIP limits.

32. When a person multi-tasks between two projects, that person is not 50% on each project. Instead, due to the cost of task switching, the person is somewhere between 20% to 40% on each project. Which of the following is not a cause behind this general loss of productivity?

A. People assigned to multiple projects are more likely to make mistakes when they multi-task.

B. People assigned to multiple projects are more likely to have competing priorities.

C. People assigned to multiple projects are less likely to remember project contexts.

D. People assigned to multiple projects are not loyal to any of the projects.

33. You are managing a software development project and need size estimates for a couple of new features. Two of the programmers on your team are most likely going to develop these new features. How will you get your estimates?

A. Ask the product owner to prioritize and estimate the features.

B. Involve the entire team to get the estimates.

C. Ask the responsible programmers to provide the estimates.

D. Use historical estimates from past similar projects.

34. Which of the following statements regarding Scrum framework is incorrect?

A. Scrum uses an iterative approach to deliver a working product.

B. Scrum is run on time-boxed sprints.

C. Scrum is a multiple-team process framework.

D. The Scrum framework consists of roles, events, artifacts, and rules.

35. According to the DSDM MoSCoW technique, the planned effort for a project targeted at "Must Have" requirements cannot exceed?

A. 0.8

B. 0.5

C. 0.7

D. 0.6

36. Which of the following Agile techniques are useful for learning and may be used in circumstances such as estimation, acceptance criteria definition, and understanding the flow of a user's action through the product?

A. Behavior Driven Development (BDD)

B. Continuous integration

C. Acceptance Test Driven Development (ATDD)

D. Spikes

37. A release burndown bar chart is more ________ than the traditional burndown chart.

A. Expressive

B. Risky

C. Agile

D. Linear

38. Which of the following actions will impact the team velocity?

A. New stories are added to the project.

B. Team moves from storming to performing stage.

C. Some stories are dropped from the project.

D. Team maintains the story points delivery rate.

39. A team is currently developing a bespoke enterprise resource planning (ERP) system for a manufacturing plant. At the start of the project that backlog was estimated to have 10,000 story points and the order of magnitude cost estimate for the project was $1M. The team has just finished the 15th iteration and has provided the following project statistics: Completed features value = $450,000; Actual costs to date = $600,000; Completed story points = 550; Planned story points = 700. What is the project's SPI?

A. 0.79

B. 1.33

C. 0.75

D. 1.27

40. Which of the following Agile approaches utilizes a technique similar to feature buffering?

A. DMAIC

B. Kanban

C. DSDM

D. Story estimating

PMI-ACP Lite Mock Exam 19 Answer Key and Explanations

1. A - Scrumban is an Agile approach originally designed as a way to transition from Scrum to Kanban. As additional Agile frameworks and methodologies emerged, it became an evolving hybrid framework in and of itself where teams use Scrum as a framework and Kanban for process improvement. There are no predefined roles in Scrumban – the team retains their current roles. [Agile Practice Guide, 1st edition, Page 108] [Value-driven Delivery]

2. D - Velocity = average story points per iteration. At the end of the 4th iteration, the team delivered 76 story points in total. The velocity at the end of the 4th iteration was 76/4 = 19 story points per iteration on average. At the end of the 5th iteration, the team delivered 100 story points in total (76+24). The current velocity is 100/5 = 20 story points per iteration on average. Further the 5th iteration throughput was 24 story points per iteration. Since 600 story points are remaining (700 – 100), at the 5th iteration throughput of 24 story points per iteration, the team would require an additional 25 iterations (600/24) to complete the project. With each iteration fixed at three weeks, this means the team needs 75 weeks to complete the project. [Agile Practice Guide, 1st edition, Page 61] [Team Performance]

3. C - On DSDM (Dynamic Systems Development Method) projects, requirements are sorted into four categories: must have, should have, could have, and won't have. DSDM refers to this sorting as the MoSCoW rules. [Cohn, M., 2006. Agile Estimating and Planning. 1st ed. Massachusetts: Pearson Education. Page 187] [Value-driven Delivery]

4. D - When the project uncertainty is low, incremental approaches, adaptive and Agile approaches can be expensive. When the risk level is low, especially with the scope of works, predictive/waterfall approaches are more suitable. [Agile Practice Guide, 1st edition, Page 20] [Problem Detection and Resolution]

5. B - In iteration-based Agile, everyone answers the following questions in a round-robin fashion: What did I complete since the last stand-up? What am I planning to complete between now and the next stand-up? What are my impediments? [Agile Practice Guide, 1st edition, Page 53] [Adaptive Planning]

6. D - The philosophy behind the use of Kanban boards is to limit the work being done in order to boost performance. [Agile Practice Guide, 1st edition, Page 103] [Team Performance]

7. C - Both burnup and burndown chart show work completed and story points remaining. The two charts are based on the same data, but displayed in two different ways. Some Agile teams prefer one type over the other. [Agile Practice Guide, 1st edition, Pages 62, 63] [Team Performance]

8. B - DevOps is a collection of practices for creating a smooth flow of delivery by improving collaboration between development and operations staff. [Agile Practice Guide, 1st edition, Page 151] [Value-driven Delivery]

9. C - Broken Comb, also known as Paint-Drip, is a person who has various depths of specialization in multiple skills required by the team. [Agile Practice Guide, 1st edition, Pages 150, 153] [Team Performance]

10. A - A retrospective leader which can be any team member chairs the retrospectives. The retrospective leadership is not restricted to the project manager or the product owner. [Derby, E. and Larsen, D., 2006. Agile Retrospectives: Making Good Teams Great. 1st ed. Texas: Pragmatic Bookshelf, Page 41] [Continuous Improvement]

11. D - Although it is desirable that all team member are physically present during the daily standups, there are always some constraints that can create impediments. In this case, the remotely located team member should join the meeting using video conferencing technology. [Agile Practice Guide, 1st edition, Page 122] [Problem Detection and Resolution]

12. C - When estimating, Agile teams do not compare all stories against a single baseline or universal reference. Instead, Agile teams estimate each new story against an assortment of those that have already been estimated. This is referred to as triangulation. [Cohn, M., 2006. Agile Estimating and Planning. 1st ed. Massachusetts: Pearson Education. Page 55] [Adaptive Planning]

13. C - If the majority of the people in the room are vacationers, that's interesting information about how people feel about their work environment. You may want to turn on a dime and make that the major topic of discussion for the retrospective. [Derby, E. and Larsen, D., 2006. Agile Retrospectives: Making Good Teams Great. 1st ed. Texas: Pragmatic Bookshelf, Page 46] [Continuous Improvement]

14. A - Although Agile Manifesto, methods and techniques originated in the software industry, these have since spread to many other industries. Agile is a mindset defined by values, guided by principles, and manifested through many different practices. As the first step, any organization wishing to embark on an Agile journey, needs to adopt an Agile mindset. [Agile Practice Guide, 1st edition, Page 10] [Agile Principles and Mindset]

15. B - When the work in progress (WIP) limits are reached, the team cannot pull further work. However, if the work gets stuck in the "Road blocks" section, further work can be pulled into the "WIP" section. This, if not managed, can soon become a big problem. You need to call a retrospective and discuss "What do we do as a team to move this work ahead?" [Agile Practice Guide, 1st edition, Page 66] [Continuous Improvement]

16. A - This is a variation of the "Mad Sad Glad" activity. During this activity, individuals use colored cards or sticky notes to describe times during the project where they were mad, sad, or glad. [Derby, E. and Larsen, D., 2006. Agile Retrospectives: Making Good Teams Great. 1st ed. Texas: Pragmatic Bookshelf, Page 62] [Continuous Improvement]

17. D - Critical path analysis is a waterfall approach. The rest of the choices are valid actions that can help in this situation. [Agile Practice Guide, 1st edition, Page 58] [Problem Detection and Resolution]

18. D - Developing the high-level model is the first stage of a Feature Driven Development (FDD) project. [Agile Practice Guide, 1st edition, Page 109] [Value-driven Delivery]

19. C - Interest rate is used to discount future amounts to present values. [Cohn, M., 2006. Agile Estimating and Planning. 1st ed. Massachusetts: Pearson Education. Page 100] [Value-driven Delivery]

20. B - A user story is finished when it can be demonstrated to meet all of the conditions of satisfaction identified by the owner. [Cohn, M., 2006. Agile Estimating and Planning. 1st ed. Massachusetts: Pearson Education. Page 201] [Stakeholder Engagement]

21. B - Points counted toward velocity are only for those stories or features that are complete at the end of the iteration. Incomplete stories are not counted toward velocity. In this case, stories that moved from "In Progress" to "Complete" will count toward the team's velocity during the iteration. [Cohn, M., 2006. Agile Estimating and Planning. 1st ed. Massachusetts: Pearson Education. Page 211] [Team Performance]

22. D - Since the changes are requested by the CEO, they need to be considered. However, you cannot just accept them. You need to take these to the product owner and only the product owner can prioritize these. [Agile Practice Guide, 1st edition, Page 41] [Problem Detection and Resolution]

23. B - The raw value of story points we assign is unimportant. What matters is the relative values. A story that is assigned a 20 should be twice as much as a story that is assigned a 10. As long as all stories are correctly relatively estimated, addition or removal of team members do not effect this estimate. [Cohn, M., 2006. Agile Estimating and Planning. 1st ed. Massachusetts: Pearson Education. Page 36] [Problem Detection and Resolution]

24. C - Since the system requirements can only be specified through a series of prototyping iterations, an Agile life cycle is best suited for the design and build phase. [Agile Practice Guide, 1st edition, Page 26] [Agile Principles and Mindset]

25. B - Acceptance Test Driven Development (ATDD) requires the entire team to get together and discuss the acceptance criteria for a work product. The team then creates the tests and writes enough code and automated tests to meet the criteria. [Agile Practice Guide, 1st edition, Page 56] [Value-driven Delivery]

26. A - Swarming is a technique in which multiple team members focus collectively on resolving a specific impediment. [Agile Practice Guide, 1st edition, Page 154] [Problem Detection and Resolution]

27. A - An epic is a very large user story that may span several iterations. Epics are decomposed into smaller user stories before being included in an iteration backlog. [Cohn, M., 2006. Agile Estimating and Planning. 1st ed. Massachusetts: Pearson Education. Page 53] [Adaptive Planning]

28. C - Measuring story points is not the same as measuring completed stories or features. Some teams attempt to measure story points without completing the actual feature or story. When teams measure only story points, they measure capacity, not finished work, which violates the Agile Principle of "the primary measure of progress is working software". [Agile Practice Guide, 1st edition, Page 66] [Team Performance]

29. D - If an iteration's scope of work has been completed half way through the iteration, this means that the stories were not correctly estimated. The root cause of the variation can be discussed during the retrospective and future estimates refined, but at this stage the team needs to consult with the product owner and include more stories to fit the current iteration. [Cohn, M., 2006. Agile Estimating and Planning. 1st ed. Massachusetts: Pearson Education. Page 244] [Problem Detection and Resolution]

30. B - Velocity = average story points per iteration. At the end of the 3rd iteration, the team had delivered 81 story points. The velocity was 81/3 = 27 story points per iteration. At the end of the 4th iteration, the team had delivered 120 story points (81+39). The current velocity is 120/4 = 30 story points per iteration. If the team maintains its current velocity and no more story points are added to the project, the team would require another 16 iterations to deliver the remaining 480 story points (480/30). [Agile Practice Guide, 1st edition, Page 61] [Team Performance]

31. C - The best practice is to move work from "WIP" column to the "Done" column in order to create capacity to move further work from the "Ready" column. Other choices are not best practices. [Agile Practice Guide, 1st edition, Page 66] [Value-driven Delivery]

32. D - People are more likely to make mistakes when they multi-task. Task-switching consumes working memory and people are less likely to remember their context when they multi-task. However, multi-tasking should not affect a person's loyalties. [Agile Practice Guide, 1st edition, Page 45] [Team Performance]

33. B - Estimating is best done by the whole team even though it may be apparent that only one or two specific team members will work on the story or task being estimated. [Cohn, M., 2006. Agile Estimating and Planning. 1st ed. Massachusetts: Pearson Education. Page 248] [Adaptive Planning]

34. C - Scrum is a single-team process framework used to manage product development. The framework consists of Scrum roles, events, artifacts, and rules, and uses an iterative approach to deliver a working product. Scrum is run on timeboxes of one month or less with consistent durations called sprints where a potentially releasable increments of products are produced. [Agile Practice Guide, 1st edition, Page 101] [Value-driven Delivery]

35. C - MoSCoW stands for must have, should have, could have, and won't have. DSDM refers to this sorting as the MoSCoW rules. Applying MoSCoW rules to project requirements ensure that the highest valued business requirements/features are developed first. No more than 70% of the planned effort for a project can be targeted at "Must Have" requirements. [Cohn, M., 2006. Agile Estimating and Planning. 1st ed. Massachusetts: Pearson Education. Page 187] [Value-driven Delivery]

36. D - Spikes are useful for learning and may be used in circumstances such as estimation, acceptance criteria definition, and understanding the flow of a user's action through the product. [Agile Practice Guide, 1st edition, Page 56] [Continuous Improvement]

37. A - A release burndown bar chart is more expressive than the traditional burndown chart. This type of burndown chart uses bars rather than lines to help distinguish the regions above and below the horizontal axis at 0. The bottom is moved up whenever work is removed from an iteration. If the bottom is below the horizontal axis at 0, it means overall work has been added to the release. [Cohn, M., 2006. Agile Estimating and Planning. 1st ed. Massachusetts: Pearson Education. Page 215] [Team Performance]

38. B - A team's velocity is an indicator of its productivity. Adding or removing stories should not affect this productivity. However, if the team becomes more productive as it moves from the "storming" stage to the "norming" stage, the team's velocity will most likely increase. [Agile Practice Guide, 1st edition, Page 61] [Team Performance]

39. A - Agile SPI = Completed story points/planned story points = 550/700 = 0.79. [Agile Practice Guide, 1st edition, Page 69] [Team Performance]

40. C - The feature buffering process that is consistent with use in the Agile process is DSDM (Dynamic Systems Development Method). On DSDM projects, requirements are sorted into four categories: must have, should have, could have, and won't have. [Cohn, M., 2006. Agile Estimating and Planning. 1st ed. Massachusetts: Pearson Education. Page 187] [Adaptive Planning]

PMI-ACP Lite Mock Exam 20 Practice Questions

Test Name: PMI-ACP Lite Mock Exam 20
Total Questions: 40
Correct Answers Needed to Pass:
30 (75.00%)
Time Allowed: 60 Minutes

Test Description

This is a cumulative PMI-ACP Mock Exam which can be used as a benchmark for your PMI-ACP aptitude. This practice test includes questions from all exam topic areas, including sections from Agile Tools and Techniques, and all three Agile Knowledge and Skills areas.

Test Questions

1. On some projects, financial prioritization can be difficult due to difficulty in estimating the financial returns on a theme. Which of the following non-financial measures can be used in such cases?

A. Prioritizing by internal rate of return.

B. Prioritizing by net present value.

C. Prioritizing by payback period.

D. Prioritizing by desirability of features.

2. Traditional project management approaches do allow changes through a formal change control process. What is the main issue with this?

A. Formal change control procedures need to be designed, documented and implemented.

B. Formal change control procedures are resource intensive.

C. Formal change control procedures are not practical.

D. Formal change control procedures discourage changes on a project.

3. Agile methods, tools and techniques deliver maximum benefit if they are applied correctly in the right environment. Which of the following scenarios provides an ideal environment for Agile teams?

A. Agile team operates in silos while the leadership isolates the teams.

B. Agile teams focus on processes and tools while the leadership focuses on individuals and interactions.

C. Agile teams are self-organized while the leadership strives to fulfil the needs of the teams.

D. Agile teams focus on delivery while the leadership focuses on quality management.

4. What is the main benefit of delivering a project in increments and discovering the requirements on-the-go versus strictly following a written specification?

A. Teams are better able to understand the true customer requirements faster and more accurately.

B. Red tape involved with upfront planning is eliminated.

C. Team size is reduced, significantly reducing the project costs.

D. When the project planning effort is reduced, the focus shifts from planning to actual work.

5. Which of the following is the correct way to plan an Agile project?

A. Desired features -> schedule -> estimate size -> estimate duration

B. Desired features -> estimate duration -> estimate size -> schedule

C. Desired features -> estimate size -> estimate duration -> schedule

D. Schedule -> estimate duration -> desired features -> estimate size

6. If all features on a project have been classified by their risk and business value, which of the following group of themes would you recommend avoiding?

A. The features that deliver high value and eliminate the maximum risk from the project.

B. The features that deliver high value but are less risky.

C. The features that have low value, especially those that are also high risk.

D. The features that have less impact on the total value and have low risk.

7. An Agile team estimated a story at 4 ideal days. If the team size is doubled, how would that impact the story size estimate?

A. The story size might get changed.

B. The story size might get increased.

C. The story size might get reduced.

D. The story size will remain the same.

8. An Agile team has collaborated with the product owner to define and prioritize user stories. However, prior to starting work on the high priority stories, what would the team still need?

A. Kanban board.

B. Definition of ready for all stories.

C. Visual controls.

D. Duration estimate for all stories.

9. You are reviewing the product backlog of an online collaboration tool and find out that most of the user stories have been assigned story points in the range of 10 to 30. Some of the user stories are typical for most of the projects you have led so far in your previous organization, however those user stories were assigned story points in the range of 50 to 150. What should you do?

A. Take this issue to the next standup and investigate why the team has underestimated the effort on the project.

B. Disregard how previous projects assigned story points to user stories and check if the relative values of story points on this project makes sense.

C. Raise a red flag and report the issue to the senior leadership.

D. Do nothing as the raw values assigned to the story points does not matter.

10. Task B can only start once task A has been completed. If I need to add a 2-day feeding buffer between the tasks, how should I schedule the tasks?

A. Add a 2-day lead to task B

B. Add a 2-day lag to task B

C. Add a 2-day lag to task A

D. Add a 2-day lead to task A

11. T-shaped people are more suitable for Agile teams than I-shaped people. All of the following are benefits of having T-shaped people on the team EXCEPT:

A. This helps in creating a cross-functional team.

B. This helps in forming smaller teams.

C. This allows teams to self-organize.

D. This removes the risk from the project.

12. Which of the following is an Agile estimation technique played by the team as a game using cards?

A. Approximating Black Jack

B. Planning poker

C. Estimating Rummy

D. Contracting Bridge

13. A project team that has managed all of its past projects on waterfall has recently kick-started their first Agile project. Due to the lack of a formal communications and resource management plan, the team is currently having issues due to lack of clear working agreements for the team. What needs to be done?

A. Develop an Agile team charter.

B. Develop detailed communications and resource management plans.

C. Develop a detailed resource management plan.

D. Develop a detailed communications management plan.

14. Which of the following techniques is ideal for requirements validation?

A. Planning poker

B. Questionnaires

C. Rolling wave planning

D. Prototyping

15. You invited your product owner to the upcoming iteration retrospective. She thanked you for the invitation and told you that she would look forward to the session and would like to adopt good ideas. Which ESVP role closely relates to this attitude?

A. Shoppers

B. Stakeholders

C. Dictators

D. Explorers

16. You are leading the development of an enterprise knowledge management system. You haven't done detailed cost estimates for each of the user stories on the project. In order to prioritize user stories the product owner can use which of the following estimates?

A. Number of iterations

B. Story points

C. Product backlog

D. Number of themes

17. Which of the following project lifecycles is both iterative and incremental in nature?

A. Agile life cycle

B. Waterfall life cycle

C. Predictive life cycle

D. Lean life cycle

18. The Kano model gives us an approach to separate features into three categories: must-have features, linear features, and delighters. What are linear features?

A. The ones for which "the more, the better" holds true.

B. The ones that have a direct relationship with development cost.

C. The ones that can be evenly distributed across project iterations.

D. The ones that need to be developed in a strict linear order.

19. Which of the following actions could impact a story's response time?

A. Prioritization of the story.

B. Size of the story.

C. Story's cost of development.

D. Story's technological requirements.

20. You want to establish a management and communication tool to visualize how a team is performing at completing the planned functionality of a release classified by themes. The Agile team has proposed using a board with a large box for each theme in the release. Each box is to be annotated with the name of the theme, the number of stories in that theme, the number of story points or ideal days for those stories, and the percentage of the story points that are complete. In Agile community, what is such a board called?

A. Parking lot chart

B. Kanban board

C. Andon

D. Poka-Yoke

21. You are leading a complex automation system deployment project. The Agile team has decided to deploy the systems in increments of value for delivery and feedback. During each iteration, the team receives feedback about how the product looks and operates. The team members then reflect upon and determine how they can optimize these processes. Which Agile techniques facilitate these activities?

A. Feedback is received during spikes while the reflection is done during backlog grooming.

B. Feedback is received during demonstrations while the reflection is done during retrospectives.

C. Feedback is received during retrospectives while the reflection is done during demonstrations.

D. Feedback is received during backlog grooming while the reflection is done during spikes.

22. An organization structured in such a way that it only manages to contribute a subset of the aspects required for delivering value to customers is known as:

A. Projectized organization

B. Value-driven organization

C. Matrix organization

D. Siloed organization

23. You have recently taken over a PMO of an organization. You have notices that the project teams are estimating all user stories of a project prior to developing the release plan. What is your view on this?

A. The user stories can be estimated prior to release planning but only once the iteration planning has been done.

B. It is a good practice to estimate all user stories prior to release planning.

C. This is okay since an Agile team can choose whatever route they want to take on the project.

D. It is not an Agile approach to estimate all user stories prior to release planning.

24. Agile is more of a ___ than a body of knowledge.

A. Framework

B. Mindset

C. Methodology

D. Process

25. You are leading a 500 story points feature-driven project. If the expected velocity is 25 story points per three-week iteration. How many iterations will be required to complete the project?

A. This cannot be determined by the information provided.

B. 20

C. 75

D. 167

26. During release planning, selecting iteration length, estimating velocity, and prioritizing user stories are some of the critical planning activities. What is the general recommendation around the correct sequence of these planning activities?

A. Estimate velocity -> Select an iteration length -> Prioritize user stories.

B. Estimate velocity -> Prioritize user stories -> Select an iteration length.

C. No general sequence for these activities is recommended.

D. Select an iteration length -> Estimate velocity -> Prioritize user stories.

27. ESVP is an activity commonly used to set the stage of Agile retrospectives. What does ESVP stand for?

A. Excellent, Super, Volatile, Pathetic

B. Energetic, Sluggish, Volatile, Passive

C. Educator, Successor, Value-added, Promoter

D. Explorer, Shopper, Vacationer, Prisoner

28. Which of the following Agile terms means an agreed-upon condition, when satisfied, means a feature is complete?

A. Acceptance constraints

B. Definition of done

C. Test case

D. Triple constraints

29. Agile projects rely on product owners to define and prioritize backlog items. How do product owners do this?

A. By collaborating with business stakeholders.

B. By collaborating with the Agile team.

C. By collaborating with the servant-leader.

D. By collaborating with the project manager.

30. During an iteration demonstration, at the end of an iteration the product owner has highlighted some performance issues with the released features. These performance issues might render the released features unusable. What should you do next?

A. Prioritize the performance issues at the top of the backlog.

B. Delete the troublesome features from the backlog.

C. Convert the performance issues into user stories and return them to the backlog.

D. Conduct a root cause analysis at the start of the next iteration.

31. Transforming from traditional to Agile approaches requires change management. This is typically considered a project on its own. If you are required to lead such a project, how would you manage it?

A. By treating the change process as an Agile project with its own backlog of changes.

B. Using traditional approaches as the organization is already aware of these approaches.

C. Using Agile approaches to establishing detailed scope, schedule and cost management plans.

D. By treating the change process as a predictive project with established project baselines.

32. Which of the following is a systematic problem-solving Agile process that collects the pertinent information on a single sheet of paper?

A. 5-Whys

B. Fishbone

C. A3

D. Scrum

33. You are leading a massive knowledge work project. Some team members have complained they have to work overtime in order to complete some of the assigned work. What should you do to resolve this issue?

A. Establish working agreements

B. Call a team retrospective

C. Establish a Kanban board and set WIP limits

D. Launch a root cause analysis

34. Mark is the project manager on an Agile project. During the daily team meeting, he reviews the iteration plan and assigns tasks to team members. He also collects reported issues and negotiates with functional managers to get them resolved. What do you think of this Agile team?

A. The team requires coaching on Agile practices.

B. The team is not self-organizing.

C. Mark is the product owner on this project.

D. Mark has got a dictatorial attitude.

35. Which of the following statements is correct for all project life cycles?

A. Each project life cycle shares the element of planning.

B. Each project life cycle allows teams to segment work into a sequence of predictable groupings.

C. Each project life cycle only provides finished deliverables that the customer may be able to use immediately.

D. Each project life cycle allows feedback on partially completed on unfinished work.

36. Your project has multiple stakeholders who have strong interest and influence on the project. What is the best strategy to manage such stakeholders?

A. Keep them informed.

B. Utilize their strong interest in grooming the backlog.

C. Involve them in all decisions.

D. Provide minimum information so that they don't create any roadblocks for the project.

37. You have been invited by your colleague to attend one of the project standup meetings. You notice that the team has got a big chart on a wall, divided into sections such as "Ready", "In Development", "Being Tested", and "Completed". What tool are they using?

A. Burndown chart

B. War room

C. Kanban board

D. Activity matrix

38. A project team was assembled to develop organizational policies and procedures using an Agile approach. The team members were selected from various departments in order to form a cross-functional team. The members coming from operations were responsible for the development, while the members coming from support were responsible for the validation of the policies and procedures. The team members were assigned to work part-time on this project, while they continued to work in their respective departments for the rest of the time. Is this team representative of a typical Agile team?

A. Yes; the team is cross-functional.

B. Yes; the team is following an Agile approach.

C. No; the team members are not specialists in policies and procedures development.

D. No; the team members are not 100% dedicated to the project.

39. In contrast with traditional project management approaches, Agile approaches focus on rapid product development rather than focusing on exhaustive planning and change control. In your opinion, why do Agile teams strive for rapid product development?

A. To reduce scope creep.

B. To meet project deadlines.

C. To obtain early feedback.

D. To reduce the number of change requests.

40. What happens when the time-box of a sprint expires?

A. The velocity increases.

B. The teams move on to the next sprint.

C. The project is terminated.

D. The project gets delayed.

PMI-ACP Lite Mock Exam 20 Answer Key and Explanations

1. D - Net present value (NPV), internal rate of return (IRR) and payback period are all financial measures. In situations where financial measures are difficult to determine, non-financial measures such as "desirability of features" can be used. [Cohn, M., 2006. Agile Estimating and Planning. 1st ed. Massachusetts: Pearson Education. Pages 81, 91] [Adaptive Planning]

2. D - There can be many challenges associated with designing and implementing formal change control procedures, however the main disadvantage is that they inherently discourage changes. Many features get delivered that users don't want just because formal change control puts the responsivity on the customer and users to identify and request the change, which is usually not a very proactive approach. [Cohn, M., 2006. Agile Estimating and Planning. 1st ed. Massachusetts: Pearson Education. Page 247] [Problem Detection and Resolution]

3. C - Quality management and focusing on individuals and interactions are the responsibilities of the project team. Operating in silos is against the spirit of Agile Manifesto. A perfect Agile environment is created when project teams are self-organized while the leadership strives to fulfil the needs of the teams. [Agile Practice Guide, 1st edition, Page 36] [Agile Principles and Mindset]

4. A - Teams can verify their work when they use small increments and can change what they do next. When teams deliver small increments, they are better able to understand the true customer requirements faster and more accurately than with a static written specification. [Agile Practice Guide, 1st edition, Page 13] [Value-driven Delivery]

5. C - The correct sequence is: desired features -> estimate size -> estimate duration -> schedule. [Cohn, M., 2006. Agile Estimating and Planning. 1st ed. Massachusetts: Pearson Education. Page 38] [Adaptive Planning]

6. C - The features that deliver low value but are high risk are best avoided. It is recommended deferring work on all low value features, especially those that are also high risk. [Cohn, M., 2006. Agile Estimating and Planning. 1st ed. Massachusetts: Pearson Education. Page 85] [Adaptive Planning]

7. A - An estimate in ideal days can change based on the team's experience with technology, the domain, and themselves, among other factors. Additional team members can positively (completing stories faster) or negatively (too many communication channels) affect the story. [Cohn, M., 2006. Agile Estimating and Planning. 1st ed. Massachusetts: Pearson Education. Page 70] [Problem Detection and Resolution]

8. B - The Definition of Ready (DoR) is a team's checklist for a user-centric requirement that has all the information the team needs to be able to begin working. [Agile Practice Guide, 1st edition, Page 151] [Value-driven Delivery]

9. B - Disregard how previous projects assigned story points to user stories and check if the relative values of story points on this project make sense. The raw value we

assign is unimportant. What matters are the relative values. A story that is assigned a 20 should be twice as much as a story that is assigned a 10. It does not matter if earlier projects assigned these user stories 120 and 60 story points respectively. [Cohn, M., 2006. Agile Estimating and Planning. 1st ed. Massachusetts: Pearson Education. Page 36] [Adaptive Planning]

10. B - A feeding buffer, like the schedule buffer, protects the on-time delivery of a set of new capabilities. This is a somewhat complicated way of saying that if your team needs something from my team tomorrow morning, my team shouldn't plan on finishing it the day before. In order to add a 2-day feeding buffer between two tasks, we add a 2-day lag to the successor task. [Cohn, M., 2006. Agile Estimating and Planning. 1st ed. Massachusetts: Pearson Education. Page 204] [Adaptive Planning]

11. D - In Agile communities, people with expertise in one domain, less-developed skills in associated areas and good collaboration skills are known as T-shaped people. For Agile projects, it is preferred to have a team of self-organizing, T-shaped, cross-functional team generalists. However, having T-shaped people doesn't remove the project risk. [Agile Practice Guide, 1st edition, Page 42] [Value-driven Delivery]

12. B - Planning poker is an Agile estimating technique. The rest of the choices are all made up terms. Planning poker is generally recognized as the best Agile estimating technique. Planning poker combines expert opinion, analogy, and disaggregation into an enjoyable approach to estimating that results in a quick but reliable estimate. [Cohn, M., 2006. Agile Estimating and Planning. 1st ed. Massachusetts: Pearson Education. Page 56] [Adaptive Planning]

13. A - Developing detailed project plans are not recommended in Agile. The Agile team charted should be enough to resolve this issue. [Agile Practice Guide, 1st edition, Page 58] [Value-driven Delivery]

14. D - A prototype is a draft version of a product that allows you to explore your ideas and show the intention behind a feature or the overall design concept to users before investing time and money into development. Prototyping is an efficient and effective way to understand and validate system requirements at the early stage of software development. [Agile Practice Guide, 1st edition, Page 21] [Stakeholder Engagement]

15. A - Shoppers want to look over all the available information and will be happy to go home with one useful new idea. [Derby, E. and Larsen, D., 2006. Agile Retrospectives: Making Good Teams Great. 1st ed. Texas: Pragmatic Bookshelf, Page 45] [Continuous Improvement]

16. B - The size of user stories is typically estimated in story points. Size of user stories is one of the critical factors considered for selection of user stories. [Cohn, M., 2006. Agile Estimating and Planning. 1st ed. Massachusetts: Pearson Education. Page 133] [Adaptive Planning]

17. A - Lean is a methodology rather than a project life cycle. Predictive life cycle, also known as the waterfall approach, requires the bulk of the planning to happen upfront and then executing the project in a single pass. Agile lifecycle, on the other hand, is both iterative and incremental as it focuses on frequent deliveries and continuous refinement of work items. [Agile Practice Guide, 1st edition, Page 17] [Agile Principles and Mindset]

18. A - A linear feature is one for which "the more, the better" holds true. These are called linear features because customer satisfaction is correlated linearly with the quantity of the feature. [Cohn, M., 2006. Agile Estimating and Planning. 1st ed. Massachusetts: Pearson Education. Page 110] [Adaptive Planning]

19. A - The response time is the time a story waits until the work starts. In Agile projects, stories wait till the higher value stories are completed. Prioritization of the stories impacts their response time. [Agile Practice Guide, 1st edition, Page 64] [Team Performance]

20. A - Such boards are known as parking lot charts. A parking lot chart is a powerful method for compressing a great deal of information into a small space. [Cohn, M., 2006. Agile Estimating and Planning. 1st ed. Massachusetts: Pearson Education. Page 218] [Stakeholder Engagement]

21. B - Feedback is received during demonstrations while the reflection is done during retrospectives. [Agile Practice Guide, 1st edition, Page 57] [Value-driven Delivery]

22. D - An organization that is structured in such a way that it only manages to contribute a subset of the aspects required for delivering value to customers is known as a siloed organization. [Agile Practice Guide, 1st edition, Page 154] [Agile Principles and Mindset]

23. D - It is not recommended to estimate everything early in the project. It is only necessary to have an estimate for each new feature that has some reasonable possibility of being selected for inclusion in the upcoming release. [Cohn, M., 2006. Agile Estimating and Planning. 1st ed. Massachusetts: Pearson Education. Page 134] [Adaptive Planning]

24. B - Agile is more of a mindset than a body of knowledge. [Agile Practice Guide, 1st edition, Page 8] [Agile Principles and Mindset]

25. B - If the project is feature-driven, we can estimate the number of iterations required by dividing the project size by the expected velocity; 500/25 = 20 iterations. [Cohn, M., 2006. Agile Estimating and Planning. 1st ed. Massachusetts: Pearson Education. Page 135] [Team Performance]

26. C - The general release planning sequence is determining conditions of satisfaction, followed by estimating user stories; then any sequence of selecting iteration length, estimating velocity and prioritizing user stories, followed by selecting stories and release date. [Cohn, M., 2006. Agile Estimating and Planning. 1st ed. Massachusetts: Pearson Education. Page 133] [Adaptive Planning]

27. D - ESVP is the abbreviation for Explorer, Shopper, Vacationer, or Prisoner. [Derby, E. and Larsen, D., 2006. Agile Retrospectives: Making Good Teams Great. 1st ed. Texas: Pragmatic Bookshelf, Page 45] [Continuous Improvement]

28. B - Definition of done (DoD) is a checklist of all the criteria required to be met so that a deliverable can be considered ready for customer use. [Agile Practice Guide, 1st edition, Page 151] [Value-driven Delivery]

29. A - The product owner prioritizes the product backlog so that the team delivers the most valuable ones first. The product owner does that by determining the items' value by collaborating with business stakeholders. The team does not determine the value of the backlog items and neither does the project manager. [Agile Practice Guide, 1st edition, Page 41] [Stakeholder Engagement]

30. C - Incomplete work is returned to the product backlog where it gets prioritized again. In most cases, it usually ends up assigned to the next iteration but automatic assignment to the next iteration is not recommended. [Cohn, M., 2006. Agile Estimating and Planning. 1st ed. Massachusetts: Pearson Education. Page 66] [Problem Detection and Resolution]

31. A - Agile approaches do not require a detailed plan to start the project. Detailed plans and baselines are recommended in traditional approaches. Traditional approaches work well when the project scope can be reasonably defined early during the project. Agile transformation is a complex project with high uncertainty. A common practice is to treat such initiatives as an Agile project with its own backlog of changes that could be introduced and prioritized by the team. [Agile Practice Guide, 1st edition, Page 84] [Problem Detection and Resolution]

32. C - A3 is a way of thinking and a systematic problem-solving process that collects the pertinent information on a single sheet of A3-size of paper. [Agile Practice Guide, 1st edition, Page 150] [Stakeholder Engagement]

33. C - The problem is hand is unmanageable WIP. The solution is to limit the WIP based on team capacity. A Kanban board can be really helpful in setting this up. A Kanban board provides a means to visualize the flow of work, make impediments easily visible, and allow flow to be managed by adjusting the work in process limits. [Agile Practice Guide, 1st edition, Page 31] [Problem Detection and Resolution]

34. B - Although Mark is assigning tasks to team members, this doesn't mean he has got a dictatorial attitude. All we can conclude for sure is that the team is not self-organizing; either due to the lack of ability or the selected management approach. Further, no information is provided that shows that Mark is also the product owner on this project. [Agile Practice Guide, 1st edition, Page 154] [Stakeholder Engagement]

35. A - A key thing to remember about life cycles is that each of them share the element of planning. What differentiates a life cycle is not whether planning is done, but rather how much planning is done and when. [Agile Practice Guide, 1st edition, Page 20] [Agile Principles and Mindset]

36. A - If many stakeholders have strong interest and influence on the project, the best strategy is to keep them informed. Simple but regular reporting in the form of performance indicators and burndown charts are very useful in keeping stakeholders informed. [Cohn, M., 2006. Agile Estimating and Planning. 1st ed. Massachusetts: Pearson Education. Page 249] [Stakeholder Engagement]

37. C - This is an example of Kanban board. A Kanban board provides a means to visualize the flow of work, make impediments easily visible, and allow flow to be managed by adjusting the work in process limits. [Agile Practice Guide, 1st edition, Page 31] [Value-driven Delivery]

38. D - Agile teams are cross-functional and they do follow Agile approaches, but they are also supposed to be 100% dedicated to the project work. In this scenario, the project team is not 100% dedicated, which is not representative of a typical Agile team. However, it must be noted that while this condition is desirable, it sometimes cannot be met. [Agile Practice Guide, 1st edition, Page 43] [Value-driven Delivery]

39. C - Change requests and scope creep are welcomed by the Agile teams as long as changes deliver value to the customer and the changes are requested by the customer. (Scope creep should not be confused with gold plating where the project team adds features that were not requested by the customer). Meeting project deadlines is a prime goal in traditional approaches while the Agile approaches focus on value delivery. Rapid product development allows early feedback to the project team. [Agile Practice Guide, 1st edition, Page 39] [Value-driven Delivery]

40. B - Time-box for a sprint or iteration is the duration of the sprint or iteration. When the time-box expires, the team simply moves on to the next sprint. [Agile Practice Guide, 1st edition, Page 25] [Problem Detection and Resolution]

PMI-ACP Lite Mock Exam 21 Practice Questions

Test Name: PMI-ACP Lite Mock Exam 20
Total Questions: 40
Correct Answers Needed to Pass: 30 (75.00%)
Time Allowed: 60 Minutes

Test Description

This is a cumulative PMI-ACP Mock Exam which can be used as a benchmark for your PMI-ACP aptitude. This practice test includes questions from all exam topic areas, including sections from Agile Tools and Techniques, and all three Agile Knowledge and Skills areas.

Test Questions

1. Most Agile teams do planning at the release, iteration and daily levels. How does an Agile team conduct daily planning?

A. Daily planning is done by the servant-leader and shared with the team.

B. Daily planning is not a recommended Agile practice and it is considered a waste.

C. Daily planning is done by the team during the daily standups.

D. Daily planning is done by the product owner and passed on to the team.

2. One of the senior team members, who is the best performer in your project, plays favorites. A few of the other team members who work closely with this team member have gotten exceptionally good appraisal reports in the past, even though they may not have deserved them. As the Agile coach, what do you need to actively do?

A. Ignore the matter since you would otherwise lose a senior team member who is key to your project.

B. Speak to the senior team member and ask them to do appraisals fairly, in accordance with the appraisal guidelines.

C. Ensure that the senior team member does not get to appraise anybody.

D. Ask all the members of your team who are appraisers of other team members to be liberal in their appraisals. This will help compensate for the appraisals the senior team member does.

3. If your cost of capital is 5%, and only one of the following projects can be executed, which of the following projects is the most lucrative assuming that all projects cost the same?

A. Project D with a net profit of $210,000 at the end of year five.

B. Project L with a net profit of $250,000 at the end of year eight.

C. Project B with a net profit of $180,000 at the end of year two.

D. Project R with a net profit of $200,000 at the end of year three.

4. What is a product roadmap?

A. The collection of stories grouped by themes.

B. The collection of stories classified by epics.

C. A Gantt chart based on user stories.

D. The anticipated sequence of project deliverables over time.

5. Which of the following models shows that during the feasibility phase of a project, a schedule estimate is typically as far off as 60% to 160% and after the requirements are written, the estimate might still be off +/-15% in either direction?

A. Pareto Chart

B. Monte Carlo Model

C. Fishbone Diagram

D. Cone of Uncertainty

6. Does establishing a Kanban board on a project influence the work being performed?

A. Yes, it reduces the lead times.

B. Yes, it decreases the cycle times.

C. Yes, it limits the work in process to increase performance.

D. Yes, it pushes the work in process to increase performance.

7. You are leading an Agile team. For the last two iterations, the team wasn't able to complete planned stories. Upon investigation, you found out that team frequently got interrupted to do bug fixes. What should you do now?

A. Ask the team members not to take on bug fixing work without your permission.

B. Ask the team members to add bug-fixes to the backlog where they can get prioritized.

C. Escalate the issue to the product owner for their immediate attention.

D. Ask the team members to take on the bug fixing work once their daily targets have been achieved.

8. A release burndown chart can be plotted in a number of formats, except as a:

A. Histogram

B. Line chart

C. Area chart

D. Pie chart

9. You have been assigned as the project manager to develop a software tool. The project is going to be delivered using Agile practices. When do you create the business case for the project?

A. In Agile projects, the business case development is considered optional.

B. At the start of the project, like any other project.

C. In Agile projects, the business case is built into the user stories.

D. Business cases are not developed for Agile projects.

10. You are managing an Agile software development project and currently engaging with the product owner to refine the product backlog. What should be your prime focus during this activity?

A. Selecting highest value requirements.

B. Collecting business requirements.

C. Optimizing project costs.

D. Reviewing processes.

11. Pair programming is a development technique in which two developers work together to develop a product. Pair programming is a technique used in which of the following Agile frameworks?

A. Scrum

B. XP

C. Lean

D. Kanban

12. Which of the following statements is most accurate?

A. Any project can benefit from a project charter.

B. Only a handful of projects benefit from a project charter.

C. Some projects benefit from a project charter.

D. Only traditional projects benefit from a project charter.

13. Project sponsors usually want to know project timelines. Agile teams usually estimate project completion using variables such as current velocity and cycle time. However, like any other estimate, this estimate has some degree of variability. Which of the following tools can help an Agile team reflect this variability?

A. Flow charts

B. Fishbone diagrams

C. Hurricane-style charts

D. Pareto charts

14. Agile teams generally use which of the following tools to keep project stakeholders informed of the project's progress?

A. Burndown charts

B. Sprint diagrams

C. Flowcharts

D. Gantt charts

15. How does an Agile team do daily planning?

A. The scrum master allocates the tasks and collects feedback during the daily scrum.

B. Each team member makes commitments to complete, or at least make progress on, specific tasks during the daily standup.

C. The scrum master conducts a series of 15-minute face to face meetings with the team members and allocates tasks.

D. Each team member emails their commitments to complete, or at least make progress on, specific tasks during the day.

16. You have recently completed a project iteration and prior to the commencement of the next iteration a few defects have been found. What should be done next?

A. Create a user story for each identified defect.

B. Escalate the issue to the product owner.

C. Hold the servant-leader accountable for all the defects.

D. Delay the next iteration until all defects have been fixed.

17. How much time should an Agile team spend on check-ins during an iteration retrospective session?

A. Five to ten minutes per participant.

B. 50% of the time.

C. Five to ten minutes.

D. 25% of the time.

18. Traditional EVM metrics can be translated into Agile terms. Which of the following is the correct CPI formula for Agile projects?

A. Completed story points/planned story points.

B. Planned story points/completed story points.

C. Actual costs to date/completed features value.

D. Completed features value/actual costs to date.

19. You are the project lead of a large IT project. A manager from a company contracted to work on the project offers you free tickets to a local sporting event. The tickets are expensive, but your organization has no formal policy regarding gifts. What is the best way to handle the offer?

A. Politely refuse the tickets.

B. Accept the tickets but notify your employer.

C. Refuse the tickets and report the offer to your employer.

D. Accept the tickets since there is no policy.

20. You are leading a team of 10 process analysts assigned to observe organizational processes and map the "AS-IS" processes. You usually arrange the process workshops and encourage two analysts to facilitate a workshop at a time. By having two analysts facilitating a single workshop, you believe that you get early feedback and early identification of process issues. What is this technique called?

A. Double lens

B. One piece flow

C. Plan Do Check Act

D. Pair work

21. Which of the following statements regarding Return on Investment (ROI) measure is incorrect?

A. ROI is a more accurate measure than IRR.

B. ROI measure doesn't factor in the time value of money.

C. ROI calculations put equal value on the money invested now and the money earned in the future.

D. ROI is commonly used by accountants to measure financial benefits.

22. You are responsible for the design and build of a resilient data center for your organization. Due to the complexity and the number of requirements, you need someone to provide the guiding direction and requirements prioritization. Ideally this role should work with the project team daily and provide product feedback and set direction on the next piece of functionality to be delivered. In Agile lexicon, this role is called?

A. Servant-leader

B. Product owner

C. Cross-functional team member

D. Scrum master

23. Which of the following is NOT an Agile methodology?

A. FDD

B. DSDM

C. PDCA

D. AUP

24. Which of the following is correct about project and team charters?

A. A project charter is an optional project artefact while the team charter is a mandatory project artefact.

B. A project charter is recommended for waterfall approaches while the team charter is recommended for Agile approaches.

C. A project charter is a mandatory project artefact while the team charter is an optional project artefact.

D. A project charter documents the project objective while the team charter documents how the team members will interact.

25. If an Agile project's Earned Value is $100,000 and the CPI is 0.8, how much the team has spent so far on the project?

A. 80000

B. 100000

C. 125000

D. This figure cannot be computed with the given data.

26. The use of iterative approaches is recommended when there is a high risk of:

A. Change of requirements.

B. Change of organizational priorities.

C. Change of environment.

D. Change of team members.

27. Which of the following is the method of collaboratively creating acceptance test criteria that are used to create acceptance tests before delivery begins?

A. SAFe

B. ATDD

C. XP

D. RUP

28. Flow-based Agile has a different approach to stand-ups than iteration-based Agile. Which of the following is NOT a typical question addressed during these stand-ups?

A. What are my impediments?

B. What do we need to do to advance this piece of work?

C. Is anyone working on anything that is not on the board?

D. Are there any bottlenecks or impediments to the flow of work?

29. You have recently been hired by an organization that is new to Agile approaches. You find out that some of the teams have developed detailed release plans and do not require iteration planning. However, they do fine-tune the release plan on a daily basis. What is your view on this?

A. Release planning becomes redundant if the team develops detailed iteration planning.

B. Iteration planning becomes redundant if detailed release plans are developed and baselined.

C. Both release and iteration planning becomes irrelevant to teams who are capable of developing accurate and precise daily plans.

D. The release, iteration, and daily plans are all important as they cover different time horizons.

30. Which of the following statements regarding the iterative and incremental life cycles is correct?

A. Both incremental and iterative life cycles allow customer feedback on partially completed or unfinished work.

B. Both incremental and iterative life cycles only provide finished deliverables that the customer may be able to use immediately.

C. Iterative life cycles allow customer feedback on partially completed or unfinished work while incremental life cycles only provide finished deliverables that the customer may be able to use immediately.

D. Incremental life cycles allow customer feedback on partially completed or unfinished work while iterative life cycles only provide finished deliverables that the customer may be able to use immediately.

31. Agile Kanban boards were inherited from Lean manufacturing systems. The Lean Kanbans were originally used for?

A. Quality assurance

B. Inventory management

C. Risk management

D. Production planning

32. Which of the following Agile events demands mandatory participation of the product owner?

A. Daily standups

B. Demonstrations

C. Estimation

D. Retrospectives

33. You have recently taken over leadership of an Agile team that is halfway through a complicated project. You have recently examined project requirements and now want to get an idea of team velocity. Which document should provide some insight on the team's velocity?

A. Kanban board

B. Burndown chart

C. Definition of done

D. Product backlog

34. You are auditing an Agile project. While reviewing the release plan, you find out some of the larger stories exist further down the project's prioritized list of work. What would be your recommendation for the team?

A. Schedule all of the larger stories for the next iteration.

B. Do not decompose the stories into smaller pieces until starting the iteration where these are scheduled.

C. Schedule all of the larger stories for the next few iterations.

D. Decompose the stories into smaller pieces but the development can wait until the assigned iterations.

35. Which of the following is a model of skills acquisition that describes progression from obeying the rules, through consciously moving away from the rules, and finally through steady practice and improvement finding an individual path?

A. Salience model

B. Shu-Ha-Ri model

C. Kaizen model

D. PDCA model

36. According to the Agile Manifesto responding to change is valued more than:

A. Following a plan

B. Contract negotiation

C. Processes and tools

D. Comprehensive documentation

37. The Agile manifesto was initially developed for?

A. Generic projects

B. Construction projects

C. User experience projects

D. Software projects

38. When Agile teams have dedicated members, which of the following benefits is usually realized?

A. Formal change control.

B. Efficient multi-tasking.

C. Increased focus and productivity.

D. Collocation.

39. Agile plans cover which of the following three levels?

A. Backlog, sprints, and spikes.

B. Release, iteration, and the current day.

C. Strategic, tactical, and operational.

D. Epics, themes, and stories.

40. At the end of the third iteration, you are asked if the release will be finished within the planned eight iterations. How can you determine the finish date using a burndown chart?

A. Reading the x-intercept of the burndown line.

B. Adding a linear trendline and reading the x-intercept.

C. Adding a linear trendline and reading the y-intercept.

D. Reading the y-intercept of the burndown line.

PMI-ACP Lite Mock Exam 21 Answer Key and Explanations

1. C - Most Agile teams use some form of daily standup meeting to coordinate work and synchronize daily efforts. Although it may seem excessive to consider this planning in the formal sense, teams definitely make, assess, and revise their plans during these meetings. [Cohn, M., 2006. Agile Estimating and Planning. 1st ed. Massachusetts: Pearson Education. Page 28] [Adaptive Planning]

2. B - As Agile coach, you need to speak to the senior team member and ask for all appraisals to be done in an objective manner. The other options are incorrect. Ignoring the matter will not help solve it. The other two options are likewise impractical. [PMI Code of Ethics and Professional Conduct] [Stakeholder Engagement]

3. D - To determine which of these projects is the most lucrative, we need to calculate the present values of all four projects and select the project with the highest PV using the formula PV = FV / (1 + r)^n. The PVs of the projects are: PV Project R = $172,768; PV Project D = $164,540; PV Project L = $169,210; PV Project B = $163,265. Project R is the most lucrative one. [Cohn, M., 2006. Agile Estimating and Planning. 1st ed. Massachusetts: Pearson Education. Page 100] [Value-driven Delivery]

4. D - A product roadmap shows the anticipated sequence of deliverables over time. Product owners are primarily responsible for developing product roadmaps. [Agile Practice Guide, 1st edition, Page 52] [Stakeholder Engagement]

5. D - Barry Boehm drew the first version of what Steve McConnell later called the "cone of uncertainty". The cone of uncertainty shows that during the feasibility phase of a project a schedule estimate is typically as far off as 60% to 160%. That is, a project expected to take 20 weeks could take anywhere from 12 to 32 weeks. After the requirements are written, the estimate might still be off +/-15% in either direction. So an estimate of 20 weeks means work that takes from 17 to 23 weeks. [Cohn, M., 2006. Agile Estimating and Planning. 1st ed. Massachusetts: Pearson Education. Page 4] [Adaptive Planning]

6. C - A Kanban board helps the team to further improve its effectiveness by visualizing the flow of work, making impediments easily visible, and allowing the flow to be managed by adjusting work in process limits. [Agile Practice Guide, 1st edition, Page 31] [Team Performance]

7. B - Bug fixing work must be added to the product backlog where it should get prioritized. [Cohn, M., 2006. Agile Estimating and Planning. 1st ed. Massachusetts: Pearson Education. Page 66] [Problem Detection and Resolution]

8. D - A release burndown chart can be shown in a variety of formats. Although a line chart is most commonly used, a histogram (bar chart) or an area chart can also be used. The pie chart cannot show the reducing story points by iterations. [Cohn, M., 2006. Agile Estimating and Planning. 1st ed. Massachusetts: Pearson Education. Page 214] [Team Performance]

9. B - The business case is developed at the start of the project, like any other project.

[Cohn, M., 2006. Agile Estimating and Planning. 1st ed. Massachusetts: Pearson Education. Page 90] [Stakeholder Engagement]

10. A - In Agile, the product owner creates the backlog for and with the team. The backlog helps the teams see how to deliver the highest value without creating waste. [Agile Practice Guide, 1st edition, Page 41] [Adaptive Planning]

11. B - Pair programming is an Agile software development technique in which two programmers work together at one workstation. One, the driver, writes code while the other, the observer or navigator, reviews each line of code as it is typed in. The two programmers switch roles frequently. Pair programming is one of the XP techniques. [Agile Practice Guide, 1st edition, Page 102] [Value-driven Delivery]

12. A - Every project needs a project charter so the project team knows why this project matters, where the team is headed and what the project objective is. [Agile Practice Guide, 1st edition, Page 49] [Team Performance]

13. C - Pareto charts and fishbone diagrams are quality management tools. A flow chart is a process management tool. Agile teams reflect estimate variability using hurricane-style burndown charts. [Agile Practice Guide, 1st edition, Page 61] [Team Performance]

14. A - A burndown chart is the most commonly used project's progress presentation tool used by Agile teams. [Cohn, M., 2006. Agile Estimating and Planning. 1st ed. Massachusetts: Pearson Education. Page 249] [Stakeholder Engagement]

15. B - The daily plan, as committed to by each participant in a team's daily meeting, is fairly precise. Individuals express commitments to complete, or at least make progress on, specific tasks during the day. [Cohn, M., 2006. Agile Estimating and Planning. 1st ed. Massachusetts: Pearson Education. Page 245] [Adaptive Planning]

16. A - A defect found later (or not fixed during the iteration it was discovered) is treated the same as a user story. Fixing the defect will need to be prioritized into a subsequent iteration in the same way any other user story would be. [Cohn, M., 2006. Agile Estimating and Planning. 1st ed. Massachusetts: Pearson Education. Page 152] [Problem Detection and Resolution]

17. C - Typically five to ten minutes are spent on check-ins. The rest of the choices do not result in efficient time management. [Derby, E. and Larsen, D., 2006. Agile Retrospectives: Making Good Teams Great. 1st ed. Texas: Pragmatic Bookshelf, Page 41] [Continuous Improvement]

18. D - Agile CPI = Completed features value/actual costs to date. For example, if the team spent $2.8M but delivered $2.2M value of features, the CPI = 2.2/2.8 = 0.79. [Agile Practice Guide, 1st edition, Page 69] [Team Performance]

19. A - The best way to handle this type of offer is to politely reject the offer. Taking gifts can be viewed as personal gain and may affect your integrity as an Agile practitioner. It may leave you and your organization open to allegations of improper conduct. [PMI Code of Ethics and Professional Conduct] [Stakeholder Engagement]

20. D - This is known as Pair Work. Pair work involves two analysts working on a single process. One person maps the process while the observer reviews, inspects, and adds value to the mapping process. These roles are switched throughout a paired session. [Agile Practice Guide, 1st edition, Page 153] [Team Performance]

21. A - Although ROI is commonly used by accountants to measure financial benefits, the ROI measure doesn't factor in the time value of money, which makes it less accurate than the IRR measure. [Cohn, M., 2006. Agile Estimating and Planning. 1st ed. Massachusetts: Pearson Education. Page 100] [Value-driven Delivery]

22. B - The product owner is responsible for guiding the direction of the product. Product owners rank the work based on its business value. Product owners work with their teams daily by providing product feedback and setting direction on the next piece of functionality to be delivered. [Agile Practice Guide, 1st edition, Page 41] [Value-driven Delivery]

23. C - PDCA (plan–do–check–act) is an iterative four-step quality management method and is not part of the Agile methodologies. [Agile Practice Guide, 1st edition, Page 100] [Agile Principles and Mindset]

24. D - Both project and team charters are optional project artefacts and the project team and the servant-leader determines if formal charting is required. A project charter documents the project objective while the team charter documents how the team members will interact. [Agile Practice Guide, 1st edition, Pages 49, 50] [Value-driven Delivery]

25. C - Since CPI = Earned Value/Actual Costs, this means that Actual Costs = Earned Value/CPI = $100,000/0.8 = $125,000. This means that the team has spent more on the project than planned. [Agile Practice Guide, 1st edition, Page 69] [Team Performance]

26. A - Iterative approaches are recommended when you suspect the requirements will change based on customer feedback. [Agile Practice Guide, 1st edition, Page 22] [Stakeholder Engagement]

27. B - Acceptance Test-Driven Development (ATTD) is the method of collaboratively creating acceptance test criteria that are used to create acceptance tests before delivery begins. [Agile Practice Guide, 1st edition, Page 150] [Stakeholder Engagement]

28. A - In flow-based Agile, the focus is on the flow of work and the team's throughput. Questions such as, "What are my impediments" are addressed during iteration-based Agile and not flow-based Agile. [Agile Practice Guide, 1st edition, Pages 53, 54] [Adaptive Planning]

29. D - Do not make the mistake of thinking that a release plan makes an iteration plan unnecessary, or the other way around. The release, iteration, and daily plans each cover a different time horizon with a different level of precision and each serves a unique purpose. [Cohn, M., 2006. Agile Estimating and Planning. 1st ed. Massachusetts:

Pearson Education. Page 248] [Adaptive Planning]

30. C - Iterative life cycles allow customer feedback on partially completed or unfinished work while incremental life cycles only provide finished deliverables that the customer may be able to use immediately. [Agile Practice Guide, 1st edition, Page 19] [Agile Principles and Mindset]

31. B - Kanban in Lean manufacturing is a system for scheduling inventory control and replenishment. [Agile Practice Guide, 1st edition, Page 103] [Value-driven Delivery]

32. B - Participation of the product owner in the daily standups, estimation and retrospectives is optional. However, the product owner is the "owner" of the product demonstrations. [Agile Practice Guide, 1st edition, Page 55] [Stakeholder Engagement]

33. B - You need to have a look at the burndown chart. The burndown chart will tell the number of story points remaining and the current team's velocity. Teams might update velocity on a Kanban board, but this is not a common practice. [Agile Practice Guide, 1st edition, Pages 61, 62] [Team Performance]

34. B - Larger user stories can exist down a project's prioritize list of work. However, as those features near the top of the list (when they will be scheduled into an iteration that is beginning) they are disaggregated into smaller pieces. [Cohn, M., 2006. Agile Estimating and Planning. 1st ed. Massachusetts: Pearson Education. Page 246] [Problem Detection and Resolution]

35. B - The Shu-Ha-Ri model of skills acquisition describes progression from obeying the rules (Shu means to obey and protect), through consciously moving away from the rules (Ha means to change or digress), and finally through steady practice and improvement finding an individual path (Ri means to separate or leave). [Agile Practice Guide, 1st edition, Page 119] [Value-driven Delivery]

36. A - According to the Agile Manifesto, responding to change is valued over following a plan. [Agile Practice Guide, 1st edition, Page 8] [Agile Principles and Mindset]

37. D - Although now applied universally across complex organizational projects, the Agile manifesto was initially developed for software projects. [Agile Practice Guide, 1st edition, Page 8] [Agile Principles and Mindset]

38. C - Although collocation of team members is highly desired, there are times when such arrangements are not possible. A project can have dedicated team members that are not collocated. Formal change control and multi-tasking are not desirable as these can potentially limit the team's agility. However, when the team members are dedicated to the project, this usually results in increased focus and productivity. [Agile Practice Guide, 1st edition, Page 40] [Value-driven Delivery]

39. B - Agile plans cover three different levels– the release, the iteration, and the current day. [Cohn, M., 2006. Agile Estimating and Planning. 1st ed. Massachusetts: Pearson Education. Page 245] [Adaptive Planning]

40. B - The burndown line will only touch the horizontal axis upon project completion. During the project, a linear trendline can be plotted to forecast future performance. The x-intercept of the trendline indicates the project completion. [Cohn, M., 2006. Agile Estimating and Planning. 1st ed. Massachusetts: Pearson Education. Page 214] [Team Performance]

Additional Resources

Exam Taking Tips

PMI-ACP Exam Facts

- There are 120 total multiple choice questions which make up the PMI-ACP exam
- 20 randomly placed "pretest questions" are included, and do not count towards the pass/fail determination
- Students have 3 hours to complete the exam
- While PMI does not publish a precise passing score, students should expect to score 65% or higher to pass the exam (65 of 100 questions)
- Students may bring blank "scratch" paper with which to draft responses, such as for formula-based exam questions.

Before the Exam

- Visit the exam location before your exam date so that you are familiar with the address and commute time, especially if you are a nervous test taker.
- Be prepared to fully utilize your blank "scratch" paper in the exam. This means that you have committed important formulas, concepts, and key facts to memory; and you are able to apply them to a blank sheet of paper in less than five minutes.
- Alleviate exam stress and anxiety by taking practice exams that attune you to the pace, subject matter, and difficulty of the real exam.
- On the night before the exam, reduce your study time to one hour or less and get extra sleep. The reduced study time and extra rest will allow your brain to better process the information it has absorbed during earlier, more intense, study sessions.

Taking the Exam

- IMPORTANT: Bring your PMI authorization letter, as well as two forms of ID, to the exam center.
- At the beginning of the PMI-ACP exam, use your scratch paper to "download" all of the formulas, concepts, and key facts you have committed to memory. To save time, perform this activity immediately after the initial computer tutorial which allots 15 minutes.
- Approach each question from PMI's perspective, not your own experience, even if the most correct response seems contrary to your "on-the-job" knowledge.
- Plan your breaks during the exam. A recommended break pattern during the PMI-ACP exam is to stand up and stretch after every 50 questions.
- Smile as you take the exam. It has been proven that smiling alleviates stress and boosts confidence during exceptionally difficult tasks. Use deep breathing techniques to further relax.
- If you have exam time remaining, review the questions you "marked for review". Use all the exam time you have until each question has been reviewed twice.

The PMI-ACP exam is a multiple choice test that asks one to recognize correct answers among a set of four options. The extra options that are not the correct answer are called the "distracters"; and their purpose, unsurprisingly, is to distract the test taker from the actual correct answer among the bunch.

Students usually consider multiple choice exams as much easier than other types of exams; this is not necessarily true with the PMI-ACP exam. Among these reasons are:

- Most multiple choice exams ask for simple, factual information; unlike the PMI-ACP exam which often requires the student to apply knowledge and make a best judgment.
- The majority of multiple choice exams involve a large quantity of different questions – so even if you get a few incorrect, it's still okay. The PMI-ACP exam covers a broad set of material, often times in greater depth than other certification exams.

Regardless of whether or not multiple choice testing is more forgiving; in reality, one must study immensely because of the sheer volume of information that is covered.

Although three hours may seem like more than enough time for a multiple choice exam, when faced with 120 questions, time management is one of the most crucial factors in succeeding and doing well. You should always try and answer all of the questions you are confident about first, and then go back about to those items you are not sure about afterwards. Always read *carefully* through the entire test as well, and do your best to not leave any question blank upon submission– even if you do not readily know the answer.

Many people do very well with reading through each question and not looking at the options before trying to answer. This way, they can steer clear (usually) of being fooled by one of the "distracter" options or get into a tug-of-war between two choices that both have a good chance of being the actual answer.

Never assume that "all of the above" or "none of the above" answers are the actual choice. Many times they are, but in recent years they have been used much more frequently as distracter options on standardized tests. Typically this is done in an effort to get people to stop believing the myth that they are always the correct answer.

You should be careful of negative answers as well. These answers contain words such as "none", "not", "neither", and the like. Despite often times being very confusing, if you read these types of questions and answers carefully, then you should be able to piece together which is the correct answer. Just take your time!

If you ever narrow down a question to two possible answers, then try and slow down your thinking and think about how the two different options/answers differ. Look at the question again and try to apply how this difference between the two potential answers relates to the question. If you are convinced there is literally no difference between the two potential answers (you'll more than likely be wrong in assuming this), then take another look at the answers that you've already eliminated. Perhaps one of them is actually the correct one and you'd made a previously unforeseen mistake.

On occasion, over-generalizations are used within response options to mislead test takers. To help guard against this, always be wary of responses/answers that use absolute words like "always", or "never". These are less likely to actually be the answer than phrases like "probably" or "usually" are. Funny or witty responses are also, most of the time, incorrect – so steer clear of those as much as possible.

Although you should always take each question individually, "none of the above" answers are usually less likely to be the correct selection than "all of the above" is. Keep this in mind with the understanding that it is not an absolute rule, and should be analyzed on a case-by-case (or "question-by-question") basis.

Looking for grammatical errors can also be a huge clue. If the stem ends with an indefinite article such as "an" then you'll probably do well to look for an answer that begins with a vowel instead of a consonant. Also, the longest response is also oftentimes the correct one, since whoever wrote the question item may have tended to load the answer with qualifying adjectives or phrases in an effort to make it correct. Again though, always deal with these on a question-by-question basis, because you could very easily be getting a question where this does not apply.

Verbal associations are oftentimes critical because a response may repeat a key word that was in the question. Always be on the alert for this. Playing the old Sesame Street game "Which of these things is not like the other" is also a very solid strategy, if a bit preschool. Sometimes many of a question's distracters will be very similar to try to trick you into thinking that one choice is related to the other. The answer very well could be completely unrelated however, so stay alert.

Just because you have finished a practice test, be aware that you are not done working. After you have graded your test with all of the necessary corrections, review it and try to recognize what happened in the answers that you got wrong. Did you simply not know the qualifying correct information? Perhaps you were led astray by a solid distracter answer? Going back through your corrected test will give you a leg up on your next one by revealing your tendencies as to what you may be vulnerable with, in terms of multiple choice tests.

It may be a lot of extra work, but in the long run, going through your corrected multiple choice tests will work wonders for you in preparation for the real exam. See if you perhaps misread the question or even missed it because you were unprepared. Think of it like instant replays in professional sports. You are going back and looking at what you did on the big stage in the past so you can help fix and remedy any errors that could pose problems for you on the real exam.

29962902R00183

Made in the USA
Middletown, DE
23 December 2018